the sanctified body

Also by Patricia Treece:

A Man for Others
Nothing Short of a Miracle

the

SANCTIFIED

body

patricia

treece

DOUBLEDAY
new york
london
toronto
sydney
auckland

Published by Doubleday

a division of Bantam Doubleday Dell Publishing Group, Inc.
666 Fifth Avenue, New York, New York 10103

Doubleday and the portrayal of an anchor
with a dolphin are trademarks of Doubleday,
a division of Bantam Doubleday Dell Publishing Group, Inc.

Diagram on page 91 based on diagrams, pages 222 and 234 of *Encounter with God*, copyright © 1987 by Morton T. Kelsey. Used by permission of The Paulist Press.

Library of Congress Cataloging-in-Publication Data

Treece, Patricia.
 The sanctified body / Patricia Treece. — 1st ed.
  p. cm.
 Bibliography: p.
 ISBN 0-385-26229-9
 1. Christian saints—Miscellanea. 2. Body, Human—Religious aspects—
Catholic Church. 3. Catholic Church—Doctrines.
I. Title.
BX4669.T73 1989
248.2′9—dc20   89-33115
                CIP

ISBN 0-385-26229-9

This book is dedicated to our human
family—
rising from the same source
called to the same bliss.

And to C. Maxwell Cade of London:
With the heart of a mystic, the
steady eye of the scientist, you
advanced human consciousness.

acknowledgments

When everyone else was telling me—kindly or bluntly—that no one would accept a book on mystical phenomena written for the human family instead of slanted to a precise market such as New Agers, Catholics, Jews, etc., three men's understanding and praise for the manuscript gave me heart. My thanks for the encouraging words to publisher Jeremy P. Tarcher of Los Angeles, editor Stratford Caldecott of London, and Anthony T. Chenevey, S.S.P., editor in chief at Alba House, Staten Island, N.Y.

To credit by name and affiliation all those archivists, librarians, heads or other officers of religious orders or other spiritual organizations, postulators or vice-postulators of Causes, and other authorities on the holy men and women of this book who assisted me is impossible here. To all of you scattered across the world in Lebanon, France, Israel, Spain, Taiwan, Holland, Mauritius, England, Mexico, Poland, Canada, Portugal, the Vatican, Belgium, Germany, Ireland, Italy, Switzerland, India, and over half the American states who helped with this eleven-year project, my deepest thanks. For those who shared their personal experiences with modern mystics or related phenomena, my wholehearted gratitude to Geoffrey Blundell and Isabel Cade of London, Charles Carpenter, M.A.P. of Sonora, Mexico, Mother Marguerite Carter, Paul Chacon, Rev. Robert Fox, Bill Landa, Antonia Moore, Katherine Morrow, Marlene O'Neill, Sister Veronica and Sister Lucy, O.C.D., Mary and Francis Levy—all of the United States. My thanks also to other interviewees, again too many to name, whose information provided important context or support for the testimonies used in the book or who introduced me to other individuals.

My gratitude also to the individuals in the greater Los Angeles Hindu, Jewish, Buddhist, Islamic, Protestant, and Catholic Christian communities who helped me with my efforts to speak of each tradition's holy people with the proper terminology and accuracy.

Three close friends assisted me, each in an area of expertise. Judith Hodgins repeatedly read segments for clarity and style. Psychologist Dr. Sheila Kalivas, who has strong psychic talents, shared a personal experiment, made research suggestions, and read the chapter on bilocation. And psychologist Dr. John Butler, who knows much about mysticism and human wholeness from personal experience, reviewed those sections in Chapter One. To each, many thanks.

There are a few individuals on whom I made unusual demands or whose response went far beyond the normal courtesy to researchers. My special gratitude to Dr. Yaffa Eliach of the Center for Holocaust Studies in Brooklyn, N.Y.; Rabbi Chaim Seidler-Feller of UCLA's Hillel Center; William A. Volk, C.PP.S. of Rome; Miss Luisa Sbragia of San Francisco; Diego Borgatello, S.D.B. of New Rochelle, N.Y.; Brother Salvatore Azzarello, C.M.F. of Los Angeles; Ruth Kent, I.H.M. of St. John's Seminary, Camarillo, Ca.; Monsignor Traino Crisan and Monsignor Jaroslav Nemec of the Congregation for the Causes of Saints, Vatican City; Joseph Elworthy, C.SS.R. and the staff of the Seelos Center, New Orleans, La.; Rev. Royale Vadakin of Los Angeles; the late Ralph Lavigne, S.S.S., and associates of the Eymard League, New York; Rabbi Robert Krause of Camarillo, Ca.; my Islamic connection Dr. Azade-Ayse Rorlich of USC; and my special friend Therese Martin and all her associates.

To the research associates of C. Maxwell Cade in London, my thanks for hospitality and useful interviews on the physiology of sanctity.

And my gratitude to Sister Veronica, O.C.D. of Eugene, Ore. for reading the entire manuscript, her useful suggestions, and her prayers.

My work gets nowhere without prayer. Lots of prayer. So my public gratitude, also, to those with whom I usually pray daily: Eva Engholm, Alice Williams, and Judith Hodgins—and to the many others from whom I frequently or occasionally begged prayers for this project. It is all of you who kept me going for over a decade. And finally my thanks to a husband and children who do not share my interest in saints but so lovingly put up with me anyway.

contents

note to the reader

Non-English names which appear in these pages are anglicized or not depending on how the individual in question is most commonly known to the English-speaking reader. Where individuals are not generally known, a few names are anglicized for ease of pronunciation; where pronunciation presents no problem, names are spelled as in the native tongue—with the exception of accent marks.

Although they appear in footnotes and endnotes referring to non-English sources, accent marks are omitted in the body of the text in foreign names, such as Andre, where English pronunciation is well established. They are used, however, for other non-English words such as Curé or Abbé, as an aid to pronunciation.

the
sanctified
body

One of Western spirituality's great masters of discernment once had some excited visitors. Breathlessly they stammered of mystical wonders they had just witnessed—a man luminous, his body levitating three feet off the floor.

"What a great saint he must be!" they exclaimed.

"Perhaps," was the dry-toned response. "Tell me, how does this fellow treat his wife? What do his children say of him?"

▲

This is a book about things—like levitation and luminosity—at which great spiritual masters such as Buddha or the just-quoted St. Ignatius Loyola look with a jaundiced eye.

And for good reason.

Get hooked on them as important in themselves, and you

set out on a long, winding path to nowhere. Yet Jesus spoke of "signs" that could foster belief in numerous realities. Acknowledged in that way, *in the crucial presence of extraordinary virtue,* mystical phenomena in any of the world's great spiritual traditions become by-products of sanctity that can inspire us to seek its source.

Besides pointing to numinous realities, the specifically bodily phenomena of mysticism also show holiness is a whole-person phenomenon. Finally bodily phenomena make it startlingly clear that, for all our physiological knowledge and careful recording of our species' "records" for speed, endurance, and agility, we still have no real idea of the outer limits of human physical potential.

That ignorance undoubtedly arises from ours being a society that does not exactly flock to observe its mystics. Michael Harner, New York professor of anthropology and a practicing healer-shaman, says we are only beginning to appreciate "the important impact" of the mind in individuals who are masters of altered states of consciousness "on what have . . . been too often perceived as questions of purely 'physical' capability."[1] Dr. Harner has shamanism in mind, but his statement certainly applies to more traditional mysticism as well.

Fortunately—or this book could not hope for understanding —we are moving closer to grasping that, as Nobel Prize-winner psychobiologist Roger Sperry has said, ideas of mind-body separation are "simply obsolete."[*] Holistic medicine, psychiatry, and psychology, popularized by individuals like Norman Cousins[†] and Bernie Siegel,[‡] testify that what one thinks and believes affects the body dramatically, as do emotions, even those hidden from the conscious mind. Conversely, from new discoveries, particularly that the human brain secretes at least

---

[*] In the 1981 *Annual Review of Neural Sciences.*
[†] See his *Anatomy of an Illness* and *The Healing Heart*
[‡] In his books *Love, Medicine, and Miracles* and *Peace, Love and Healing*

thirty or forty chemicals—among them mind-altering "drugs" such as the hallucinogen dimethyltryptamine—the body's role is suddenly apparent in areas that used to be seen as purely mental. The world is ready to see at last that "there is no such thing as a purely mental, spiritual, or bodily illness or triumph, but only a living event taking place in a living organism."* That acknowledgment will give us a whole new understanding of the bodily side of mysticism.

Another help is the post-Materialist view of matter and reality. Here astronomers and quantum physicists join hands with the world's mystics. For instance, a philosophical premise of quantum mechanics is that all the things in our universe (including us) that appear to exist independently are actually parts of one all-encompassing organic pattern. Thus astronomer Sir James Jeans could explain the universe as more like a "giant thought" than anything else. This concept is strikingly relevant both to certain mystical phenomena that suggest a psychic connection even between strangers and to the teachings of many of the world's mystics that God is in all, causes and maintains all, and is, in a twentieth-century phrase, "the very ground of being."

Working with subatomic particles, researchers find they defy conceptualization or visualization, two things mystics often claim about numinous realities. Scientists in the era of Materialism claimed the universe was a giant puzzle they would gradually solve. Quantum mechanics investigators more humbly find the very nature of their subject ensures that only partial aspects of it can be grasped. The mystic, who laughed at the old boast that the puny human mind could encompass reality, smiles in agreement.

Finally, quantum physicists note that a tiny reality, the sub-

---

* I paraphrase the German clinician Leo Mohr, author of *Handbuch der inneren Medizin* (Berlin, 1911–19)

atomic particle, is either an energy wave or a particle of matter, depending upon how one looks at it. If matter can be seen as having such qualities of energy as fluidity, this makes certain experiences of mystics much more reasonable. So does the understanding we owe Einstein that space and time are only mental constructions by which we deal with a reality that cannot, in fact, be so neatly boxed.

Under Materialist science, for something to be two opposing things, such as energy and matter, was nonsense. Today the vanguard of science prefers the more open-minded view expressed by Gary Zukav in his book on quantum physics *The Dancing Wu Li Masters:*

> The more clearly we experience something as "nonsense," the more clearly we are experiencing the boundaries of our own self-imposed cognitive structures . . . , the prearranged patterns . . . we have superimposed on reality. "Nonsense" is . . . unintelligible because we have not yet found that point of view from which it makes sense.†[2]

One area still unintelligible to many people—and which hopefully this book will bring new light on—is the way soul functions affect mind and body. By soul I mean that eternal aspect of personality through which God nourishes the whole person. Because the concept of the soul affecting body and mind isn't exactly in general circulation, let me give a few examples.

For years in Western societies, people who "sat around meditating" were thought to be engaged in purely spiritual activity. Then in 1957 Walter Hess described the relaxation response. The opposite of the fight-or-flight syndrome of stress, its physiological features included reductions in heart rate,

---

† I have changed the order of two phrases but not the meaning.

blood pressure, respiratory rate, blood cortisone and lactate levels, and muscle tone. There were positive increases too, some intelligible only to medical personnel but others, such as warmer hands, recognizable to anyone. All this, it was discovered, was happening in the bodies of proficient Eastern or Western style meditators. And it was not happening to those just sitting around or sleeping. In other words, it was the soul activity, not plain old inertia, that produced physiological benefits.

In the sixties and seventies at Harvard Medical School Herbert Benson and Keith Wallace began investigating Transcendental Meditation (TM), the Hindu meditation technique that was sweeping the country. Using electroencephalographs, it was now possible to prove that the brain is also positively affected in meditation. For a time, articles proliferated on the benefits of the alpha and theta brain waves of meditation. Again, these were not the brain waves of ordinary relaxation in front of the television or of sleep.

Then Dr. Wallace, now at Maharishi International University (MIU), compared TM meditators to nonmeditators on the basis of blood pressure, hearing, vision, cardiovascular fitness, and breathing efficiency. He concluded that people who meditated twice daily for over five years are physiologically twelve to fifteen years younger than those who do not meditate.[3] MIU biochemist Ken Walton confirmed that levels of the brain chemical serotonin rise during TM meditation. Serotonin is thought to play a critical role in reversing depression.

Although one must have a healthy skepticism about any studies done for self-promotion by an organization itself rather than by outside investigators, Wallace's work at MIU seems to have simply continued his Harvard research. It is also joined by other studies indicating *any* form of *positive* meditation benefits the body and emotions. For instance, pioneer mind-body researcher, British psychologist-physicist and Raja yoga master C. Maxwell Cade treated anxiety states by biofeedback, minimal psychotherapy, and instruction in meditation. Using techniques from Soto Zen Buddhism, Sufism, yoga, autogenic and progressive relaxation training, the Divine Love Meditation of Swami Prakashanand Saraswati, and TM, he found all produced physical and emotional benefits if practiced regularly and correctly. (He also noted that entered into *only* for those mental and physical effects, meditation still may also "induce soul consciousness.")[4]

Jonathan Lieff, director of psychiatry at Lemuel Shattuck Hospital in Boston, where he works with handicapped patients, says that the rosary (which he calls "one of the oldest and best tools"), TM, or other forms of positive meditation comfortable for the belief systems of his patients have helped them literally throw away canes or crutches or even speak when they had been mute.[5]

Five years of experiments as long ago as the 1950s at California's Redlands University demonstrated the healing power of prayer that is practiced with complete honesty and expectation. A striking case in this Protestant pastor/psychologist-led experiment involved a man named Klaus whose daily half dozen grand mal epileptic seizures were only the start of problems that included hospitalizations for palsy, nervous breakdowns, and alcoholism. Bitterly hostile, according to a diagnostic psychological profile, Klaus had severe marital, sexual, and financial problems as well. Dismissed by both psychiatry and medicine as "hopeless," he entered prayer therapy although he was an atheist. Nine months later, he had not suffered a single seizure, and new psychological tests showed "a man simply remade."[6]

The Redlands findings are supported by a 1989 report in the *Journal of the American Medical Association.* Studying hospitalized heart patients, researchers found those prayed for suffered fewer complications.[7] And my book *Nothing Short of a*

Miracle details physical healings through prayer alone of people "past medical help" with every type of condition.

Many mind-body studies that never mention the spiritual still show its importance. Take, for instance, the time-pressured Type A personality filled with "free-floating hostility." Linked to heart disease by cardiovascular researchers Meyer Friedman and Ray H. Rosenman, the Type A syndrome can be summed up as not loving one's neighbor because of not loving oneself as a child of God whose worth is independent of dollars earned or amount produced.

The soul is linked to human sexuality as well. One of the popular national women's magazines—which one now eludes me—several years ago published a wide-ranging survey of reader sexuality. The editors noted that the women who said spiritual matters were important to them were also the women who had the most satisfying marital sex.

Each particular spiritual path, at least in advanced practitioners such as monks, even leaves its unique imprint on the body: Work at Harvard and again at Tokyo University showed significant differences on E.E.G. monitors during different types of meditation. Yoga consciousness, for example, proves quite different physiologically from Zen consciousness.[8]

So, yes, mind-body separation is obsolete, but even more true, as St. Antony the Great (251–356) saw centuries ago: "Life is union and junction of these three: body, mind and soul."[9]

The body plays a central role in the spiritual life, or what I prefer to call by broader terms like the ascent to wholeness or human development. In the body, "every prayer, however secret and however interior it may be, will be mirrored," says French Trappist Andre Louf. This constant interaction between the mind-soul (speaking in mystical terms, he calls it the heart) and the body Louf terms *the* typical feature of authentic

Christian prayer.[10] Or I would say of all authentic prayer. For as Jacob Needleman says, from Judaism but for us all, "the discovery of universal meaning is . . . an experiential, bodily and emotional event requiring three-dimensional sacrifice and need."[11]

The body's contribution to human spirituality takes many forms. I think of the yogi's emphasis on breath and postures, the dervish's or Hasidic's dance, or certain shamanistic spiritual initiations involving the endurance of physical pain. The one thing every spiritual tradition I know has in common is that in all authentic mystics from the Sioux Black Elk to the lotus-postured monk, in the thrust toward God the body is as seriously trained as the mind or soul. "Give your blood and get the spirit,"[12] one early Christian desert father puts it for them all.

This training in no way necessitates mind-soul war on the "less worthy" flesh. We need not join Gnostics, Manichees, Shakers, and others who think spiritual progress demands the physical "give way to spirit," so that growing toward God, the body drops behind as a butterfly sloughs off her cocoon. The view of this book is the holistic one‡ that the body, too, is a butterfly. It becomes as sanctified as mind and soul. Or as good old St. Antony says "in the end the whole body in both (its) struggles . . . and the tranquility of prayer, will become one with the mind and the soul."[13]

Over seventeen hundred years later a researcher on brain states, using the most sophisticated instruments yet devised to track brain functioning, concurs with the desert father, at least regarding moments of mind-body unity through "the tranquility of prayer." Cade writes that expert meditators focusing on a body function such as breathing can be shown via biofeed-

‡ Born in the Western world in Judaism and carried over into Catholicism, this view has prevailed in both traditions but not without struggle at times.

back monitoring to eventually merge their self-consciousness with the focus of their attention. He says:

> Here then, is the scientific explanation of the mystical practices of all ages in which the so-called separate entities of mind and body become directly unified in consciousness: voluntary-involuntary sensory channel overlap causes mental and physical awareness to merge in a single identity that is not perceived as either mind or body *because it is both simultaneously*[14] [his italics].

In the more permanent higher consciousness of holiness, Abbé Louf explains a state he terms "resurrection life begin[s] to flower and bear fruit in the body."[15] Put another way, the flesh, too, shares in cosmic consciousness or maximal human development.

However we phrase it to fit our mental matrices, most of us know nothing of maximal development, cosmic consciousness, or resurrection life. A good way to picture the lowlier life we lead is a study that situates humanity on a ladder of well-being. On the lowest rungs are those mired in resentment, self-pity, and anxiety who see themselves as unhappy and rate their health and vitality as below average. Others agree, even judging them "not particularly likeable and not very good-looking." This correlation continues up the ladder: As individuals see themselves as happier, they feel healthier and more energetic, while others find them more likeable and better looking. But when we come to the realm of ultimate wholeness in mind, soul, and body, suddenly the ladder of well-being is no longer pertinent. On its highest rung stands not the saint but a well-integrated, basically happy person who enjoys good health and knows herself likeable and physically attractive, facts seconded by others. From this point to cosmic consciousness or resurrection life, extending the ladder is ineffectual. Instead we must simply step off it into thin air and enter another dimension. If not, perfect popularity, perfect physical beauty, and perfect health would be the marks of holiness. Instead in this mystical dimension the Sufi is as apt to be stoned as salaamed, the zaddik sought eagerly for healing today may fall to the same crowd's pogrom tomorrow. So much for popularity. As for the body, the focal point of this volume, neither of the ultimates to which flesh can aspire, beauty nor perfect health and vitality, pertain, except in the sense Nobel Prize winner Mother Teresa of Calcutta demonstrates, that where there is authentic holiness a face which would dismay a beautician can be strangely appealing and an aged, exhausted body outlast youth.

Clustering about this sanctified body, we find exotic characteristics. By no means will each be found in every holy person. The human body in sanctity retains its tremendous range of response, with some physiogomies much more apt to physically evidence holiness. Thus the sanctified body will inevitably reflect its mystical life by unusual energies, but to varying degrees. And only in rare cases will it levitate. Only because, when they show up, these characteristics, if genuine, are most often associated with holiness may the physiology of sanctity be said to include luminosity, inexplicable energy, the perfumes of sanctity, expanded sensory perceptions, levitation, transportation, bilocation, and certain characteristics of the holy corpse, including, at times, incorruptibility.

To examine these topics cursorily trivializes, sensationalizes, or scatters perplexities. Expanded sensory perceptions and characteristics of the holy corpse each require a volume to do them justice. To examine the other six phenomena is the work of this book.

If a friend falls wildly, madly in love, we have no doubt of the lover's existence even before we see the individual. The phenomena in this book flow out of a mad love affair too. (I speak in the concepts of the Judeo-Christian tradition, my treasured, adopted Catholic faith in particular but I hope in a universal spirit.) At least the best analogy for sanctity seems that of a great, mutual human passion. The person giving off visible light or rising from the floor is enraptured, that is, caught in an ecstatic moment of love. This points, to me, to a numinous Lover. Of course, lonely people have faked the existence of a lover. And there are people who fake mystical phenomena. There are also individuals who take a lover for sinister purposes. There are dark mystics as well. This book is not about the frauds or the phenomena of darkness; it is about the joyous phenomena that flow from authentic holiness.

What is authentic holiness? Jewish Kabbalah scholar Leo Schaya defines it as "the human being . . . purified and penetrated by the divine."[16] From this you can see that just as the touchstone of alcoholism is not "Does she have cirrhosis of the liver?" but "Does she drink obsessively?" the touchstone of sanctity is never "Does he bilocate?" but "Is his prayer life deep beyond comprehension, his virtues heroic?"

Those virtues will generally include (remember, *in heroic proportion)* such things as large-mindedness, optimism, a realism that sees beyond the narrow concerns and illusions of contemporaries, inner joy that is not dependent on things "going well," courageous adherence to moral values even in immoral societies, a steady good-naturedness, spiritual wisdom (which may resemble foolishness to nonmystics), simplicity, almost always a strong sense of humor, and always great humility,* a trait that has nothing to do with lack of healthy self-esteem.

But more than any of these qualities and more than any physical manifestation, passionate love is the infallible sign of

---

* Writer John V. Sheridan points out "humility" comes from *humus,* meaning "grounded," "and connotes a fundamental realism, an authentic appreciation of our creaturehood, our talents, and our limitations." Humility and humor, he adds, are closely related *(They Touched Me,* p. 97).

holiness—love for God and love for the entire human family down to its least loveable member. This is not "niceness" but "foolish and unreasonable" passion that risks ostracism or worse to do good even to "bad people"—the invaders of one's homeland, the torturers of one's kin—all those "legitimate" enemies cheerfully hated by exemplary religious people of every persuasion. It is the Jewish girl nursing the wounded Palestinian in spite of the hate in his eyes *because* he is a child of God; the German Lutheran mother hiding a Jewish child in 1940 Berlin *because* every child belongs to God; the white Southern Baptist putting his own fragility between the KKK mob and their prey—and doing it without hating, only pitying and humanly fearing the men in the mob—*because* the black man, like the white persecutors, is God's precious creature; the black Pentecostal boy in South Africa dragging a white bigot from a burning house, knowing if the man were conscious he would spit on his rescuer. In short, it is love in its ultimate and humanly incomprehensible form.

No wonder its practitioners are often considered nuts, extremists, even traitors. They have come to the humanly absurd position of loving and pitying their own torturers, like Dutch Protestant Betsie ten Boom (1885–1944) who, dying in Ravensbruck concentration camp for sheltering Jews, lamented not for herself but for the spiritual misery of her Nazi jailers.[17] Or another Dutch saint, Carmelite Titus Brandsma. Used as a lab animal in experiments by the Nazis in Dachau, he begged his tormentor to take and use his rosary. She snarled, "I can't pray," but before she killed the Catholic priest their encounters had begun her transformation.[18]

It was by the purity and magnitude of his love, of course, that he redeemed her. Impossible? Hasidic Jews maintain the most mundane act, if one were holy enough, could redeem the world.

Spilling over with goodness because he or she is "penetrated by the divine," the saint inevitably draws others. Malcolm Muggeridge has described his first BBC interview with Mother Teresa of Calcutta in 1967. She had no presence, no charisma. Yet when the tape aired, it received an overwhelming response from people who wrote, "This woman speaks to me as no one in my life has ever done." Speaking of a saint she visited in India, a close friend of mine of Jewish background comments of the holy Hindu: "I just love to be with her; she somehow gives me the sense that God is real, that I am cared for by the divinity—in short, that all is well."

How does one get to be the kind of person we call a "saint"?

To answer that, let's summarize the process in mystical terms, again in psychological language, and finally by a physiological description. Speaking mystically, the ascent to sanctity is a series of encounters in which an individual experiences God as the answer to his deepest hungers. Suddenly or gradually the individual falls in love with this great Lover. Typically, after a period of infatuation, disenchantment (called "the dark night of the soul" by medieval mystics) sets in. The lover seems cold, demanding more than one can give. Yet life alone is miserable, meaningless. Gradually it becomes clear the lover is not the problem. It is I, one mourns, who am deficient in love and will have to change if the relationship is to become what it can be. Now begins a transformation Kabbalah masters call a "deep probing of the heart." Often long and painful, it takes courage and commitment, for there are darkness and demons to be faced in one's own depths. Those who persevere see with new eyes that what the Lover asked was only to be loved unselfishly for more than what one could get from the relationship. Overwhelmed by the lover's faithfulness, forbearance, sheer goodness, and beauty, one finally surrenders. Loving the other at last more than oneself in the mystical or ego death, one delights to say, "Do with me as you will"—and discovers, not slavery, but bliss.

▲

In psychological terms, healthy growth starts where one is loved and consequently learns to love. This its gateway, there is much more to wholeness. To achieve individuation, one term for the height of psychological development, it is necessary to become conscious of deeper levels than the mask one presents to the world or even the fuller person one reveals to intimates. One must confront the unconscious aspects of personality one hides from oneself as "bad" or "undesirable." This "shadow side" must be humbly acknowledged and ultimately transformed and integrated. Moreover wholeness involves a life-or-death struggle within the personality to overcome the ego with its lifelong cry "Me first." As egotism dies, the authentic Self emerges and, enlightened by its hard-won consciousness, discovers a meaning to life larger than self-aggrandizement. At the heights of wholeness, life is lived altruistically and empathetically at the service of higher values.

Now let us look at the development of sanctity physiologically. Roger Sperry's split-brain studies at Cal Tech in the 1950s and 1960s began talk of left- and right-brain personalities. Although it turns out one cannot so neatly pinpoint the site of "left" and "right" lobe functions,[19] it is still useful to recognize the two types of consciousness: one handling verbal, analytical, time-sequential processes and another visual-spatial, holistic, and intuitive functions. Obviously access to both modes is a higher use of the brain. C. Maxwell Cade showed† that individuals with psychological problems such as phobic states, anxiety neuroses, and interpersonal failures show over-reliance on one type of consciousness, most often the verbal, analytical. Both developmentally speaking and literally, that is

† By a multichanneled double electroencephalograph designed to instantaneously mirror each hemisphere's brain waves.

physiologically, as seen in their electroencephalograms, such individuals are lopsided.[20]

Steps in self-development awaken the undeveloped lobe.[21] As these same individuals learn‡ healthier patterns of behavior, their electroencephalographs move toward the more balanced and integrated use of the brain hemispheres which characterizes maturer individuals. At the high level of psychospiritual consciousness-maturity he calls "lucid awareness" or "the awakened mind," Cade found, for instance, that the brain waves from the two hemispheres are in beautiful symmetry.[22] At a certain point the hemispheres seem to communicate reciprocally or integrate, as well.[23] Literally then, as one becomes better balanced or more integrated, this is mirrored physiologically in the brain. Or to put it from the physiologist's opposite viewpoint, expanded consciousness results from expanded brain use.

Meditation and contemplation—major means of transformation—also induce brain symmetry.[24] As Cade put together a hierarchy of states of consciousness based on physiology, his many monitorings showed that fledgling meditators cannot long maintain this symmetry when they once more "face life."[25] Advanced meditators, however, gradually learn to carry over the symmetrical state into their postmeditation periods, with increased tranquility and "ability to cope."[26] Obviously this is, physiologically speaking, an important step in the transformation process that ends with sanctity's "divine imperturbability" in all situations. And such results from meditation indicate that those like psychiatrist M. Scott Peck* who

‡ Because some people think biofeedback can make meditators "instant mystics," Cade emphasizes there are no shortcuts to the demanding process of self-transformation.

* See his *The Road Less Traveled: A New Psychology of Love, Traditional Values and Spiritual Growth.*

say the movement toward God and the movement toward psychological wholeness "are one and the same" are correct.

In the most spiritually advanced subjects tested, such as Hindu swami Prakashanand, the ordinary brain state is that "lucid awareness" of advanced meditation (this did not falter in the swami's case, even when he engaged a physicist in intense intellectual debate).[27] In other words, under such an individual's active mind processes is a layer of continuous contemplation, as described by centuries-old mystical classics such as *The Practice of the Presence of God.* Physiologically, mystics' claim to live on two levels (the spiritual and the mundane) at the same time is a fact.†

It is pertinent that progress toward this level of maturity keeps involving the use of more of the brain. For instance, Jung's "transcendent function"‡—the rare power to consciously choose one's mode of consciousness through a "higher mind"—involves more than accessing and integrating the two hemispheres; Jung found the "higher mind" in the brainstem.[28] The reticular activating system (RAS) is "the gateway to all forms of meditation . . . and higher states of consciousness," while the limbic system just above it, Cade feels, is responsible for many of the phenomena* experienced in those altered states which are the mystic's home territory.[29]

At the highest levels in Cade's hierarchy of states of consciousness, he notes that psychologists and other interpreters of these states are only using new terminology "for what is

† See another striking example of this in Menninger Foundation researchers Dr. and Mrs. Elmer Green's 1970 work with Swami Rama, a yogi from Rishikesh in the Himalayas described by William Johnston in his *Silent Music* (pp. 107–8).

‡ Cade thinks it is in "transcendent function" that conscious and unconscious mind contents tend to unify *(The Awakened Mind,* pp. 49–50).

* Among those he enumerates, out-of-body sensations, for instance, may relate to ESP and to the lowest levels of bilocation (as well as certain unconscious counterfeits of true bilocation); while feelings of floating and/or flying may have a similar bearing on at least imagined levitations.

actually mysticism."[30] It is in these as yet barely charted but physiologically verifiable states, where "paranormal ability and psychic events" are standard, that the phenomena of the sanctified body occur.

To sum up all three ways of looking at sanctity, it can be said that saints are the ultimate in human development, the furthest reaches on the long, arduous journey from self-centeredness and lopsided, minuscule use of the brain to its fullest use in a psychospiritual wholeness that extends beyond itself to numinous realities.

In a sense, as St. Therese of Lisieux has said, on this journey "everything is a grace." Yet paradoxically, it is equally true that the saint learns hope by fending off despair, faith by wrestling with desperate need, and heroic levels of charity by overcoming bitter temptations to hate. Or as Judaism's Schaya puts it, "If God is the first cause of this transformation, man is its second. . . . One cooperates actively in the process of being . . . sanctified."[31]

To encounter God is to be transformed by joy as well as struggle. Some of the saints I speak of in these pages at times feared they would die of joy; electroencephalographic studies combine with older medical evidence that they were not faking bliss: euphoria and various forms of ecstatic trance are real. And it is at least one of them—often called rapture—that produces many of the striking physiological manifestations of sanctity.

▲

For immediacy and better verification of the facts of those manifestations, I focus this book on sanctified bodies from the nineteenth and twentieth centuries. My criterion for nineteenth-century saints is that they lived their spiritual maturity in that century.

Where do I find these? Certainly there are genuine saints the world over. I can point to Sufi saints, Hasidic saints, Pentecostal saints, Tibetan lama saints, American Indian saints, yogic saints, Bahai saints, Methodist saints, and on through the whole great macrocosm of sanctity in the human family.

There is sanctity throughout humankind, I believe, because wherever an individual reaches out with all his being to God, God responds. Still if I may be facetious on the subject, the electroencephalograph has proven what bigots always knew: All traditions are not "the same." Remember, yoga and Zen consciousness even differ in their physiological effects (p. 7). Not only different, some roads to God seem harder. Buddhism and Hinduism, for instance, doubt their paths can be traveled in one lifetime. And some paths—from the old human sacrifice religions to recent cults that bloody human freedom or West Indian imports that slaughter animals in voodooistic rituals— smack of darkness.

Of course when we get away from the great world religions' concepts and traditions, we find mystics, looked at purely in regard to their experiences, are often to a striking degree sisters and brothers under the skin.

That being the case and with so much genuine holiness out there, it may shock you when I explain that, while I will refer to saints from *all* the great world traditions, including shamanism, *any time I think I can speak with accuracy,* the preponderance of my examples will be Catholics. Remember, this is not a book about saints or religion; it is a book about the human body as it is affected by holiness. For that, we don't need equal numbers of examples from every tradition as much as we need examples we can authenticate according to our Western standards of evidence and proof.

Let me address right out the question of hidden agendas on my part. Since I am a Catholic convert, the obvious question is do I wish to shanghai you into my faith? Let me borrow my reply from Mother Teresa of Calcutta, whose organization is made up of Hindus, Moslems, Sikhs, Jews, western agnostics and others, as well as her fellow Catholics. She says: "Oh I hope I am converting. I don't mean what you think. I hope we are converting hearts. What we are all trying to do . . . is to come closer to God. We become a better Hindu, a better Moslem, a better Catholic, a better whatever we are, and then by being better we come closer and closer [to God]."* And she adds that each of us must accept the God that is in our mind.

With that in mind let me explain why I have so often staggered gratefully into the arms of one tradition. To do so I borrow a technique of Hasidic spirituality and tell you a tale:

One long ago summer I found myself a Protestant observer at a papal audience. "Why couldn't I have come to Rome when the saint was alive," I grumbled to myself "instead of having to see this ugly, old, fat man." The ugly, old, fat man was John XXIII, who was soon to delight the world with his obvious holiness. As to my penetrating insight that his predecessor was a saint, my data, I blush to admit, consisted entirely of that pontiff having been thin with a somewhat melancholy look. Hopefully today I have more insight; but let's not bank on it.

Yes, there are living saints who could fill me in firsthand on the sanctified body. But they won't. They try to hide such manifestations lest someone focus on them, not God. "Mystics" willing to be interviewed about their levitations are dark frauds like the late Jim Jones of Guyana massacre fame or crazies and con artists whom fear of libel leaves unnamed. What our human family needs is a multifaith, unbiased Institute for the Discovery of Human Sanctity. Unfortunately there is no such thing.

* Dorothy S. Hunt, *Love: A Fruit Always in Season: Daily Meditations by Mother Teresa,* Ignatius Press, San Francisco, 1987, p. 49, quoting Desmond Doig, *Mother Teresa: Her People and Her Work,* p. 136.

But out of its Western rationalist tradition and acceptance of the supra-rational as a real factor in spiritual life, Catholicism over the centuries has developed a science par excellence for the detection of authentic holiness and accompanying mystical phenomena within its ranks (it would be amusing but the height of arrogance, after all, for Catholics to tell the Buddhists, Methodists, or any other group who their models of holiness should be). Beginning with the taking of testimonies under oath from those who knew a candidate across all the years, phases, and geographical locations of his life, the whole stringent quasi-juridical apparatus, with its well-defined stages under carefully established norms and specified modes of inquiry, is a godsend to a work like this.

Success of a Cause, as the overall investigation of an individual is titled, requires (as well as suprarational evidence†) reams of firsthand testimonies of "heroic virtue." (I have described the foremost virtue, heroic love. The others are those recognizable in authentic saints the world over.) What it all adds up to for our purpose is authentication that these are the phenomena of *sanctity,* not frauds like Jim Jones' staged "miracles of healing" or M. Lamar Keene's "levitations."

Another vital factor for our purposes is the careful attention given to the question of mental health, particularly in the presence of mystical phenomena. In spite of the ever-accumulating evidence that holiness is the acme of psychological wholeness, there are still many intelligent people, including writers on sanctity and spiritual leaders of every tradition, who maintain mystical phenomena are signs, not of numinous realities or the outer limits of human potential but of "complex neuroses"— or at least a "limited neurosis" that causes delusion in just one area.

Such critics find plenty of ammunition. To mention only one

---

† Described in the introduction to my *Nothing Short of a Miracle.*

phenomenon, visions, every year in the Catholic Church alone local bishops are investigating at least two hundred supposed apparitions. Almost all of these will be dismissed as looney tunes: crowds kneeling before a "heavenly sign" that turns out to be intersecting shadows, or a self-proclaimed seer who is psychotic.

With religion and spirituality perpetually rubbing shoulders with mass hysteria and individual lunacy, I feel a stringent need to prove that the mystical phenomena of even genuine holiness are at the opposite end of the human spectrum from psychosis or neurosis. Since there's no way I can Rorschach test the world's saints, Catholicism's investigation on just this point becomes my most workable way to show bodily phenomena in genuine saints point to the outer limits of human potential, not to the outer limits of neurosis.

For those who wonder if I am giving Catholicism too much credit on this point, let me quote a twentieth-century pope:

> That mental health is one of the fundamental goods from the viewpoint of nature is obvious. But it is just as clear that such health is also fundamental in the religious and supernatural sphere. In fact the full development of religious values and of . . . sanctity . . . is inconceivable if an individual does not start out with a healthy mind.‡[32]

Catholic readers, aware that Vatican curia do not always listen to popes, may wish more. For them I present author Peter Rohrbach, who posed to himself the "fundamental ques-

‡ My own research concurs: Those medical men, whether believers in supra-natural realities or not, who were physicians to saints invariably left comments that this man or woman was "maximally healthy psychologically." Of course, this did not keep the same saints from drawing epithets like "weird," "extremist," or "nut" because of their wholehearted living of spiritual values in nonspiritual societies.

tion: whether *any* canonized saint could possibly have been a neurotic or psychotic?" In an article by Father Gabriel of St. Mary Magdalen, for many years consultor to the Congregation of Rites working on "innumerable Causes" Rohrbach found his answer. Father Gabriel says that any signs of psychological imbalance in a candidate immediately precipitates a very careful investigation. "It is not actually possible to find a case in which proceedings [toward official sanctity] . . . continued," he testifies, adding that he could point to various Causes that failed "because of doubts of this nature which were not satisfactorily resolved."[33]

But could just enough neurosis slip through to cause otherwise holy people to have strange bodily symptoms? I think not, for the presence of bodily phenomena elicits painstaking scrutiny on just this point.

Please note no one is saying a neurotic can't attain "some degree of holiness."* And with sanctity and wholeness the latter stages of a *process,* obviously a future saint may be a neurotic but those who attain the heights honored by official beatification or canonization will have been healed along the way. Take, for instance, British writer-artist-therapist Caryll Houselander (1901–54), who may one day be canonized. Child of a disturbed single parent, Carryl was a self-confessed neurotic whose love of God and humanity grew to the point it healed, not only her own neurosis, but—according to the testimony of psychiatrists who called her to work with their patients—the neuroses of others.

---

* If crippling anxiety forbids perfect trust and self-abandonment, for instance, there may be compensatory virtues such as compassion and humility. The reason this can never reach canonizable magnitude is that the essence of sanctity is a love that expresses itself in *heroic* trust, *heroic* openness, while neurosis is, by definition, a blockage in such self-giving. Or, to quote Rohrbach's summation of an article by Jesuit psychologist Richard P. Vaughn in which holiness and neurosis are contrasted, "The neurotic . . . [too] involved in himself, simply cannot maintain the evenness of disposition, the gentle charity, [and] the self-forgetfulness required of *heroic* [italics mine] virtue ("Neuroticism and Perfectionism" in *Review for Religious,* March 1960, pp. 93–101, quoted in Peter-Thomas Rohrbach, The Search for St. Therese, p. 129).

I have no doubt the authentic saint of any tradition is mentally sound. But considering the pervasiveness and the intensity of contrary allegations, I am grateful I can assure you that the preponderance of mystical phenomena in these pages cannot be attributed to even modest mental imbalance.

A third factor in my using so many Catholic exemplars is that the entire mountainous materials of a Cause are permanently archived in various places. You can imagine what this means to a researcher only if you are as painfully aware as I that genuine material can be so incomplete, offensively over-credulous, or mocking that it seems false, while complete fabrication may be beautifully detailed and judiciously presented. If this volume took eleven years, it's because I needed that long to consult many of those archives, either to verify with those who have the original material accounts of phenomena found in books or interviews or to obtain published or unpublished materials. Another plus is that most of this archival material is in European languages I read. In the languages of the Far and Near East or shamanism, I could verify nothing.

Some Catholics in this book are so recent that the official investigation is incomplete. On these figures I still have ample material, thanks to the tradition's passion for fastidious, if discreet, record-keeping on those it sees as future canonization candidates. I think of the nineteen volumes on St. John Bosco, much of it collected behind his back while the saint was still alive. Or of the student who in the 1930s prepared a testimony in case he didn't live through the Holocaust to personally swear to Max Kolbe's holiness.

A final reason I offer so many Catholic examples is that while their investigators do not automatically write off mystical phenomena or other supra-rational elements† before crying "Miracle," rational explanations are always sought first. This

---

† They are, in fact, required in a Cause, as God's stamp of approval.

is another help to me, for, as I see it, most bodily phenomena have a psychophysiological basis and only on rare occasions exceed the outer limits of human potential. Thus I want to keep on them the critical eye of analytical thought until that reaches its limits. In that analytical mode, at times I present what the experts who guide Causes' evaluations of mystical phenomena say, as well as what science and/or medical research, authorities on mysticism, my own holistic ideas, and mystics themselves offer on each phenomenon.

Nevertheless while I value rational investigation enough to spend eleven years assembling verified testimonies, authenticated events, and pertinent analytical materials, I am not a rationalist and make no pretense of living in that narrow band of reality. I do not intend to cramp either of us by forced and unprovable explanations for every event. Sometimes there is little science, mystical theology, or anyone else can say. Gerard Baillie, born in France in 1941, is an example of what I mean: At two the child went blind from bilateral chorioretinitis and double optic atrophy. At school age, he was accepted into the Institute for Blind Children in Arras because his medical records revealed total, incurable blindness.

Asking the intercessory prayers of Mary, whom Catholics revere as their greatest saint, in 1948 Gerard was taken to Lourdes, a Marian shrine in southwestern France.

"Just let him see enough for a normal life" had been his mother's prayer, she says, for years. On the second day at Lourdes, the eight-year-old and his mother were doing a holistic meditation outdoors, moving along a trail where statues represent Christ's redemptive acts. Suddenly the child, whose mother led him by the hand, bent over and picked up a piece of wood. Then looking up at his mother, his face broke into a smile, and he exclaimed, *"Ah, ma mere, que tu es belle!"* [Oh Mama, how beautiful you are!]

After years of destruction of the internal tissues of the eyes

24

and total atrophy of the optic nerves, Gerard could see again. Not perfectly but enough to easily permit "a normal life" and regular school. Tests verified this. Tests by various eye experts also show bilateral chorioretinitis and double optic atrophy. In other words, Gerard sees with eyes which, physiologically speaking, are blind.[34]

How do I explain this? I don't. Besides my wish not to bore either of us to death trying, picking the genuine supra-rational event to pieces by linear thought is useless: I can prove Gerard Baillie cannot see by flawless logical analysis.

But Gerard still sees.

In this book there will be other mystical events that rise phoenix-like from the ashes to which logic reduces them. These force recognition that there are realities which belong "to the abyss where science stops."[35] In those depths we can be profoundly affected—our lives even changed—by matters about which, to paraphrase a sigh of the Upanishads, words of analysis would only weary us.

notes

1. Michael Harner, *The Way of the Shaman,* p. xviii.

2. Gary Zukaw, *The Dancing Wu Li Masters,* p. 117.

3. Wallace has authored or co-authored articles on the physiological aspects of meditation in *Science* (1969), *American Journal of Physiology* (1971), and *Scientific American* (1972), among others. See an excellent overview of meditation's effects in Kenneth R. Pelletier's *Mind as Healer, Mind as Slayer.*

4. C. Maxwell Cade and Nona Coxhead, *The Awakened Mind,* pp. 203–18 for examples and 154–55.

5. *Los Angeles Times,* Dec. 27, 1981, Part VII, pp. 24–25.

6. The Redlands prayer experiments are detailed in the book on the subject, *Prayer Can Change Your Life,* by William R. Parker and Elaine St. Johns.

7. *Los Angeles Times,* Jan. 23, 1989, Part I, p. 2.

8. For a description of these experiments and their significance, see William Johnston's *Silent Music: The Science of Meditation,* pp. 28–29 and 37–41.

9. *Early Fathers from the Philokalia,* trans. from the Russian by E. Kadloubovsky and G. E. H. Palmer, p. 31.

10. Andre Louf, *Teach Us to Pray,* pp. 60–61.

11. In his foreword to Leo Schaya's *The Universal Meaning of the Kabbalah,* p. 4.

12. *Apophthegms,* Longinius, no. 5, quoted by Louf, op. cit., p. 62.

13. Living before the Catholic-Orthodox schism, he is regarded as a spiritual master by both. Quoted here by Louf, op. cit., p. 61.

14. Cade and Coxhead, op. cit., p. 97.

15. Louf, op. cit., p. 62.

16. Schaya, op. cit., p. 167.

17. See *The Hiding Place* by her sister Corrie ten Boom, who survived the camp.

18. She came forward to testify in favor of his 1985 beatification.

19. Cade and Coxhead, op. cit., pp. 7, 225.

20. Ibid. See case studies, pp. 208 and 211, for examples.

21. Ibid., p. 7. See previous note as well.

22. Ibid., p. 106.

23. Ibid., pp. 49, 226.

24. Ibid., p. 39.

25. Ibid., pp. 55–56.

26. Ibid., pp. 103–5, 107–8, 112.

27. Ibid., pp. 165, 201.

28. Ibid., pp. 49–50 and 7.

29. Ibid., pp. 7–12.

30. Ibid., p. 115.

31. Schaya, op. cit., p. 124.

32. In Peter-Thomas Rohrbach's *The Search for St. Therese,* p. 127.

33. Ibid., p. 128, quoting Gabriel of St. Mary Magdalen, "Present Norms of Holiness" in *Conflict and Light* (New York: Sheed and Ward, 1953), p. 167.

34. Officially documented at the Lourdes Medical Bureau (there are no religious criteria for physicians) and by his own physicians. The case is reported in several books, most recently Protestant Ruth Cranston's *The Miracle of Lourdes,* pp. 227–33.

35. Archaeologist Loren Eisely was quoted by *Baltimore Sun* editorial writer Richard H. Gilluly in an article titled "Body and Soul" which I clipped from the *Los Angeles Times* about 1978.

2

luminosity

In the summer of 1930 I found myself at Assisi, around the last of June or the first of July. At the Sacro Convento [of St. Francis] I ran into [a Franciscan] . . . a rather tall fellow with a beard, nice-looking. . . . Seeing that he wore a beard I imagined he was a missionary, something I had desired but which problems with my eyes had made impossible. I asked him if he worked in the missions and he replied affirmatively and introduced himself as Father Maximilian Kolbe.* He conversed with me about the Madonna. . . . Speaking . . . with great enthusiasm, he became, as I watched, transfigured in a diaphanous form, almost transparent, and surrounded by a halo of light, all

---

* After his death (never during his life), Kolbe was accused of anti-Semitism. See note p. 146 on this point.

of which lasted while he spoke. . . .† I found myself
trembling with a sort of fear, filled with confusion—so
moved that tears came to my eyes.[1]

Testimonies like this one on nineteenth- and twentieth-century holy people fill the following two chapters. In an age of
religious rationalism, occasional luminosity in the sanctified
body is embarrassingly well documented. Studiously ignored
in recent centuries, the phenomenon in earlier ages was often
called the halo. I do not adopt this term because it implies, to
most people, light only around the head. On those admittedly
rare occasions when bodily luminosity is visible to the naked
eye of one or more onlookers, testimonies show light often
surrounds a saint's entire body.

Bodily luminosity is related to the so-called Shekinah (from
Hebrew for glory) Light,[2] which appears to be a universally
accepted sign of God's presence. God's eternal state of glory,
so much easier to feel than define, makes English dictionaries,
like Hebrew ones, stumble toward words like "splendor" and
"radiance."

In religious traditions of every type, light is intimately associated with the divinity, God or divine messengers often appearing as light alone. In a study of shamanism, famed religious historian Mircea Eliade says so-called primitives "feel a
relationship between the condition of a supernatural being and
a superabundance of light." Eliade points out a Tatar people
who call their chief god "White Light," while for another shamanistic people, the Ostyak, "the celestial being's name has
the primitive meaning of "luminous, shining, light."[3]

Islam's mystics, the Sufis, too, have seen God as Light. In
their theology, in fact, it is from God as Light that Muham-

† Bruno Borgowiec, Auschwitz prisoner-interpreter in the penal block, saw the saint's
body immediately after his 1941 murder in the concentration camp and has left written testimony that the Polish mystic's corpse, too, "radiated light."

mad was created as the Primal Light existing before the first man and all other prophets.[4]

Hinduism's *Upanishads* speak of God's "transforming His white radiance into His many-colored creation."[5] And tales from Buddhism's saints contain references to divine light. Take, for instance, the tale of the sainted eighth-century Japanese Empress Komyo:

> Pious and humble, this lady vowed to wash the bodies of a thousand beggars; she had bathed nine hundred and ninety-nine when the last appeared before her as a loathsome leper. Without a sign of repugnance the Empress bathed him. When she had finished, a glory of light radiated from his body and he ascended heavenward.[6]

The Kabbalah of Judaism tells of creation rising out of God's "luminous fullness," the light of His "divine radiation" filling the cosmos.[7] Jewish prophet Ezekiel saw God (Ezekiel 1:4) as "a huge cloud with flashing fire enveloped in brightness. . . ." And in the middle of the eighteenth century, the founder of Polish Hasidism the "famous saint and mystic Israel Baal Shem"[8] (d. 1760), more commonly called simply the Baal Shem Tov ("Master of the Holy Name") saw the Shekinah at times.[9]

In 1899 Moslem and Christian Lebanese, from peasants to a regional official, kept reporting they saw a great light hovering over the communal grave where a white-bearded old Maronite-rite monk, a man his fellows considered "drunk with God," had been buried the previous Christmas Day. These incidents led to disinterrment of the body (unembalmed, uncoffined, and half-buried in mud, it was found incorrupt) and were the first of many mystical phenomena which led eventually to Charbel Makhlouf's canonization in 1977 as his rite's first official saint.[10]

Modern mystics still experience God in Shekinah light. A

nun, Sister Cairo, briefly shared a room with Mother Frances Cabrini (1850–1917) before the penniless young foundress of the Missionary Sisters of the Sacred Heart boldly came to the United States to build orphanages, hospitals, and schools on behalf of other equally impoverished Italian immigrants. Asleep in their shared room, Cairo woke in the middle of one night to find the lampless room flooded with light as Mother Cabrini prayed.

Awed, the suddenly wide-awake Cairo asked "Do you see that?"

"It's nothing. Go back to sleep" was her answer. But the next day Cabrini, who would become the first American citizen to be canonized by the Catholic Church in 1946, arranged things so that from then on she would pass her nights alone.[11]

Less reticent, Protestant healer-mystic Agnes Sanford (1897–1982) naively tells in her book *Creation Waits* how the unpainted shack where she prayed in New England "became so full of the light of the Lord" that her tiny grandson exclaimed "Who's in here?"[12] Agnes also recounts in her autobiography *Sealed Orders* how after she had given a conference to ministers outside Sydney, Australia:

> One of the ministers went back to the little chapel at the edge of the bush to take a snapshot. The altar was bare, the cross being high above it in the window. . . . There was no sunlight, no electric light in the chapel, and no flashlight on his camera. But the photograph showed a ball of gentle light softly gleaming in the center of the altar. When on my departure I showed this snapshot to a lady at the Sydney airport, she said simply, "Quite. I saw that light in the cathedral while you were lecturing."[13]

Malcolm Muggeridge has written of this light in the Home for the Dying run by Mother Teresa of Calcutta in that city and his BBC cameraman captured it, somewhat, on film.[14]

It appears that the presence of God as Light in our time is found in the environs of Mother Teresa, the bedroom of Frances Cabrini or the prayer shack of Agnes Sanford because of the holiness of such people. The light in the Sydney chapel, too, seems connected to Agnes—perhaps a divine seal of approval of her ministry. But the Shekinah light is also seen at times in circumstances which have nothing to do with saints. A couple I know well some years back were bathed in this light when on a retreat during a time of intense marital turmoil. The experience remains baffling to them, if oddly consoling. It did not make them compatible, they admit; yet somehow it inspired hope.

If the Shekinah appears where and to whom it will, including the non-holy, one may assert confidently that the non-holy do not *emit* light clearly—at times dazzlingly—visible to onlookers in ordinary states of consciousness and with no special psychic gifts. Only of those in the most intimate relationship to God may it be said, as the learned St. Bonaventure (1221–74) explained of St. Francis of Assisi, that "the extraordinary illumination [occasionally] around his body was witness to the wonderful light that shone within his soul."[15]

One of Islam's mystics, a Sufi named Najmoddin Kobra, who died the year Francis was born, linked such luminosity to purity of heart. He says: "When the circle of the face has become pure, it gives off light." This condition can eventually, he says, encompass the Sufi's entire body which, "submerged in purity" now, too, will emit light. Uniquely among mystics I am acquainted with, Kobra also says "the mystic has a feeling (by his awareness of the supra sensible) of flashing lights irradiating from his face" or "from his entire person."[16] While I see no reason this could not occur, this awareness of luminosity does not seem to be the norm.

The name of the Hindu saint Paramahansa Yogananda (1893–1952), often reporting his assessment of other spiritual figures from India, will appear so often in these pages that he may seem my "token Hindu." I refer to him because Yogananda is the only swami of whom I can say (1) I know him through his own writings in English, not writings about him by others or through translation and (2) I am personally familiar with the spiritual organization he founded. Neither during his lifetime nor since his death has there been any taint of opportunism or impropriety concerning either. Therefore, Yogananda is a figure I put before you with confidence that he was neither fraud nor nut. Even as a youth, he wanted to dedicate himself to the search for spiritual wisdom, but obeying his father, he graduated—barely, for he had no interest in worldly subjects—in 1914 from the University of Calcutta before becoming a Hindu monk. Three years later he founded his first school, where the spiritual would be presented as "the central fact of existence." As Swami Yogananda, he came to the United States in 1920. Throughout the country he packed auditoriums, as he made the spiritual legacy of Hinduism, minus its more parochial aspects, available to the West. The Self-Realization Fellowship he founded in California in 1925 (today it has spread to many areas of the world) tries to unite the essence of all faiths, especially Hinduism and Christianity in a universal way to spiritual growth. Orthodox Christians such as myself must say that, out of his Hindu background, Yogananda at times gave very unorthodox meanings indeed, to individual Christian scriptures and beliefs. Nevertheless this early ecumenist did achieve the universality of the true mystic as he proclaimed that God is love and calls all people to love through service to the human family. Christians, Jews, and non-believers have all joined Hindus in acclaiming his sanctity. In 1977 the government of India, issuing a stamp to mark the quarter-century anniversary of his death, called Yogananda one of India's "great saints" who followed the ideals of love for God and service to humanity. Yogananda knew the Shekinah Light from his visions. And Yogananda writes in his *Autobiography* of nineteenth- or twentieth-century Hindu saints such as Lahiri Mahasaya (1828–95) and others I will mention in later chapters who were at times seen "haloed by glorious light."[17] Hinduism's term for this spiritual luminosity is Brahmic Splendor.

The earliest Western example of bodily luminosity comes from Judaism. Chosen by God for one of the human family's most extraordinary destinies, Moses personally received the Ten Commandments from Jahweh "face to face" on Mount Sinai. The Torah (Exodus 34:29–35) says:

> As Moses came down from Mount Sinai with two tablets of the commandments in his hands, he did not know that the skin of his face had become radiant while he conversed with the Lord. When Aaron, then, and the other Israelites saw Moses and noticed how radiant the skin of his face had become, they were afraid to come near him. Only after Moses called to them did Aaron and all the rulers of the community come back to him. Moses then spoke to them. Later on, all the Israelites came up to him, and he enjoined on them all that the Lord had told him on Mount Sinai. When he finished speaking with them, he put a veil over his face. Whenever Moses entered the presence of the Lord to converse with him, he removed the veil until he came out again. On coming out, he would tell the Israelites all that had been commanded. Then the Israelites would see that the skin of Moses' face was radiant; so he would again put the veil over his face.

Scholar-writer Yaffa Eliach tells me the luminosity which marks "a person of great spiritual distinction"—a term she prefers to saint—in Judaism is termed Meor Panim (literally "lighted face").‡ Shmuel Joseph Agnon, winner of the Nobel Prize for Literature, has spoken of this phenomenon in a twentieth-century Israeli mystic. Agnon said of modern Palestine's first Chief Rabbi, Abraham Isaac Kook that he had "a face shining, translucent with goodness."[18]

For Christians the best-known example of luminosity is the incident in Jesus' life called the Transfiguration (Matthew 17:1–2):

> Jesus took Peter, James and his brother John and led them up on a high mountain by themselves. He was transfigured before their eyes. His face became as dazzling as the sun, his clothes as radiant as light.

Added to this report were those like the one (Acts 6:15) of the earliest Christian martyr, a man known for his holiness named Stephen, that his face was that "of an angel."

Did the halos drawn around saints' heads for centuries in Western art originate from personal testimonies by those who had seen saints luminous? Were they originally non-verbal testimony to the reality of this mystical phenomenon?

Possibly. Stephen is only one of many saints of various traditions who die, illumined, in ecstasy. Obviously this is usually a very private moment with only intimates in attendance. However, during Christianity's first three hundred years, many Christians were tortured and killed publicly. Some of these individuals, like Stephen, went to their deaths in ecstasy, their observable radiant joy, in Morton Kelsey's words, arousing "the wonder . . . of those who saw them die."[19] From

‡ There are many references to this in the tales told of the eighteenth-century Baal Shem Tov, See Dan Ben-Amos and Jerome R. Mintz, *In Praise of the Baal Shem Tov,* pp 28, 30, 50, 79, 136, 243.)

radiant martyrs and transfigured saints *could have come*—obviously I conjecture—the halo in western art.

If the first nimbus was drawn as a way to represent luminosity, this literal depiction must have ended rather early. This could have occurred over the years following the conversion to Christianity of the Roman emperor Constantine (288–337), when whole tribes and peoples were commandeered into the Christian faith on the grounds that as the king believes so must the people.* Many new "converts" knew little of Christian spirituality, especially in areas where few could read. How easy for such people to see several tiled or painted representations of Christ or saints with aureoles and conclude the halo was the way artists indicated holiness. With public martyrdom ended, few individuals would ever catch a saint in those generally private rapturous moments when illumination occurs. At some point, the assumption that the halo in art stands for sanctity, not luminosity, would become correct. Today certainly, if there ever was a literal meaning, no hint of it remains.

▲

Still, in the past hundred years evidence that the human body has the potential, at least under certain conditions, to emit light has been piling up. For some it may be reassuring that the evidence has been primarily offered by groups and individuals who have nothing to do with studying or proclaiming saints.

South American Jivaro shamans told anthropologist-shaman Dr. Michael Harner that in a drug-induced trance state, they perceive light being emitted by fellow shamans in the same ecstatic state. This luminosity is noticeable, they say,

---

* Previously, to join the new religion meant investing three years in spiritual preparation (such people were called catechumens) before being allowed full membership. Obviously the new situation, for a long time, greatly lowered the overall level of spirituality, as it must wherever a religious tradition is forced upon people. To this day there are unfortunate legacies in areas of the world from these forced, often politically motivated conversions, whether to Catholicism, Protestantism or Islam.

particularly in a "crown" from the head. In his book *The Way of the Shaman,* Dr. Harner reproduces the drawing of "a golden halo around the head of a Jivaro shaman in an altered state of consciousness drawn by another Jivaro shaman."[20] So to the Jivaro, then, their most advanced members, the shamans, have the potential to emit light in psychically exalted circumstances.

In the nineteenth century, perhaps as a reaction to the efforts of Materialism and dispensationalism† to eliminate "non-rational elements" from Western spirituality, trying to contact the dead through seances, or Spiritualism, became popular. Spiritualism led to investigatory bodies, such as the Society for Psychical Research in England in which the boldest men of science and religion (Arthur Conan Doyle and England's Cardinal Manning were two) joined hands, however gingerly, that had not met for two centuries. Open to the possibility that supra-rational, nonmaterial things might be real, these researchers were told by people with psychic gifts that everyone is surrounded by "a colorful emanation," an outline of light in shifting intensities that the speakers variously termed the aura, vital field, energy field, etc. Invisible to the ordinary eye, the aura could be seen, they said, by psychically gifted individuals like themselves.

An aside about people with psychic gifts, because psychics have been confused with mystics: Like good coordination or an eye for color, inborn psychic abilities are a spiritually neutral gift that may be used for good or ill and may belong to a saint, a fine, a mediocre, or a thoroughly messed-up person. As longtime psychic-researcher, magician, and Episcopal priest William V. Rauscher points out, someone "can be psychic but not necessarily spiritual or even ethical."[21]

---

† The tenet of certain Christian groups that miracles and mystical phenomena were given to the early church "to get it started," that is as a special dispensation, but cannot occur today.

How can mysticism, the state of human spiritual development where an individual moves increasingly into union with the divine by dying to egotism, be confused with innate psychic ability? It happens because con artists at times get away with dubbing themselves "psychics," then faking what they call "mystical phenomena" (former Spiritualist minister M. Lamar Keene exposes some of these tricks in his autobiographical *The Psychic Mafia*). The distinction is also clouded by one fact of spiritual development: As individuals grow spiritually, at a certain level they begin to show psychic abilities *as a side-effect*.[22] In great saints the sanctified mind regularly evidences clairvoyance, telepathy, etc., a situation quite different from—but easily confused with—common psychic abilities.‡ I can only reiterate that psychic is *not* a synonym for mystic.

To return to the aura, while it was immediately debunked as pseudo-scientific nonsense by many, this was probably less because it was implausible and more because of the intellectually suspect people who touted it. A few scientific researchers, however, brought to the world's attention by Sheila Ostrander and Lynn Schroeder (whose two books on psychic researches[23] are my sources for the next five examples) took the idea seriously. One was Englishman Dr. Walter Kilner of St. Thomas Hospital in London. Early in the twentieth century, Dr. Kilner attempted to find this human light emanation systematically. "Using glass screens stained with dicyanin dye," he believed he perceived "a colorful area of radiation about six to eight inches around the human body." He agreed with psychics that this aura was "affected by disease, mood, hypnosis, and other factors."[24]

‡ A major difference is the greater reliability of the saint's gifts than the psychic's. As early investigator Sir Oliver Lodge maintained and University of Southern California (UCLA) studies have seconded, the innate psychic gift is fragile, its reliability varying with factors such as an individual's energy level. In those who sell their services or gain prestige by their psychic utterances, conscious or unconscious padding or plain fraud is common, according to Lodge and others. My in-progress work *The Sanctified Mind* explores the mental phenomena of sanctity.

Then in the 1930s in Russia, scientist Alexander Gurvich announced experiments showing that living things generated energy or light, although this could be seen only from its effects.[25]

Thirty years later a second Russian at Moscow University had better equipment. By using highly sensitive light amplifiers (photoelectronic multipliers) used to track stars by astronomers, biophysicist Boris Tarusov found extremely faint rays of light emanating from plants, animals, and even, in infinitely tiny rays, from single cells.

Further studies in 1972 with plants showed the rays varied according to an organism's condition, revealing illness before the plant showed "any physical sign."[26]

Even work on heat convection currents surrounding the human body revealed a "pulsing envelope of warm air from one to three inches thick" which shows up as a halo on photographic plates, using a nineteenth-century German technique known as Schlieren photography.[27]

Most telling of all was work with another specialized type of photography. Called Kirlian photography (after the Russian couple Valentina and Semyon Kirlian who invented it), this technique enabled researchers for the first time to place individuals in a high-frequency electric field and effectively photograph energy as it emanates from the human body. This force field found around people (and all living things) again corresponded to what psychics termed the aura. Again, it increased or decreased according to the physical condition, emotions, and other variables. If, for instance, a leaf was plucked and photographed at intervals, the brilliant and colorful emanations gradually decreased until they faded out entirely as the leaf withered and died.[28] And individuals who can heal or relieve pain in others by laying hands on them have been photographed at UCLA and elsewhere showing the normal emanation from their hands increases during healing activity.[29]

Shamans, investigators of Spiritualism, psychics, and scientific researchers in England, Russia, Germany, and the United States—none can be accused of trying to prove that saints can be luminous. And those who study saints do so to examine holiness, not the phenomena which may accompany it. But observers of saints, too, have amassed much evidence of the human body's capacity to emit light. Speaking for the many witnesses over the centuries whose under-oath testimonies to the Congregation for the Causes of Saints tell of halos of light, Cardinal Lambertini* (1675–1758) wrote in *De servorum Dei beatificatione et beatorum canonizatione,* still the most authoritative Catholic work on the bodily phenomena associated with sanctity:

> It seems to be a fact that there are natural flames which at times visibly encircle the human head, and also that from a man's whole person fire may on occasion radiate naturally, not, however, like a flame which streams upward, but rather in the form of sparks which are given off all round; further, that some people are resplendent with a blaze of light.[30]

Can the invisible-to-the-ordinary-human-eye aura posited by many offer a physiological explanation for the visible emanations at times associated with saints? I believe it can. Purely as a theory, mind you.

To back up for a moment, research I mentioned and other studies—which limited space forces passing over—generally agree that (1) the human body, like all living things, emits an energy or light; (2) this pulsating sheath changes with such conditions as health, energy levels, emotions, etc.; and (3) it is usually invisible to the unassisted human eye.

Assuming for the moment these assertions are correct, luminosity in the sanctified body becomes only an intensification of

* Afterward Pope Benedict XIV.

a physiological characteristic of all living things—the saint at the outer limits, in this too, of human potential.

Those who claim to see auras report they are composed of one or many colors, which again vary with conditions. Anger or other negative emotions are said to muddy the aura's colors. It would seem appropriate that the luminosity of the holy is always reported as the opposite: clear or white light.

A possible key to how ordinarily unseen auras of the unsanctified body might become the visible luminosity of the sanctified I found unexpectedly in a statement of psychics studied by another medical investigator, Shafica Karagulla, M.D. Dr. Karagulla's subjects divided the aura into three energy fields, which is unimportant for our purposes. Then they declared: When an individual comes into the presence of a well-beloved person, all three of his energy fields are intensely brightened; the entire aura becomes "scintillating and bright."[31]

Not all saints become luminous.† And those who do are certainly not luminous all the time. The sanctified body bursts into light only in moments of ecstasy or rapture.‡ And what are ecstasy and rapture but encounters of the most passionate kind with the one the saint loves above all?

If linking the aura with the luminosity of the sanctified body for a theory that there is a physiological explanation for luminosity offends you, you can think of the phenomenon of luminosity another way. Suppose a sponge is dropped into water. Each remains a separate entity but the sponge is saturated with water. Squeezed, it emits water. Similarly, a saint is one who is in union with God, that is, saturated with the one who

---

† As far as we can tell, anyway: see the incident (pp. 37–38) involving Mother Cabrini for an indication of how a saint's private moments usually elude our observation.

‡ The explicit tie of luminosity to rapture is not limited to Christian tradition. For instance, it is said of the Baal Shem Tov that he was "in such great rapture that his face glowed" as he immersed himself in a mystical commentary on the Torah [Dan Ben-Amos and Jerome R. Mintz, *In Praise of the Baal Shem Tov*, p. 79].

in all traditions is somehow Light. Consider a rapture a gentle squeeze and you have another way of describing luminosity.

There is also another position, my own, which says simply that even if the idea of the aura is one day disproven, the fact remains indisputable that people can glow with happiness. So it seems physiologically sound to propose that the ecstatic sanctified body, rapt in communion with the divine who is perceived as Light by almost every tradition, at times goes further and shines in a more striking fashion.

▲

Whichever idea one finds attractive for explaining the luminosity of the sanctified body, there appears a spectrum when we examine our human family. At one end, if we assume auras exist, are all of us whose emanations are visible only to gifted individuals or through special aids such as Kirlian photography. Then there are individuals who momentarily glow out of love: The "radiant" brides and "beaming" grooms of small-town wedding reports certainly exist. Rarer are the instances where to onlookers very good people may appear more or less radiant when praying in church, synagogue, or ashram. Finally come the bursts of radiance of those who are not just good but saints. These illuminations may range from a gentle glow suffusing the face to dazzling brightness that fills a room.

Here the spectrum ends, for it is untrue that the greater the luminosity, the holier the saint. As I said earlier some bodies are more resistant to the physiological effects of rapture. And for another thing, saints are only too prone to beg God to diminish anything that they find is making them noticeable. Finally, God's ways are not so easy to sort out.

It is also a fact that in a group of onlookers, some people will see light around a saint while others will not. There appears to be no correlation whatsoever between belief or lack of belief, spiritual maturity or lack of it, and such sightings. They are as apt to occur to a person with no interest or belief in such things as to anyone else. To go back for a moment to the stoning of Stephen, the saint's ecstatically luminous face—that of an angel, scripture says—did not stop the people who believed they were righting an outrage to God from stoning him. I conclude that the onlooking Jewish Christians saw Stephen's luminosity, the devout people stoning him did not.

I can testify to a modern example of the same strange disparity myself. Some years ago I attended a lecture at a Protestant church near my home. The speaker, in modern ecumenical fashion, turned out to be a Jesuit, Father Ralph Tichenor (1908–83), a man I had never seen and knew nothing about.

Having seen him a number of times after that night, I can say the old Jesuit's face was usually beaming with love and goodwill. However this night as I listened to his simple talk (I recall particularly the joy with which this college professor spoke of being willing to be accounted a fool for Christ), I saw more. Father Tichenor was suffused by a yellowish-white light which streamed out to me. The light was warm and sweet (I know light cannot be sweet but it was). As this light touched me, I said to myself, "I'm being healed."

The lecture over, I felt I should thank the speaker in spite of the fact I had no idea what had been healed. But as he was surrounded by people, embarrassment overcame a strong sense of gratitude, and I went home without a word (months later when I did have a chance to rush up to him in a corridor at Loyola Marymount University and thank him, he murmured something about the goodness of God, showing not the slightest curiosity to know where, when, or of what I had been healed).*

A few weeks earlier I had been rushed by ambulance to the emergency hospital with what was apparently a gallbladder

---

* This lack of ego—giving all credit to God and seeking no details that might give one any impetus toward self-congratulation—is typical of the holy.

attack, according to the attending physician (no x-ray was taken once it was decided I was not undergoing a heart attack). For a long period I had suffered more and more misery with chest pains and abdominal pain following eating or even bending over. I soon learned my mother's family is full of people whose gallbladders have been removed. My internist's diagnosis was hiatus hernia. Almost every one of my living relatives have that condition as well. Whether gallbladder or hernia, I had a problem. For instance, gardening was out, for if I stooped or squatted my abdomen immediately bloated and pains stabbed my chest.

Until my experience with the luminous priest. After that night, it was back to pulling weeds with vigor.

The experience had intimate spiritual benefits as well.

Yet when I asked others who were present that night for their impressions of the sweet streams of light, I was shocked to find only one other person had seen anything at all.

Although I am not a rationalist, I find some mystical phenomena too much to believe. Because of Father Ralph Tichenor, luminosity is never a problem.

notes

1. Testimony of Ricardo Bandini in 1951, found in *Posito super virtutibus,* Rome, 1966, Vol. 2, pp. 268–69.

2. A Christian source is *The Interpreter's Dictionary of the Bible,* Vol. 4, pp. 317–19. A Jewish explanation of the term "Shekinah" will be found in *The Universal Meaning of the Kabbalah* by Leo Schaya. See particularly p. 21. The Shekinah is often identified with the spirit of God, according to Arnold J. Band, professor of Hebrew and comparative literature at UCLA.

3. Mircea Eliade, *Shamanism: Archaic Techniques of Ecstasy,* p. 9.

4. Fazlur Rahman, *Islam,* p. 142.

5. *The Upanishads,* translations from the Sanskrit, p. 91.

6. Told in Oliver Statler's *Japanese Pilgrimage,* p. 121.

7. Schaya, op. cit., pp. 67–68. See also pp. 79, 163.

8. Gershom G. Scholem, *Major Trends in Jewish Mysticism,* p. 325.

9. See one incident cited in Dan Ben-Amos and Jerome R. Mintz, *In Praise of the Baal Shem Tov,* pp. 45–46.

10. Information furnished by the Monastery of St. Maron, Annaya, Lebanon. See their French-language biography *Charbel* by Père Paul Daher, pp. 9, 13–14.

11. Saverio De Maria, *Mother Frances Xavier Cabrini,* p. 173. This account, authenticated by the Order, is by one of the saint's close companions.

12. Agnes Sanford, *Creation Waits,* p. 22.

13. Agnes Sanford, *Sealed Orders,* p. 252.

14. Malcolm Muggeridge, *Something Beautiful for God,* pp. 41, 44–46.

15. Bonaventure's *The Life of St. Francis,* p. 275.

16. Laleh Bakhtiar, *Sufi,* p. 117.

17. Paramahansa Yogananda, *Autobiography of a Yogi,* p. 374.

18. Quoted in Herbert Weiner's *9 1/2 Mystics,* pp. 328–29.

19. Morton Kelsey, *Healing and Christianity,* p. 132.

20. Michael Harner, *The Way of the Shaman,* p. 29.

21. William V. Rauscher, "The Mystical and the Psychical," from *Frontiers of the Spirit,* pp. 16, 20.

22. Research using electroencephalographs to measure the brain waves of various states of consciousness appears to correlate with this observation of authorities on mysticism. See *The Awakened Mind,* C. Maxwell Cade and Nona Coxhead.

23. Sheila Ostrander and Lynn Schroeder, *Handbook for PSI Discoveries* and *Psychic Discoveries Behind the Iron Curtain.*

24. See Walter Kilner's *The Human Aura,* reissued in 1965, University Books, New Jersey.

25. Ostrander and Schroeder, *Psychic Discoveries Behind the Iron Curtain,* pp. 411–12.

26. Ostrander and Schroeder, *Handbook of Psi Discoveries,* p. 93.

27. Ibid., p. 133.

28. *Psychic Discoveries Behind the Iron Curtain,* pp. 200–13.

29. Peter Tompkins and Christopher Bird, *The Secret Life of Plants,* p. 223.

30. Prospero Lambertini (Pope Benedict XIV), *De* [servorum Dei] *beatificatione et* [beatorum] *canonizatione,* Book 4, Part I, ch. 26, n. 21, quoted by Herbert Thurston, S.J., in *The Physical Phenomena of Mysticism,* p. 163.

31. Shafica Karagulla, *Breakthrough to Creativity,* p. 159.

3

word pictures

Luminosity is the part of the movement of love constantly streaming between saint and God that occasionally bursts into visible fire, like lava from time to time bubbling over the side of its volcanic cauldron. In the most intimate rapturous moments of their love affair with God, many saints become luminous, at least to some degree. Luminosity, then, is one of the commonest bodily mystical phenomena.

You can check this out in a sampling of saint's biographies. Even if you wisely confine yourself to books which aim to portray a real, struggling human being in order to avoid any pious excess, you will almost invariably find reports like this one from a twentieth-century, highly uncolored biography of the nineteenth-century mystic St. Peter Eymard:

> They could never forget Father Eymard's reverence when he knelt in adoration at the foot of the altar. His

ascetic features appeared luminous; a certain heavenly something suffused his whole person. . . . He was so transfigured that he seemed no longer of earth.[1]

or descriptions like this from the well-researched, authoritative work on St. Jeanne Thouret (1765–1826):

She used to pray with such fervour that she was so to say absorbed in God. All her senses, both external and internal seemed suspended, and her face took on a radiant beauty.[2]

Even the account of Mother Cabrini (p. 46, note 11), written without any sensationalism by one early associate, contains at least half a dozen discreet references to times when this spiritual pioneer of social justice "became surrounded with a gleaming splendor, which was the projected reflection of that supernatural love which shone in her soul more purely than the clearest crystal."[3]

A visual phenomenon, luminosity cries out for film or photograph of enraptured saints. Yet prayer of this type by its very nature rarely takes place where there are many witnesses, and never poses for its portrait. Even though we are dealing with nineteenth- and twentieth-century figures, I can offer you only word pictures.

Picking up the idea of a spectrum from the previous chapter, the beginning accounts will be those of the lowest possible level that can be associated with luminosity. Since the face of a young girl asked to her first prom may elicit the same description as the physical evidence of prayer in these lower degrees, you may exclaim, "Is this all?"

Granted if you are looking for something clearly inexplicable, requiring suspension of cause and effect relationship, you will find these first descriptions woefully lacking. Even then you might consider that one may feel quite differently *seeing* what words like "radiant" and "aglow" attempt to describe. If however you can accept, however tentatively, a physiology of the sanctified body which, while it can stretch into the miraculous, much of the time is merely the outer limit of human potential, that is, a supra-development of innate human capabilities, then these initial low-level examples, banal as they can sound, in the context of a saint's life and holiness become important.

Their low level of luminosity, in fact, is their value, showing that as the bride's radiance comes from her happiness, so illumination is usually a natural physiological reaction to joy in God, culminating at its heights in the immeasurable bliss of spiritual rapture.

As the chapter moves into the more striking cases of luminosity (do not confuse this with any ranking of sanctity), the reader will see the first use of words indicative of the extraordinary, like "transfigured" and "supernatural." I offer no guarantee, of course, that every user means precisely the same by such words; some sincere witnesses, even testifying under oath as many are, tend temperamentally to overstatement, just as others are prone to understatement.

Further, at the levels of luminosity where we are dealing with the full-blown phenomenon of the sanctified body, to the emitted radiance of the ecstatic saint in union with the divine may be added the nonphysiological, that is, exterior, Shekinah Light. As I said at the opening of this chapter, luminosity is part of the movement of love that at a certain level of holiness constantly streams between saint and God and in some, occasionally bursts into rapture. Sometimes witnesses (see p. 66 for an excellent example) cannot tell whether the saint is emitting light or is bathed in it.

In looking at luminosity—or any phenomenon of the sanctified body—by itself, we are doing something artificial. As Sir Julian Huxley says:

> Though for certain limited purposes it may be useful to
> think of phenomena as isolated statically . . . , they are
> in point of fact never static: they are always processes or
> parts of processes.

All mystical phenomena are part of the ongoing process of a
particular individual's ever-developing* spirituality. To help
keep this in perspective, the first time I refer to any saint who
has more than the most passing role in this book, I try to
sketch enough of his or her life and charisms to situate whatever phenomenon is under discussion in the only picture where
it has its true meaning—in the panorama of a life and holiness.
(As these biographical details cannot be repeated each time the
mystic's name comes up, highlighted entries in the index at the
back of the book indicate these pages for easy referral.)

▲

Daughter of a wealthy and illustrious Italian family, Teresa
Valsé-Pantellini turned her back on a life of pleasure and ease
to become a nun. Further, instead of joining an upper-class
order that would value her fine education and many gifts, she
entered an order that had been founded by an illiterate† barely
a quarter of a century earlier. The Daughters of Mary Help of
Christians consisted almost entirely of peasants and spent itself
for the sort of people Teresa's class barely knew existed. After
heroic labor in one of Rome's worst slums, still only in her
twenties, Sister Teresa died of tuberculosis in 1907. Her Cause
was introduced in 1944.

Exceptionally humble—her life's motto, revealed reluctantly on her deathbed, was *to pass unnoticed*—Teresa tried
never to appear extraordinary; nevertheless, she had been

---

* Even saints, it appears, must go forward or begin to shrink spiritually.
† St. Maria Mazzarello, guided by St. John Bosco, founded the order as the feminine
arm of the Salesian religious family in 1872.

drawn from her early years to God above all else. When she was only a teenage student and no one suspected she hoped to become a nun, her older cousin and his wife visited Teresa at her upper-class boarding school, the Sacred Heart College at Poggio Imperiale. It was December 8, 1895—for Catholics, the Feast of the Immaculate Conception. The schoolgirls were having a procession to celebrate Mary's conception in her mother's womb free of original sin so that she might fittingly one day become the mother of Christ.

> The visiting cousin glanced around for his cousin and was profoundly impressed by her facial expression and the angelic attitude of her entire person. Teresa was holding a lily in her hand and seemed to be in such close union with God that she appeared radiant, even though by nature she was always very pale.[4]

Only twelve years later, her life's work accomplished, she lay dying. Longing to see God, the young mystic moved toward the next life by choice. The dead co-founder of her order, St. John Bosco, then not yet canonized, had appeared to her three months earlier to offer a cure. She sent him, instead, into the next room of the infirmary, where Sister Giovanna Lenci (ill for ten years) saw the dead man, was cured on the spot, and got up to work for another thirty years without recurrence of her illness.

Now the nuns praying by Teresa's bedside noted that, even exhausted and physically suffering, she exuded the serenity of the mature mystic. Almost lifeless, suddenly her emaciated face lit up and in a resonant voice she repeated three times, "Paradise!"

> Her face [was] heavenly. Those who were present felt as if they had been electrified. Their whole attention was

fixed on that face which *seemed to be illuminated from within* [italics mine].[5]

Shortly after this rapture in which she saw Jesus, Don‡ Bosco, and the Virgin Mary "waiting" for her, Teresa died like a child going to sleep.

▲

"I felt myself in another world . . . saw myself in the centre, as it were, of an immense globe of fire,"[6] wrote Jacob Libermann (1802–52), a young Jew from Alsace, of the moments of his baptism as a Catholic on Christmas morning, 1826, in Paris. Without writing home, the newly named Francis Paul Mary Libermann entered St. Sulpice seminary to study for the priesthood. There one day he was handed a letter from his father, a rabbi. The poor man had just discovered that this son on whom he had pinned so many hopes to follow —only more brilliantly—in his footsteps was no longer pursuing the rabbinical studies that had brought him to Paris but had become a Christian. It was not an age of Christian-Jewish understanding. The heartbroken father's words, bitter and excoriating, seared his son, who, like youths immemorial, had given no real thought to the effect of his actions on his family. Young Libermann came face to face with that reality now. He suddenly saw what he had done to his father and shared something of the older Libermann's agony. Shortly after this emotionally rending incident, the young man suffered his first epileptic seizure.

The attending physician, who usually found dealing with a newly diagnosed epileptic's mental state as much of a task as treating the disease, was struck by Libermann's psychospiritual equilibrium.[7] In an attitude we ordinary folk cannot readily grasp—and which undoubtedly owes much to his roots

‡ The Italian title of respect given to priests.

54

in Judaic spirituality as well as to his new Christian faith—Libermann called his illness "a great treasure,"[8] since God, in his view, had permitted (if not sent) it to confirm him in a life of the lowliest sort of poverty and devotion, for he was now barred from the priesthood and vowed to follow no secular profession.

Out of pity he was kept on at the seminary as a kind of handyman. It was soon noticed that the seminarians sought him out for counsel and whispered among themselves, "The little Jew is a saint."[9] One of them later recalled that being around Francis Libermann led to catching "the holy contagion of virtue." The seminarian in charge of assigning chapel adoration times always paired his own name with the epileptic's. He described Francis in prayer before the tabernacle as having "a face on fire."[10] There is also a testimony that one day while Libermann was serving at mass in the humble position of altar boy a "flame [likely the exterior Shekinah Light] was observed over his head"[11] by some in the congregation.

Seeking God alone, fourteen years later things worked out so the mystic was not only ordained but founded an order of missionary priests in his following final decade. August Schwindenharmmaer, a member of the new congregation not given to flights of fancy, was present at Francis' death. He wrote a letter to Jacques Laval (pp. 115–19) and the other far-flung men who counted Libermann a spiritual father describing how at the end the mystic was in a state in which "his eyes really glowed with life" and "he appeared to be listening to someone and hearing celestial harmonies that swept him up in ecstasy." "His face drawn by suffering and the approach of death," says the observer, "assumed such an expression of indescribable love and tenderness that it almost seemed to be radiating shafts of light."[12]

▲

St. Therese of Lisieux (1873–97) is the type of saint understood universally. Like the Hindu who spends years in the
lotus posture on the inner quest or the Orthodox Jew whose
life's work is done under a prayer shawl or hunched over the
Torah, Therese did not found orders, build hospitals, or heal
the sick. Rather than doing big things, she became enlarged
herself by doing small things heroically without notice or applause.*

Her gifts to God were things like never complaining about
the convent food and never complaining about her reward for
not complaining which was to be regularly stuck with all the
old, dried-up stuff no one else would eat.

The youngest child of a husband and wife who are both
candidates themselves for beatification and canonization, Therese confided she never wanted any extraordinary phenomena
in her life.[13] It was after her death, she said, that she planned
to go about doing good until the end of the world. And it is
after her death, not in her lifetime, that the miracles and extraordinary phenomena began.

But there are a few testimonies of low-level luminosity. In
the testimonies given under oath of the Process for Beatification are reports by those present when the spiritually precocious eleven-year-old made her First Communion. The second
oldest of her four sisters said Therese looked "like a seraph" or
"like someone who no longer lived on this earth." Struggling
to express herself, she insists, "I have seen a great many devout young girls on their First Communion day but this was
something different."[14] Another sister seconded this testimony,
remarking, "I thought I was looking at an angel rather than a
mortal creature."[15] The two much older sisters of the five Martin daughters also recalled how a year before that day Therese
had suffered a mysterious illness which was suddenly cured

---

* When Therese died at age twenty-four of tuberculosis, another Carmelite remarked,
"Whatever will we find to put in her obituary?"

when the ten-year-old went into "radiant" ecstasy and had a vision of the Virgin Mary.[16]

Later there was the young man who saw the pretty, blonde teenager walking with her father. "Look at Miss Martin," the young man cried, "she's like an angel!" Then he made the strange prediction that she would be canonized some day,[17] which makes clear that he did not mean "angel" in the simple sense of appreciating Therese's good looks. A shy and sheltered youngest daughter of the French bourgeoisie, Therese did not know any young man well enough for him to predict her canonization. Indeed I think it would not be far off the mark to say she did not know any young men, period. Nor were there rumors circulating about her sanctity. Those clustered about her father, Louis Martin, after the early death of her mother. If the townspeople noticed Therese at all, it was only as the pretty child who made such a sentimental picture accompanying the much-loved white-haired widower on his afternoon stroll.

It seems to me that the young observer's cry that Therese looked like an angel, followed by his strange prophecy, may indicate he saw about her a luminosity similar to that I saw around the Jesuit (see pp. 44–45). My conclusion may certainly be incorrect, however, so let us pass on to an instance which is clearer.

In 1888, when she was fifteen years and three months old, by a hard-won and much-criticized special dispensation, this spiritual genius entered the austere order of contemplative nuns known as the Carmelites, whose work is to pray and sacrifice for their church, the human family, and the world. Another novice later testified that when they were cleaning the chapel together, Therese knelt before the tabernacle, rapped on its door, and said, "Are you there, Jesus? I beg you to speak to me?" Then she put her head against the tabernacle for a few moments. When she came away, her companion testified, "her face was transfigured and shining with joy."[18]

Finally, there is the incident which took place in 1895 when Therese had become a full-fledged Carmelite of such mettle that, at age twenty-two, she was in charge of the spiritual formation of all novices. In the strength of her extraordinary love for God, she wished to make a special sacrifice of herself for others. To weed out motives of masochism or spiritual pride, permission for this sort of thing is required among Carmelites. Therese went to the convent prioress, who happened at that time to be her older sister, Pauline. In Pauline's testimony, "When she asked me this, her face was all lit up, as if she was on fire with love."[19]

▲

In the Italian-language chronicles of the Congregation of the Most Precious Blood there are descriptions of some of the frequent raptures and ecstasies of their founder St. Gaspar del Bufalo. Known throughout his lifetime as a miracle worker who healed, levitated, and bilocated, Gaspar in some of his rapturous states was *"tutto infiammato nel volto*[20] [all afire in the face]." Testimonies also mention the characteristic ardor with which, his face shining, he preached missions in areas where, in the nineteenth century, the Christian faith had practically died out until his arrival. Like so many saints, he seems to have also died in a state of ecstasy. St. Vincent Pallotti (d. 1850), present at Gaspar's deathbed, wrote that the dying man's face "shone"† with such sweetness and peace "it awakened a desire for death," and that Gaspar died "as if immersed in the joys of Paradise."[21]

▲

Teresa, Francis, Therese, even St. Gaspar del Bufalo, are in no way extraordinary manifestations of luminosity but display the

---

† *"Nel suo volto risplendeva tale dolcezza, ilarita e tali segnali di pace."*

low-level variety that links more spectacular illuminations to the natural flush of human happiness. With the next anecdote, however, we come closer to luminosity of a higher type. Notice the witness's use of the word "supernatural," which has not appeared in any description so far.

Venerable Vincent Morelli (d. 1812) was archbishop of Otranto. His secretary Clement Boccardi testified:

> When I was with the Servant of God during a visitation of the diocese in the Castignano dei Greci'im house of the deceased Mr. Antonius Marini, I looked one morning into the Servant of God's bedroom, which contrary to his usual ways, he had not left yet. I observed the room illuminated with a radiance which to me appeared to be neither candle nor daylight—especially not candlelight owing to my observation in the course of the night that no candle had been lit because I slept in the adjoining room. The scene held a surprise for me, but I kept my counsel and reflected whether *the light emanating from his person*‡ might not be of a supernatural nature. Presently I was approached by the master of the house, and told that he had looked through a keyhole of another door, and had observed the Servant of God on his knees surrounded by light. This convinced me that the illumination which I had seen in the room had not been due to the light of day or candlelight, nor some other natural source but *to a supernatural action.* The master of the house was a prudent man, highly esteemed for his moral rectitude, possessed of a capacity for clear judgment.[22]

The Franciscan evangelist Blessed Leopold of Gaiche (near Perugia, Italy) was known for his preaching and his gifts as a

‡ Italics mine.

confessor. He died in Spoleto on February 4, 1815. Among the testimonies given under oath before his beatification is this by a fellow Franciscan, Father Pacificus of Assisi:

One night a lay brother, Damian from Appignano, who has since died, happened to be in the church. Next morning he told me that during the night he had observed the venerable Servant of God Father Leopold at prayer in the church surrounded by Light. . . . I wanted to observe the nature of the incident the Brother had described to me. Consequently I went to the church [that night] before the arrival of the Servant of God, Father Leopold and, in order to remain unobserved, I seated myself in a confessional. This confessional was located in the back at the rear portion of the church, giving me an excellent view of whatever transpired.

Approximately an hour after I had taken my seat in the confessional, the venerable Servant of God entered the church, went down on his knees before the Blessed Sacrament and began to pray. I was able to observe this quite well because the Sanctuary light lit up the tabernacle. I watched the Servant of God, after his absorption in prayer for approximately an hour. With arms outstretched, face turned toward the Blessed Sacrament, he was irradiated with Light which filled the entire church. This illumination had a radiance something like that of a full moon. I observed that it could not have emanated from the Sanctuary light as that had already been there but had not radiated such an unusual brightness, nor did it so afterwards when the [other] glow faded away. Neither could it have been the light of the moon, as it was dark outside and one could no longer see the radiance in the church after that marvel had ceased. At the same time, I had the positive assurance that this extraordinary Light could not possibly have been a figment of my imagination. Because it had lasted for about half an hour, I had debated with myself what it was that was taking place, yet I could not get myself to contradict what transpired before my eyes. . . . During the time that the Servant of God had been illuminated with Light he repeated twice or three times: "Heaven, heaven, how beautiful you are!"[23]

notes

1. Martin Dempsey, *Champion of the Blessed Sacrament,* p. 94. The saint's order has furnished me with much material from the Process, all in French except for this accurate but more popularized biography.

2. Francis Trochu, *Saint Jeanne Antide Thouret,* p. 326. Furnished by her order, Trochu's works are always taken from Process testimonies and other authoritative documents.

3. Mother Saverio De Maria, *Mother Frances Xavier Cabrini,* pp. 351–52.

4. M. Domenica Grassiano, *My Decision Is Irrevocable,* pp. 28–29. Provided by the saint's order, this is based on the Diocesan and Apostolic Processes.

5. Ibid., p. 142.

6. Eily MacAdam, "Venerable Francis Libermann of the Holy Ghost Fathers," p. 9. Furnished by Fr. Farrell Sheridan of the order.

7. Ibid., p. 14.

8. Ibid.

9. Ibid.

10. Ibid., p. 13.

11. Ibid., p. 14.

12. Adrian L. van Kaam, *A Light to the Gentiles,* p. 296. The author is a member of the saint's order.

13. In a conversation with her sister Céline, in whose Process testimony it is found. See Christopher O'Mahoney, ed., *St. Therese of Lisieux by Those Who Knew Her, Testimonies from the Process of Beatification,* p. 157.

14. Ibid., p. 44.

15. Ibid., p. 88.

16. Ibid., p. 87.

17. Ibid., p. 213.

18. John Beevers, *Storm of Glory,* p. 105. Based on the authentic documents, this is the best English-language biography.

19. O'Mahoney, op. cit., p. 46.

20. Amilcare Rey, *Gaspare del Bufalo,* Vol. 2, p. 491. This copiously documented work from the original sources was furnished by William A. Volk of the order's Rome curia.

21. Ibid., p. 209.

22. Wilhelm Schamoni, *Wunder sind Tatsachen,* p. 243. This book is a compilation of Process testimonies and other authoritative reports, such as this one, on mystical phenomena.

23. Ibid., pp. 242–33, quoting *Summarium super virtutibus,* Rome, 1831, p. 485.

4 ▲

"illumined with supernatural light"

On a rainy summer afternoon in Evansville, Indiana, in 1902, a sixty-eight-year-old nun was dying. Born July 29, 1834, to a prominent family in Italy, Mother Mary Maddalena (born Annetta) Bentivoglio had been the sort of child who ages parents rapidly. Her father, a count and papal general, once looked up in St. Peter's in Rome to see his four-year-old contessa perched on a ledge of masonry over a hundred feet off the floor.* Left at home, the child had made her way to the chief church of Catholicism, climbed by a fire ladder to the roof, and found this wonderful "seat."[1] There were similar escapades before she made what seemed the unsuitable choice to become a Franciscan Poor Clare cloistered nun dedicated to the purely interior adventures of prayer. As would be expected of this lively, energetic soul, at first she found some aspects of

---

* The nave is 150 feet high, the dome 400 feet.

convent spirituality so tedious she wanted to fling the prayerbook away. But she did not.

Instead those who knew her testify the vibrancy which had once carried a four-year-old to dizzying heights carried the woman to spiritual heights. Her strong sense of humor helped, no doubt, especially when she and a blood sister brought their cloistered order to the United States only to be sent packing a number of places, even bishops growling that "nuns who just pray are un-American."

Now as she ended her life, the Poor Clares had their prayer houses in Omaha and New Orleans as well as Evansville all bulging with young American women interested in spiritual adventures and "prayer work." Mother Maddalena's request to die on the bare floor like Francis of Assisi, the cofounder of the order, had not been totally refused. She lay on the floor on a sack of straw as all twenty-three of the Indiana group crowded into the tiny room for the passing of one many Americans regarded as a saint.

Their individual testimonies tell how all at once Mother Maddalena's eyes became "like the enraptured eyes of a child that suddenly beholds the Christmas tree."

"I observed," wrote one sister, "that her eyes were on the crucifix. Her face became radiant and it was more beautiful than I had ever seen it in life." This observer, sure that Mother Maddalena saw "something extraordinary," which indicates an ecstasy, thought the dying woman "was getting well."

Another explains at length how she tried to deduce some natural explanation for "the light upon Reverend Mother's face." Her pragmatic-American testimony goes into the shuttered windows, the pouring rain outside, and the candle that cast limited light to rule out any non-mystical factors. A sister who had never seen anyone die wondered ingenuously if everyone lit up like this at death.

One onlooker saw a light emanating from the crucifix that Mother Maddalena was raptly gazing on in ecstasy. This nun says carefully, "I saw an illumination in the face of the dying Mother; but I do not know whether it emanated from her face or was a reflection from the light on the crucifix."[2]

Estimates range from thirty-five to forty minutes that Mother Maddalena Bentivoglio was illumined, from without or within or both, before, closing her eyes and smiling, she died as gently as a breath.

Twelve sisters, perhaps those farthest from the bed, saw nothing of any of this, which those investigating took as a sign that it was not a natural phenomenon, since natural light is seen by any sighted person. Her Cause is under way.

▲

Giuseppe Sarto (1835–1914) is known to the world as Pius X, to his church as St. Pius X, a mystic who often worked miracles, particularly of healing. The son of devout and hard-working but very poor Italian peasants, Sarto had to beg door to door for the funds for his seminary expenses. The boy who felt it an immense honor to be a simple country pastor ended up pope but never lost his simplicity or humility. In that socially snobbish era, someone once rebuked Pius that his habit of chatting with the Vatican gardeners, was lowering the papal dignity, only to receive the disconcerting reply, "But how can you tell who is higher in the eyes of God?"

Don Luigi Orione (1872–1940), who was beatified by Pope John Paul II in October, 1980, said of the earlier pope, "On more than one occasion the countenance of Pius X seemed to me as though illumined with a supernatural light."[3]

▲

A saint who rose to world fame from depths of poverty and obscurity even greater than the origins of Pius X is Blessed Andre Bessette (1845–1937), whom the world press dubbed— to his intense chagrin—"the wonder worker of Montreal."

There are plenty of testimonies the French-Canadian saint was luminous at times, although many descriptions make it impossible to say with certainty whether he was emitting light or bathed in Shekinah Light.

Eusebe Viau testified under oath (before a subsidiary tribunal collecting data as part of the Beatification Process) in Providence, Rhode Island, to the gradual cure of his adopted daughter from blindness after a visit by Brother Andre. Then he added, "When one saw Brother Andre pray, almost always on his knees, his face was transfigured, almost angelic."[4]

Late each night, after ministering to the sick all day, the frail Andre made the physical-mental-spiritual meditation Catholics call "The Stations of The Cross." Friends accompanying the old man sometimes saw the tiny figure in the black cassock "touched by a supernatural radiance." There is also the taxi driver who for a period brought the healer home from his sick calls. He insisted that each time he drove him, he saw "an aureole" about Brother Andre's head.[5]

Paul Corbeil, a Canadian, told the tribunal gathering information for the Process of Beatification:

> One night I accompanied Brother Andre to his little chapel. [After our prayers] at the moment when he was locking the door with a key, I saw him remain in that attitude for several seconds [indicating he was gripped by an ecstasy]. As he stood there immobile in the obscurity of the night, he was illumined by white rays of light like those one sees in the paintings of saints. That tableau made an absolutely unforgettable impression on me.[6]

Some years later another friend, Adelard Fabre, saw a similar phenomenon. Perhaps an instance of the exterior Shekinah, it is impossible to say with absolute certainty the light did not originate in the saint. Fabre swore:

I saw Brother Andre kneeling in the Oratory. He was enveloped by light. . . . I was standing a few feet, maybe six, from him. Brother Andre was in the light; I was not. The stream of light covering a distance of twenty feet stopped† at Brother Andre. There was no light in the Oratory except the lamp before the sanctuary. Far back, some votive candles were burning. The statue of St. Joseph [the saint to whose prayers Brother Andre attributed his cures] was in obscurity, but the luminous rays seemed to come from it. I had a feeling that the statue was going to fall from the main altar toward Brother Andre. I went to Brother Andre and touched his arm to warn him and lead him away but [because most likely he was rapt in ecstasy] Brother Andre didn't speak or budge. Terrified, I went to the sacristy hoping to find Brother Ludger, . . . but he had gone to his room. As I left to go get Brother Ludger I looked again into the chapel. Brother Andre at that moment had moved to the altar of the Holy Virgin, next to the main altar. He was still enveloped in light.

I found Brother Ludger who came with me to the Oratory. When we arrived there Brother Andre had left the altar of the Holy Virgin and was going to his room. The light had disappeared.

Brother Ludger and I discussed whether the light could have been rays of moonlight. But there was no moon that night.[7]

Fabre says some Holy Cross religious tried to convince him he had imagined the light, but he was so certain of what he

---

† The onlooker's interpretation. It could have started there as well. Compare a clear example of Shekinah Light: Once several people coming to bring Brother Andre from his stall back of the altar where he had stayed to pray after the rest left, saw that part of the chapel full of clear light—"alive" they called it—while Andre prayed, unaware, his eyes shut. [The incident is described by writer Katherine Burton in her *Brother Andre of Mount Royal*, p. 157. Ave Maria Press, Notre Dame, Ind., 1943.]

had seen it kept him awake all night. Three weeks later he again saw the kneeling, praying Andre with a large area of light above his head.[8]

▲

Polish Franciscan communications genius St. Maximilian Kolbe (1897–1941) is best known for his selfless heroism at Auschwitz where he volunteered to die for a condemned prisoner who cried out for his wife and children. Actually the saint's death in the Nazi concentration camp was only the final act of self-giving in a life spent for others out of love for God. In reading over a thousand pages of Process testimonies and interviewing people who remember Kolbe well,‡ I found the usual paradox of sanctity: Kolbe is remembered as the most unassuming and simple of men, and yet there are those who were willing to swear under oath they saw him at times illuminated. For instance, Brother Luke Kuszba who lived with him at the communications center that Kolbe founded near Warsaw recalls that "it was impossible to take your eyes off" the priest during his visits before the chapel tabernacle several times a day. Kuszba many times observed Father Maximilian say mass. He says flatly: "He appeared illuminated by an unearthly radiance."[9]

A priest friend of Kolbe's is more cautious. He uses the word "transfigured," which while it literally indicates extreme luminosity is sometimes understood to mean far less and thus offers a certain intellectually safe ambiguity. The friend remembers arriving at the friary and heading for "the poor little chapel."

> In a few minutes Father Max burst in through the sacristy door not noticing me kneeling in the back in the dark

‡ For my biography of this saint, *A Man for Others* (Harper & Row, 1982, reprint OSV, 1986)

under the wall. With admiration I observed his faith, his humility; with his whole being he prayed alone in the chapel before the [tabernacle]. . . . As I gazed upon the transfigured father in prayer, I began to tremble from the soul stirring impression he made.[10]

Another more explicit witness is Father Francesco Giusta, general secretary for the missions of the Conventual Franciscans during the period Kolbe spent six years starting a Christian communications center at Nagasaki, Japan. Giusta recalls Kolbe during a visit the saint made to Rome in the 1930s.

I was invited by Father Max to visit a confrere, a professor in our Theology faculty at S. Teodoro, who was distinguished for his piety and culture, an invitation which I readily accepted. We met in a small classroom and a [spiritual] conversation began at once. . . . I spoke very little because I felt myself very small stuff in comparison to the two confreres, especially small before Fr. Max whose words, peaceful and mellow-voiced, showed great delight. If I remember correctly he spoke with particular force and fervor on Mary's active participation in the life of the mystical body. . . . There was nothing ostentatious or artificial in his words. Rather he spoke with the simplicity of a child and at the same time with the certainty of a man inspired.

My wonder, already great by what I had heard, grew as my eyes took in the expression of his face. It was illuminated from time to time by an enchanting serene smile, a physical manifestation of the intimate mystical joy of one who while still on earth, feels rapt by the view of some heavenly beauty. And meantime his expression, habitually sweet and profound, was lit with a strong light *(lampeggiava di vivissima luce).*[11]

Finally, there is the Beatification Process testimony by someone who only met Father Kolbe once. The first-person account of Ricardo Bandini (I translated his Italian) opened these chapters on luminosity (see pp. 29–30).

▲

A gay young woman who laughed in St. Peter Julian Eymard's (1811–68) face when he foretold she would become a mother superior had a startling experience later in her first meeting with the saint. I translate the words of Mlle. Amade from the French:

> I turned around and was astonished to see the priest's face all alight *(toute rayonnante)* with beauty. In the visitor's parlor he had seemed sad but here in the chapel he was as transfigured with the smile of an angel. His features were stamped with a sweet beatitude. He appeared so strikingly handsome that I barely recognized him . . .[12]

Other witnesses remarked of this miracle worker, whose life was spent raising the spiritual level of his native France in times of turmoil, that "whenever he said mass he seemed transfigured." "One would think he already enjoyed the beatific vision [of heaven]," one observer put it. "So transformed was he [at times]," says another, "that he hardly resembled himself."[13]

All three spiritual organizations Eymard founded (an active order of priests, a contemplative group of nuns, and a confraternity for lay folk) were dedicated to fostering devotion among his fellow Catholics to the Christ of the tabernacle. When Eymard himself prayed before the tabernacle, many besides the surprised young woman left reports that "his ascetic features appeared luminous," while "he was so transfigured that he seemed to be no longer of earth."[14]

▲

An obituary of Francis Luyckx (1824–96), a Flemish Benedictine known as Abbot Paul, said the priest's life was best
summed up in the phrase *"transit benefaciendo* [He went
about doing good]." Known for his tireless preaching of the
love of God, he was called a saint by a bishop he served under,
an estimation echoed by many he healed, guided, and inspired.
Like Eymard, Abbot Paul had the ability to read hearts—and
sometimes minds—and could see the future in many cases.
Besides the stacks of crutches, canes, back braces, and other
paraphernalia in Termonde* abbey that testify to his healings,
there are reports of other types of miracles as well. Father
Albert Peleman of the Belgian monastery, with whom I have
corresponded about Father Paul, is careful never to use the
word "saint" prematurely (if an Order tries to "promote"
someone for sainthood by such accolades, that terminates a
Cause). Still, Peleman assures me of the esteem Father Paul
still enjoys three quarters of a century after his death, not only
among his fellow Benedictines, who in 1960 disinterred his
body† from the order's crypt and reinterred it in solemn cere-
monies inside the church, but also among the steady stream of
pilgrims who visit the grave to ask the saint's prayers.

Translated from the original Flemish, the one biography
available in English is by a layman friend of Father Paul's who
wrote not long after the holy abbot's death. Peleman says Edward van Speybrouck would never have been untruthful but in
his admiration for Father Paul, he may have fallen prey to
exaggeration. After that careful reply, my informant assures
me that Speybrouck's is a fine book. To be on the safe side I
have also relied on the German-language biography by a Bene-

---

* This should be Dendermonde, but as the only English biography says Termonde, I
use the latter to avoid confusion.
† Found incorrupt.

dictine, Benedik Stolz. The panegyric preached at the time the abbot's body was reinterred incorrupt sixty-four years after his death, convinces me Father Paul's "wonders" are not fabrications. However the reader is notified that the accounts of Father Paul's deeds, carefully recorded by contemporary witnesses, have not yet had the benefit of stringent investigation by the Catholic Church's Congregation for the Causes of Saints.‡

Among reports on Father Paul's luminosity carried by both Stolz and van Speybrouck is a letter dated June 26, 1908, from a priest in Bruges, Belgium, who had consulted Abbot Paul during Eastertide 1882. Although later events proved the wisdom of the advice the abbot gave him, during the meeting the visitor's opinion of Father Paul was not so favorable. He writes:

> At first I said to myself, "This monk is too simple, I have yielded to an illusion." But when he accompanied me to the door, he spoke a few words in Flemish on the love of Jesus Christ, with such marks of enthusiasm that I turned around to look at him (for he had made me walk ahead of him . . .) He was no longer the same man: *he was transfigured.*[15]

Depending on how the priest was using the word, this may have been at least a low degree of luminosity, or perhaps far more. Five years later in 1887, on a trip:

> Father Paul put up at the house of an old invalid lady at Schaerbeek. At seven o'clock in the evening there was a reunion of the inmates of the house, including besides the old lady, a sister who nursed the patient, a young lady

---

‡ His monastery has not opted to pursue a Cause yet, feeling both "the tenor of the times and their available resources" make it advisable to wait.

from Ghent, and another lady. The sister, having asked the Rev. Father to say a few words on the great subject of which he loved to treat best of all, namely, the love of God, as soon as he had begun his discourse, all at once saw him *transfigured. His face had become white as snow, while a brilliant aureole surrounded his head and lighted up the room in an astonishing manner* [italics mine]. Father Paul appeared to be quite rejuvenated. With an eloquence simple and sublime, he kept his audience spellbound communicating to all the burning love which overflowed from his heart . . . until eleven o'clock at night.[16]

A year later:

Father Paul was dining at the house of a lady in Bruges. As the servant in the middle of the repast reentered the room she suddenly uttered a cry of astonishment as she looked at the Rev. Father. The hostess, at a loss to understand such unusual conduct, demanded an explanation, saying "What's the matter with you? Surely it is not the first time you have seen the Rev. Father Paul." But the servant, confused and speechless, was unable to explain herself. The fact is that she saw Father Paul all rejuvenated, appearing to be not more than about thirty years of age (he was sixty-four), *his head surrounded by a brilliant aureole about a foot in diameter* [italics mine]. When Father Paul met the servant after dinner, he asked her why she had made such a noise. "Why, because you had a star on your head," replied the servant, who had not yet recovered from her surprise. "Yes, yes, that is all right," Father Paul said . . . and walked away.[17]

No doubt he was sorry he had asked. A final witness wrote Father Paul's biographer (no date given):

> Being at the church of the Benedictines in Termonde
> and seeing there how the Rev. Father Paul gave to the
> people a relic to kiss, I saw to my great astonishment, a
> shining aureole surrounding his head.[18]

It is a paradox that the joy of the saints, their "net which
catches souls," is often found in lives full of suffering. St. Julie
Billiart's life (1751–1816), for instance, reads like one of the
old dime novels. It is filled with poverty and partings as well as
such drama as Julie's hairsbreadth escape during the French
Revolution, hidden in a cartload of hay while a frenzied mob
searched for her, howling to add "a saint's head" to the grisly
trophies they paraded on pikes. Yet her French countrymen
today, recalling none of this, dub her rightfully "the smiling
saint," while those who lived with her knew that the halo, like
the mysterious joy of the saints, is a real thing.

> Every morning, in spite of age and infirmities, break of
> day found her kneeling in chapel absorbed during the
> space of an hour in the deepest contemplation, the fire
> which burned in her soul betraying itself by the supernatu-
> ral glow on her countenance. Numbers of eye-witnesses
> have deposed to her often being rapt in ecstasy. . . . At
> such times her head was surrounded by a halo of light. For
> a long time, the Servant of God was unconscious of this
> marvel; as soon as it came to her knowledge, she adopted
> a larger veil, so arranged that she could drop it over her
> face during her prayer.[19]

Her cofounder of the Notre Dame de Namur Sisters, an
order which, with its several offshoots, teaches in many countries of the world, including the United States, was Mère St.
Joseph Blin de Bourdon, a French aristocrat who bowed before the sanctity, in the person of Julie, of a peasant. In Mère

St. Joseph's memoirs she writes of her friend, "Her face was veritably inflamed by her living faith and ardent love for Jesus Christ. It was not simply the recollection of a devout and pious person praying, but her countenance was supernaturalised."[20]

▲

The Curé d'Ars' (St. Jean Marie Vianney, 1786–1859) love for God, in the nineteenth-century idiom of his witnesses, "enkindled in him a fire that caused his eyes to flash and his countenance to burn" while he said daily mass."[21] Because "at that hour his whole person became, as it were, transfigured" and some onlookers saw his head surrounded by a halo, Vianney used to instruct the orphans he supported "not to look at the priest when he was at the altar."[22]

> In March, 1852, at about half-past one in the morning (his usual hour to begin work), the Curé summoned to the confessional before everyone else, Soeur Clotilde, a young nun of the Congregation of the Child Jesus. The light of only one candle lit up that corner of the chapel of St. John the Baptist. But when Vianney opened the shutter of the confessional, his penitent saw him wholly enveloped in a transparent and unearthly radiance.[23]

She barely managed to make her confession.

> In 1849 Mlle. Marie Roch, of Paris-Montrouge, came to consult M. Vianney. After a long delay she finally succeeded in getting close to the confessional; in fact, she was even able to peer into the dark corner where the saint was seated, and this is what she beheld. The holy priest's face seemed to project two fiery rays, his features being completely hidden by the brightness of their light. . . . Mlle. Roch gazed at it [his luminous face] for at least eight or

ten minutes, when it still shone with undimmed radiance.*[24]

The Abbé Gardette, a priest who visited Ars with his brother, testified under oath that he saw the curé's forehead "encircled by an aureola" and "his countenance transfigured."[25] Longer examples, particularly relating to some of his visions, can be found in the definitive biography by the Abbé Francis Trochu, using the Beatification Process and other first-hand testimonies.

▲

Imagine a handsome, curly haired Italian of amazing physical strength (he could hammer a nail into wood with his bare fist), immense charisma, and intellectual brilliance and you have St. John Bosco (1815–88), Italian evangelist, educator, and father to slum children.

There are a number of witnesses that Don Bosco was occasionally luminous. Philip Rinaldi (1856–1931), Bosco's third successor as head of the Salesians and a candidate for canonization himself, testified that as a teenager going to Don Bosco for confession "in the small dark sacristy behind the main altar, he suddenly became aware of a radiant light about the priest's head, much like a halo around the head of a saint."[26] The boy was so amazed he could only stare speechlessly until the saint, with a smile, urged he get on with his confession.

In the fall of 1877 Rinaldi saw the priest again during a holiday celebration. Don Bosco spotted him in the crowd and, in a typical gesture, invited the teen to dinner with a group that included a bishop and other dignitaries. Following the meal, the saint lingered in the dining room to chat with the

---

* She was too overcome to enter the saint's confessional. But the next day he stopped and spoke as though she had consulted him, as intended, about a certain matter.

youth, who had never thought of becoming a priest. As a result of their conversation, Philip Rinaldi entered the seminary.

> Toward the end of the interview, Don Bosco, who had suddenly become silent, seemed to compose himself in prayer. He sat motionless, his head bowed, his hands crossed over his chest. Soon his face began to radiate a light which gradually became brighter, brighter even than the sunlight that streamed through the window. After a few brief moments, he became his normal self again, [and] resumed the conversation.[27]

Salesian Father Paul Albera spoke of three times when in bright daylight he saw Don Bosco's eyes become "luminous and, as it were, emit flames." Albera reported that the light, more intense than any natural illumination, enveloped Don Bosco's entire body on each of those occasions.

In December 1878 a youth named Evasio Garrone and a second altar boy named Franchini saw Bosco become enraptured as he said mass.† At the elevation "an aura of Paradise" lit up his face and the whole chapel, Garrone said. Two other times when Bosco said mass Garrone saw the same thing occur.[28]

Father John Baptist Lemoyne, later Bosco's biographer, wrote of his own experience on three evenings during the last year of the saint's life:

> Don Bosco's face seemed gradually to become radiant until it appeared to be luminously transparent. Startled, I went to the window to see whether there might be a light in the playground which reflected on his face. But there was no light. This happened on three consecutive nights. The . . . [light] would increase until his face became re-

---

† See a description of the levitation that occurred in these raptures on p. 286.

splendent with a strong and beautiful light; then it would slowly diminish.[29]

Called "another Curé d'Ars" by his bishop, Jean Edouard Lamy (1853–1931) of the Haute Marne region of France near Paris is another simple parish priest who appears to have been illuminated at times. One woman who had never seen Père Lamy before was in a group to whom he made a comment on Mary, the Mother of God. The thought of Mary, whom he often saw in his visions, must have triggered an ecstasy, for in the words of the onlooker:

> He stopped and looked upward. . . . His face became translucent like a block of alabaster lit from within. Old as he was, I saw him go young and handsome like a man of thirty. I saw wrinkles disappear. . . . I no longer saw his spectacles. There was no sparkling light about his head but an inward light which made his face transparent without dimness, without any shadow about either the nose or the eyes. I saw him young and beautiful. That lasted five or six seconds, perhaps more. I don't know. He was looking lightly into the air in front of him. Imperceptibly all became normal again and he went on talking as before.

Concerned that she might have hallucinated, at the end of the service the witness asked the stranger next to her if by chance she had seen anything peculiar. The answer was a description matching her own.[30]

Count Paul Biver, Lamy's friend and biographer, reports three or four other cases where the priest became "suddenly enlightened," as Biver's translator from the French awkwardly phrases it. The most striking of these took place on the road between the towns of Le Pailly and Violot.

Worn out, the walking priest sat down on a heap of stones to rest. As he prayed there, passersby saw him so luminous that some cried out, "The priest is on fire, the priest is on fire!"[31]

▲

In September and October 1902 in New Orleans a tribunal was taking those preliminary testimonies that start a Cause. Among those answering questions put to them under oath were Peter Maus, a Bavarian-born sixty-five-year-old wagon driver; Caroline Cestac, a forty-eight-year-old widowed businesswoman who was a New Orleans native; and Catherine Kielmeyer, a fifty-five-year-old German-born seamstress. I extract a few lines from each of their memories of the genially lighthearted and very holy priest who had died in their city thirty-five years earlier. Father Francis Xavier Seelos‡ (1819–67) had served in New Orleans only a year but his memory had not faded.

Caroline Cestac had been about thirteen when Seelos was in New Orleans. She recalled:

> When he came [to the school she attended] the school seemed to be illuminated by a certain supernatural light and he appeared to be surrounded by rays of celestial light.

Catherine Kielmeyer had been twenty. Her memory:

> Whenever I saw him standing at the altar, he seemed surrounded by a splendor of light.

She spoke to her father about this, Kielmeyer remembered, and far from telling her she was imagining things, he said, "Father Seelos is certainly a great saint."

‡ See two chapters on Father Seelos and his gifts of healing in my book *Nothing Short of a Miracle.*

Teamster Peter Maus had been thirty. He recalled:

> Shortly before his death [Father Seelos] was called to
> come to me, because I was in bed from an attack of the
> yellow fever. As he came into my room, I saw him sur-
> rounded by a shining light. I had the perfect use of my
> senses, and there was no light in the room before he came
> in, and there was no one with him who carried light."[32]

I have told (pp. 44–45) of my own experience with a luminous individual. A few years later I learned there had been
another at times luminous mystic in the greater Los Angeles
area.

Good-humored Father Aloysius Ellacuria (1905–81) was
known for "inspiring others to be good" and for gifts of healing that sometimes sent even "terminal illness" packing. People I have spoken to tell of occasionally catching the stocky,
little Basque in ecstasy. Some who knew him also insist Father
Aloysius at times evidenced the odor of sanctity. There are
even witnesses to the rarest bodily phenomena of mysticism,
such as levitation and bilocation. Like almost all the genuinely
holy, the Spanish-born priest was also criticized and misunder-
stood—and even had to leave California for a period. Without
any reference to the mystical phenomena others speak of, the
Claretian Congregation to which he belonged affirms "Father
Aloysius was a very good and holy priest who touched many
people with his ministry." Many he healed or encouraged look
to the day when the holiness they saw in Aloysius Ellacuria
will be officially recognized by his Church. To mention only
two instances of luminosity, a fellow member of Father Ellacuria's Claretian order, Brother Salvatore Azzarello, has
told me about the time the holy old priest joined the Azzarello
clan at a sister's home for a special Italian religious feast
known as St. Joseph's Table and blessed all of them with a
picture of their dead mother. At that moment, says Brother

Salvatore, "I felt something open up, as if another immense world entered—something indescribable." Brother Salvatore's sister, Antonia [Lee] Moore, says at the same time, she saw light surround the praying saint. Others in the family, they wish to make clear, saw nothing.[33]

Father Aloysius' former secretary, Charles Carpenter, today a priest of the Missionaries of Perpetual Adoration in Sonora, Mexico, reports that another priest who hadn't seen Father Aloysius for perhaps thirty years went to a meeting and saw him there. This onlooker told Father Carpenter that from Father Aloysius' "face there seemed to radiate a kind of luminosity—it was not just a spiritual [nonmaterial] light," he insisted. "Light was physically shining out from Father Aloysius."[34]

notes

1. Albert Kleber, *A Bentivoglio of the Bentivoglios,* p. 12. This book, by the Vice-Postulator of Bentivoglio's Cause, is from the original documents.

2. Ibid., pp. 219–20, reporting the firsthand testimonies of various Poor Clares.

3. Orione's witness is given in *Saint Pius X* by Hieronymo Dal-Gal, p. 180.

4. See an English-language account of this Process testimony in Alden Hatch, *The Miracle of the Mountain* (New York: Hawthorn Books, 1959), p. 120.

5. Andre got wind and, displeased, interrogated one of them, according to testimony of J. Pichette, Oct. 10, 1958, reported in Étienne Catta's *Le Frère André et l'Oratoire Saint-Joseph du Mont-Royal,* p. 847. The taxi driver's comment to Dr. Lamy was reported to Catta Sept. 12, 1958. See Ibid.

6. Ibid., quoting *Summarium,* p. 109, 120.

7. Ibid., pp. 845–46, quoting *Summarium,* pp. 331–32 and 77–80.

8. Ibid., quoting *Summarium,* pp. 81–83, 332.

9. See Kuszba's testimony in this writer's *A Man for Others,* pp. 68–69, a work based solely on the Process and other firsthand recollections of Kolbe by those who knew him.

10. Ibid., pp. 39–40, citing testimony of Father Anselm Kubit.

11. Ibid., pp. 71–72.

12. Un Religieux du Très Saint Sacrement, *Le Bienheureux Pierre-*

Julien Eymard, Vol. 2, p. 270. This definitive work was loaned to me by the Eymard League.

13. Albert Tesnière, *Saint Peter Julian Eymard,* p. 30. This work, published by the Eymard League, is a condensed version of Eymard's life, again from the primary sources.

14. See endnote 1, in the previous chapter.

15. Edward van Speybrouck, *Father Paul of Moll,* pp. 75–76.

16. Ibid., pp. 158–59.

17. Ibid., pp. 157–58.

18. Ibid., p. 157.

19. A Member of the Sisters of Notre Dame, *The Life of Blessed Julie Billiart,* pp. 256–57. This out of print authorative life, based on primary sources, was loaned to me by the Notre Dame Sisters, Thousand Oaks, California.

20. *Vie de Julie Billiart par sa première compagne, Françoise Blin de Bourdon, ou les mémoires de Mère Saint Joseph,* p. 280.

21. The testimony of General des Garets, is found in Francis Trochu's *The Curé d'Ars,* p. 527, citing the statement made to one Chanoine Coubé from *Panégyrique du B. Vianney,* Aug. 6, 1918.

22. Ibid., citing either des Garet or other Process testimony, p. 950.

23. Trochu, op. cit., p. 530. All Trochu's material is from authentic documents or the Process.

24. Ibid., pp. 530–31, quoting *Annales d'Ars,* May 1915, p. 383.

25. Ibid., p. 543, quoting the *Procès Apostolique ne pereant*, p. 237.

26. Peter M. Rinaldi, *By Love Compelled*, p. 18. This biography of Rinaldi by a fellow Salesian and relative relies on the original testimonies.

27. Ibid., p. 27.

28. John Baptist Lemoyne, *Memorie biografiche*, Vol. 13, p. 897. I have also consulted the English-language version to check my translation.

29. The personal testimony of Salesian priest John Baptist Lemoyne, author of three works in Italian on his mentor Don Bosco, can be found in English translation in Edna Beyer Phelan's *Don Bosco: A Spiritual Portrait* (Garden City, N.Y.: Doubleday, 1963), pp. 336–37. This out-of-print work was loaned by the Salesians, New Rochelle, N.Y.

30. Paul Biver, *Père Lamy*, p. 176, from the first-person testimonies of those who knew Lamy.

31. Ibid., p. 177.

32. *Copia Publica*, New Orleans, 1902: Peter Maus, Session VII, Sept. 25, folio 91v; Caroline Cestac, Session VIII, Sept. 30, folio 97v; Catherine Kielmeyer, Session IX, Oct. 2, folio 101v–102r.

33. Interviews in 1988 and 1989.

34. Carpenter's Nov. 3, 1988 taped reminiscences of Father Aloysius.

5 ▲

another source of energy

My brother and I slept in the same room from our earliest years, and our parents only lodged us apart when I was 12 and he was 15. From the moment that I began to observe things about me, until I was 12, I have never once seen him in his bed. He was all night praying, kneeling on his stool without support. . . . I never once woke without seeing him in this attitude. Never for years have I seen his bed unmade. Perhaps he lay down one time or another, I could not swear to it, but I never once saw him lie down.

The sister of Père Jean Lamy continues her testimony:

Yet we were working hard, he and I, during the daytime. Twice a week we used to go [on foot] together to sell . . . [farm products at a town six miles away] loaded up to the limit;* and he working in the fields from morning until night, and he even broke stones on the high road.[1]

"The priest is on fire!" onlookers once cried before the intense luminosity of Père Lamy. His sister's testimony of his nights hints Lamy evidenced another bodily phenomenon of holiness: recharging the body through prayer rather than sleep.

▲

In the Italian friary at San Giovanni Rotondo an American priest was present when:

> Padre Pio spoke at the dinner table about the time he was sick with stomach trouble for eight days. He took nothing but a little water during the whole illness. [Someone] . . . told him to weigh himself after he got up from his eight days' fast. He had gained! . . . Padre Pio laughed heartily. . . . "I think I'll have to eat more to reduce!"[2]

Amusing story, but can a man be so well-nourished without touching food that he gains weight? Medical men puzzled over the case of Padre Pio, the twentieth-century mystic-stigmatic. Dr. Giuseppe Sala, his doctor in the 1950s when the *New York Times* described the saint as "hale and hearty" with "a tendency to corpulence," said simply, "No normal man could eat as sparingly as he did and live."[3] Shaking their heads over cases like Pio's and Père Lamy's—there is more to be said about each—saints' doctors join mystical theologians in speaking of "another source of energy" they term "supra-natural" (above nature) or, more often, "supernatural" (understandable only in reference to God).

---

* Reminiscing, he once put this at thirty to forty pounds apiece.

What they mean is simply that the human body requires food and sleep to survive. Yet saints often evidence discrepancies between intake of food and rest and outgo of energy which cannot be explained except by the thesis that they tap into another energy source that does for them what food and sleep do for you and me. At least to some degree or at some period in their lifetimes, this phenomenon appears to be experienced almost universally among saints. Certainly it is the bodily phenomenon I find the commonest.

While it may take even more striking form than in the anecdotes on Padre Pio and Père Lamy, most often it is more subtle.† Padre Pio's joke to his fellow monks is also an exception: He felt safe with the friars; usually saints are silent or resort to generalities on their food and sleep habits. Supranatural energy, then, is a phenomenon we must infer from observation of a saint's habits. Where such details are lacking, we remain in the dark. Père Lamy had his own bedroom as a parish priest. Did he continue his extraordinary night prayer vigils? We don't know.

Energy, of course, comes primarily but not exclusively from food and sleep. Hinduism's Hatha Yoga, for example, teaches ways to energize the body through exercise and more efficient breathing techniques. When psychologist-physicist-Raja yoga teacher C. Maxwell Cade treated clients with an assortment of problems (p. 14) through a triad of biofeedback, meditation techniques, and minimal psychotherapy, they found new energy in every case study I read.[4] Psychotherapy alone may energize an individual sapped by the hard work of keeping the lid on emotions.

---

† Typical is an entry in the diary of the widely loved Pope John XXIII. On November 28, 1940, during a spiritual retreat, he writes of experiencing "a renewal of energies, physical as well as spiritual." On the same day he notes that "often" after going to confession, he rises from his knees full of joy and gladness which also express themselves "in the renewed physical rigour and energy of . . . [my] body." *(Journal of a Soul,* pp. 246–47).

It is not unreasonable to propose that saints, who are not in thrall to draining hate, rage, or neurotic anxiety, make better physiological use of the food they eat and relax more deeply when they do sleep than we less maximally integrated personalities. Cade's electroencephalograph shows the altered brain states that occur ever more steadily with the rise up "the ladder of consciousness" into holiness are states where the brain wave patterns are those of deep relaxation and peace even in the midst of grueling or challenging activities. I mentioned (p. 15) Swami Prakashanand who maintained the brain patterns of profound meditation while engaged in debate with a physicist. Jesuit William Johnston in *The Still Point: Reflections on Zen and Christian Mysticism* says anyone meeting "a genuine Zen monk will attest to an exquisite imperturbability," which precise readings on Tokyo electroencephalographs verify as real and again in no way inhibiting the mind from "precisely perceiving" (and dealing with) both outer and inner stimuli.[5] What Christians call "the peace that passes understanding" is similarly unruffled by ceaseless activity in Protestant, Catholic, and Orthodox mystics. I found this very characteristic of media genius Maximilian Kolbe when gathering testimony from roughly a hundred people, of many faiths or none, who knew this saint. And it showed up in electroencephalographic patterns in a one-shot testing of individuals gathered for a contemplative retreat at a Catholic convent in northern California.[6]

Am I saying that what is sometimes called "supernatural energy" is no more than a physiological aspect of holiness? To a degree, yes. In the factors just mentioned, we observe physiological participation in the total person's wholeness or what the early Christian fathers called "the resurrection life." It is highly probable that certain altered states of consciousness experienced by the holy will one day be definitely shown to fulfill the crucial functions for which sleep is necessary in other people. In London in 1985, for instance, I interviewed researchers into the brain patterns of advanced meditation. One of these, Geoffrey Blundell, spoke of some very rare subjects (a Tibetan Buddhist Namki Norbu was one) who show the dream response of extreme relaxation on an electroencephalograph during their daytime meditation. These people can get by with only four hours' sleep a night, I was told.

To picture the saint as a physiologically more efficient or perfect machine, a sort of fakir par excellence, is, however, not the whole story. For one thing, like Padre Pio with his eight-day stomach upset, at least the large group of Catholic saints often have severe digestive problems of one sort or another. One mystical theologian I read intimated this particular disability was typical of the holy Catholic.‡ So much for the tidy theory that explains supra-natural energy by ultra-efficient utilization of food, the saint as digester extraordinaire. We can only remind ourselves that when we entered the paradoxical realm of sanctity, we stepped off the ladder of ascent into another dimension: Perfect physiological efficiency is not one of the invariable marks of sanctity. Finally, while saints know a state of serenity and utilize prayer techniques that *must* have positive effects on their sleep and food utilization patterns*, there are saints who gain or maintain weight while leading active lives, without eating at all and/or without any sleep, as far as one can tell.†

‡ In their introduction to the legends about the founder of Hasidism *In Praise of the Baal Shem Tov,* editor-translators Dan Ben-Amos and Jerome R. Mintz refer to "bowel irregularity" as connected with the Jewish righteous, at least at the end of their lives, pp. xxv–xxvi.

* A news article *(The Tidings,* December 9, 1988) mentions in passing of a group of thirty-one nuns: "One sister is now 103, thirteen are in their 90s and thirteen are in their 80s." Because these were women who had rigorous work lives and, vowed to poverty, ate "whatever was cheap"—the Jello and Wonderbread diet—this hints at the vitalizing effects of a spiritual life-style and prayer.

† Having myself once fallen asleep standing up in a packed train, I think a saint could doze off even kneeling upright, the position in which Père Lamy prayed all night as a boy.

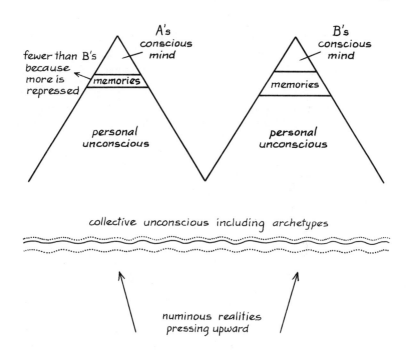

Based on diagrams on pp. 222 and 234 from *Encounter with God* by Morton T. Kelsey.

There we face two possibilities: Either sanctity and its prayer life changes the body so drastically that food and sleep are no longer necessities, or the prayer states of holiness open the sanctified person to an exterior, numinous source of energy.

We cannot yet verify the first possibility. Regarding the latter, there are conjectures about how this may happen. One I find fits well—purely as a theory, mind you—with mysticism in general springs loosely from the work of Swiss psychologist Carl Jung. Many readers are familiar with this idea which I must express here in simplified terms, directing those who wish a deeper discussion to Jung's works or exponents of these ideas like John A. Sanford and Morton T. Kelsey.

Below the workaday mind thinking of projects, weather, relationships, etc., this theory says, is the unconscious mind where our forgotten personal history, in all its trivia and richness, is stored. Below that is a layer Jung called the collective unconscious, where minds are, at least potentially, connected (See figure p. 92). From this reservoir, shared by the entire human family, well up into the individual mind archetypes or universal symbols, which represent pretty much the same thing to everyone regardless of time or place. Creative people, it is theorized, make space for material from this layer in their consciousness, creating drama, paintings, and other products that either enrich or poison our human race as they tap into its light or dark forces. From somewhere in these depths or, more likely, below them bubbles up the authentically numinous.

This numinous reality—God some of us call it—at times seizes the initiative, bursting through the layers into a consciousness trapped in the mundane. For most people, movement from living life superficially—that is, almost exclusively on the top layer of workaday consciousness, is more gradual. As the spiritual slowly takes root and narcissistic concerns no longer fully occupy consciousness, bit by bit or with a rush, in dreams and awake, the mind fills with material from the next lower layer, the personal unconscious. Breakdown or breakthrough depends on successfully handling this encounter. Every religious tradition has its failures, those whose self cannot stand firm against the onslaught. William Johnston, for instance, spoke to two Japanese psychiatrists familiar with the so-called Zen madness of that tradition.‡[7] Quite apart from religious delusion patients, American mental institutions have

‡ Johnston theorized that Zen, particularly through its use of the deliberately nonrational koan, creates "an artificial psychosis." The psychiatrists at Tokyo University agreed with him that Zen satori—enlightenment—"is often found by successfully passing through a psychotic experience."

their share of those experiencing a psychotic break with reality following a period of intense spiritual seeking.*

The personal unconscious having been dealt with (bypassed, annihilated or integrated depending on one's tradition), usually with the help of a spiritual guide, the mind is again free to fill with the material pressing in from deeper levels. In a sense the process is without end: Something is always welling up† as space is made available. The spiritual seeker is kept busy making space by integrating important material and skimming off the extraneous. This skimming and integrating is the "work," in at least the lower stages, of Zen, Catholic, Hindu, Hasidic, and other mysticism. And this is so whether one speaks from the aspect of asceticism, conversion, or other facets of the transformation—sudden, or more, often, gradual—of the sinner or unenlightened into "the one who knows," the spiritually "awake," the "whole"—the saint.

At the point of mysticism, one is empty enough to be flooded by the deepest layer, the numinous, shimmering reality of light and energy and, mysteriously, tender love we call so inadequately by the word God. "Now no longer Paul lives but Christ lives in me!" the early apostle cried, trying to articulate a situation irreducible to words or concepts. Welling up now, to return to our supranatural energy, is some degree of the limitless energy of the divine nature.

As always, examples of this energy are not limited to the saints of Catholicism who are my special area of expertise. There are explicit tales of saints supernaturally sustained while fasting or without sleep in all major traditions. And there are

* As with the Zen psychosis, psychologist Sheila Kalivas, who works at a state mental hospital, tells me, the psychotic break in many cases here, too, is a religious experience leading to growth and increased personality strength.
† While always new material, this may be only in the sense of being more profound. A life may circle around the same questions or problems for years. But if the individual is growing spiritually, these will be dealt with on an ever-deepening, that is, more transcendent, level. One theorizes that at the heights of mysticism such personal matters are long left behind or, as some traditions put it, "The ego is annihilated."

even more *implied* references to a relationship between holiness and functioning on meager sleep and/or food.

For instance American rabbi Herbert Weiner writes in his book *9 1/2 Mystics* of non-Hasidic Jewish mystics: *"matmidim* who held candles in their hands to prevent themselves from falling asleep during . . . all-night study vigils, and ascetics who wore hair-shirts and fasted [totally meaning they ate one day a week] from one Sabbath to another."[8] Weiner also notes that "in Hasidic tradition, rebbes‡ do not usually sleep."[9] Investigating his tradition's mysticism, he tells about visiting the Israeli synagogue of the spiritual followers of a deceased charismatic personality called Reb Arele. Rabbi Weiner says that the man who took him to visit this twentieth-century-born Hasidic sect in the Meah She'arim section of Jerusalem "vowed that he had spent several days and nights with the [groups'] rebbe and [had] never seen him sleeping."[10] Catnaps, adds Weiner, "do not count," being seen as moments when the Hasidic leader's soul ascends to spheres from which it returns with fresh spiritual inspiration.

In this vein, Weiner also writes of the twentieth-century Jewish spiritual master, the revered head of the Lubavitcher Hasidic movement, Menachem Mendel Schneersohn (1902–)* of New York, whom Weiner interviewed twice in the mid-1950s. Told by Schneersohn's secretary that the rabbi saw people three times a week, with appointments beginning at eight in the evening and going until three or even five in the morning, Weiner asked if the rabbi slept during the day after these interviews.

He was told the rabbi spent his days directing the spiritual movement's worldwide activities.

‡ From an Aramaic word for "our superior," this title of respect may be given a male teacher in an Orthodox school. Most usually it honors a Hasidic spiritual leader who may—or may not—be an ordained rabbi.

* I recommend Schneersohn's second dialogue with Weiner for those seeking either examples of modern Jewish mysticism of the first rank or of genuine Hasidic holiness.

"When does he sleep?" Weiner insisted.

His answer, he says, was a "slightly mysterious smile and a shrug."[11] While I can't present this as *proof* of anything, *allied to the rabbi's widely recognized holiness,* it is suggestive. And at the very least the incident clearly shows there is a Lubavitcher tradition of spiritual energy related to holiness.

From *Hasidic Tales of the Holocaust* comes another twentieth-century testimony that again implies the concept of supranatural energies is very much part of Jewish tradition:

> When the Rabbi of Belz, Rabbi Aaron Rokeach . . . stayed in the Bochnia ghetto . . . [during the dislocations caused by the Nazis invasion of Poland and persecution of the Jews] many of the ghetto inhabitants came to him to ask for a blessing and to seek his advice. The frail rabbi [in his early sixties], who slept no more than two hours a night, and survived on a few sips of coffee and a glass of milk smuggled in . . . did not turn away a single soul. He offered comfort and solace to all who came to him, never mentioning his own great tragedy, the loss of his entire family.[12]

On this starvation diet and inadequate sleep, Rabbi Rokeach not only bore his own tragedy and the pains of all who came to him but made a dramatic escape to Hungary and lived until 1957.

Shamanistic peoples join Jews, Sufis, other Moslems, Hindus, and Christians in seeking and believing they act as a conduit for explicitly supernatural sources of energy for their own personal sustenance/renewal and to help others. In *Nothing Short of a Miracle* I sampled the mountain of evidence that saints are plugged into a supernatural energy source that often heals others as well as themselves. Sioux holy man Black Elk will have to represent this enormous topic here.

Praying for a seriously sick child, he felt "the power coming through me" and knew the boy could be helped. Through an interpreter, Black Elk explained regarding this and other healings:

> Of course it was not I who cured. It was the power from the outer world, and the visions and ceremonies had only made me like a hole through which the power could come. . . . If I thought that I was doing it myself, the hole would close up and no power could come through.[13]

Every spiritual tradition of the human family also recognizes the wisdom of self-discipline for spiritual purposes in regard to food and sleep and other needs of the body. I make a point of this since Western society has recently emphatically rejected self-denial of any sort.

To mention food first, shamans like Black Elk fast for days at a time to facilitate contact with what the Sioux visionary called "the things of the other world." Black Elk offhandedly mentioned having only water for four days before an important ceremony.[14] The Japanese Buddhist holy man Gyosho of Koya abstained totally from his country's staple food, rice, and all other grains. An admiring visitor wrote, "His spiritual energy seems to be at a very high level" and wondered, "Has he attained Buddhahood in his own body?"[15]

Fasting is also among the four religious duties of Islam. The whole Moslem world each day during the entire month of Ramadan is to forgo eating or drinking until sundown for spiritual purposes. On Yom Kippur devout Jews fast to express regret for the sins of the past year and to gird themselves spiritually for the coming months. The Torah reveals that Jewish leaders historically proclaimed periods of repentence which included fasting by the entire community, while individual Jews, particularly today among the Orthodox, use the fast as either a sign of personal repentance or simply to come closer to God. Many of the Hindus popularly acclaimed as saints are ascetics, while all devout Hindus fast from meat, like many Buddhists, out of a spiritual reverence for life. The theories expounded by the world's faiths as to why one practices self-denial regarding food will vary; so will details of how long or how much to fast. Buddhists, for example, have told me that Buddhism, with its emphasis on moderation, is against fasting. Yet Buddhist discipline in this area appears extremely ascetic to the Western observer: That Buddhist monk sitting long hours in the difficult lotus posture, I am told, eats no meat, fish, dairy products, or eggs in China, Korea, or Vietnam. Even living in the United States, Theravada Buddhist monks I spoke to eat nothing from noon until the following 6 A.M. except for liquids (Lay Theravada Buddhists keep this eighteen-hour fast, too, on certain days of the lunar month). Mahayana Buddhists in California tell me they fast only a little less rigorously. They take a small amount of vegetables and rice—not a formal meal—in the same eighteen-hour period. Zen Buddhism exacts "tremendous effort" from the body, fasting and more:

> The eyes . . . concentrated on a single point . . . lack of sleep and insufficient food; the pain in the legs [so] excruciating . . . that perspiration breaks out over the whole body; the disciple has been beaten with the master's stick; perhaps he has been . . . struck across the face."[16]

All this merely part of the search for enlightenment, satori. Whatever the human family's theologians *say,* then, in the doing serious students of every great faith find the life of the spirit calling them to some self-denial (if not to the degree of Zen) in regard to food and drink, to say nothing of the body's other needs.

Without running through the details of each tradition's customs in regard to what the early Christian fathers call vigils, i.e. the curtailment of rest in favor of prayer, this practice, too, while varying in degrees and theories, seems to spring from a universal impulse. Perhaps the quiet and chance for solitude of night facilitates the altered consciousness of profound prayer. Perhaps this kind of prayer is more natural at night because it is closer to the consciousness of sleep than to daytime, workaday brain states. Perhaps, as some claim, fatigue helps one break through into other realities.

Whatever the reason, even nonsaints who are serious spiritual searchers may be drawn to spend portions of the night in prayer. Thomas Merton in *The Seven Storey Mountain* admits beginning to get up at night and pray even before he entered a Trappist monastery where such vigils are routine. Rabbi Weiner writes of twentieth-century Hasidics of the Bratzlaver sect in Jerusalem who arise in the middle of the night to go out into the desert. There, each man alone, away from the noise of day and his relationships, is encouraged to cry out aloud to God. Through this vigil, Bratzlavers believe a man "can dig into himself . . . [asking] for a lighting up of the darkness . . . [to] see with the clarity of a child and rediscover the goodness of God, the holiness of his commandments, and the wisdom of his saints."[17]

In the same vein when he was a confused young man of no particular spiritual tradition just down from Oxford, Bede Griffiths spent an entire night "kneeling on the floor, fighting against sleep and keeping my mind fixed on the figure of Christ." Although the next morning he felt "worn out and hopeless . . . [and] did not know what was to become of me," as he was leaving the room an interior voice said "You must go on a retreat."[18] He hurried to a nearby Anglican church to ask if there was such a thing as "a retreat." Told one was beginning that morning he enrolled and underwent a conversion experience which led him to Anglicanism, then Catholicism and a Benedictine monastery and finally to life in India's first Catholic ashram as a Hindu-Catholic bridge builder.[19] Besides those in Griffiths' autobiography *The Golden*

String, significant twentieth-century vigils are reported in Pentecostal Demos Shakarian's *The Happiest People on Earth* and David du Plessis' *A Man Called Mr. Pentecost,* among many others which could be mentioned. In these chapters we will see saints robbing sleep and rest time, not only for prayer vigils, but—like the Lubavitcher rabbi—also to serve God in others.

When we look at my area of expertise, the Catholic saint, one thing is immediately apparent: The roots of every Catholic saint's ascetic practices lie in Judaism as that heritage was carried into Christianity by Jesus Christ, who taught that certain goals are achieved only by prayer and fasting and at times passed his nights in prayer. Once his disciples, worried over Jesus' fast, urged, "Teacher, eat something," only to receive the mysterious answer "I have food to eat of which you do not know." When the puzzled group began querying one another as to whether someone had brought him food, Jesus explained in his typically cryptic fashion that he had not eaten physical food. His food, he told them, was "to do the will of God and God's works in the world."

Did this mean being buoyed up by one's mission, the kind of self-forgetfulness found in many people dedicated to a cause—however mundane or unworthy—outside themselves? Or is a mystical energy source insinuated as a supplement to, or even substitute for, the body's usual fuels, food and rest? I believe the latter, for after the resurrection and Pentecost, the earliest Christians, hitherto weak and vacillating in spite of their dedication to Jesus, appear charged by something—or someone they call the Holy Spirit—and reveal a new energy which sustains them through persecution, beatings, imprisonment, and fearsome deaths. From these apostles to living figures like Mother Teresa of Calcutta, there exists in this tradition, *as in others,* a chain of personal admission and/or onlookers' testimonies of holy men and women who work prodigiously for God while mysteriously upheld in spite of—chosen or unchosen—food and rest deprivation.

It is the holiness, not the deprivation, that is of import. Anorexia and manic states of sleeplessness demonstrate that giving up food and rest per se, while beneficial to a point, can pass that point to enter a morbid area. In a later chapter on saints "who live on God," that is, do not eat at all in the usual sense, the fact is confronted that there are individuals, most often women, and always invalids, whose total fast for years, believed genuine, is theorized to spring from rare physiological factors related to invalidism or from complicated neuroses. Neither situation has any spiritual or supernatural implications. These individuals (only Europeans and Americans were studied) include Protestants and Catholics of varied nationalities. Suffice here to make the point that, as much as we know, there is still a lot more to learn about human functioning. What at first glance looks angelically spiritual may be neurotic or a physiological quirk of invalidism; what at first glance is "sick" *where there is holiness* may be spiritually sound.

That paradoxical truth will help face the charge of our era that asceticism of any tradition is bizarre and unhealthy, saints abusing their bodies by starving them of food and rest. Certainly Christianity has at times suffered from anti-body, pro-spirit ideas ("beat the one to free the other"—derived from the Greeks, not the Jews) that the early church thought rejected for good when Gnosticism and Manichaeism† were condemned for their view that the spirit must war on the intrinsically evil body. Because it feeds on both self-hate and a per-

---

† Gnosticism held man is flesh, soul, and the divine spark (spirit). Humanity is divided into three classes, representing each of these. The fleshly group can never be saved. Only for the third, the Gnostics (from *gnosis,* meaning "knowledge"), is salvation certain. Gnosticism later merged with Manichaeism, which preached conflict between the realm of God, represented by light and *gnosis* (now termed "spiritual enlightenment"), and the realm of Satan, symbolized by darkness and the world of material things, including the body. The soul of man suffered from contact with physical matter, including women—earthy creatures who are part of Satan's forces. (Jesus never had a body at all; He only gave this "illusion.") For spirit to overcome body, celibacy was necessary. Groups like the Shakers came out of such ideas.

verse kind of egotism, the anti-body philosophy will always be around in one disguise or another. At the end of the seven-teenth-century, a fresh outbreak of anti-body, antimateriality harshness again attempted to warp Catholicism, as Calvin's theology (through movements such as Puritanism) in the six-teenth and seventeenth centuries was twisting Luther's Refor-mation. Catholic Bishop Cornelius Jansen of Ypres taught, like the Gnostics and Manichees, that Christ only died for a spiritual elite, while "fleshly" types could never be saved and free will was nonexistent. His so-called Jansenist philosophy was condemned by the Church, but its harshness and extreme anti-body asceticism left traces in Catholic spiritual training for more than a century. Some of the saints who died in the first half of the nineteenth-century show its touch (see mention of Gaspar del Bufalo's mortifications, p. 151), only redeemed by the love which warmed and motivated them. Unhealthy mortifications, as St. Therese of Lisieux warned those she spir-itually trained later in the century, have about them the cold aura of pride.

▲

What is a saint's asceticism—that is, self-discipline in pursuit of spiritual ends—all about? The original goal, according to Byzantine-rite Catholic priest George Maloney, is simple—and would be agreed upon, I add, by writers from many tradi-tions: to bring the whole self (soul, emotions, intellect, and body) to God. On the one hand, this means keeping out of one's life whatever hinders, such as blatant consumerism, glut-tony, various misuses of one's sexuality, spiritual laziness, etc. Equally it means adding whatever helps one grow from ego-tism into humble surrender to God's healing love and conse-quent offering/opening of oneself as an instrument through which He can love and serve others.

The saints, of course, are beyond this type of asceticism.

They have torn out by the roots whatever stood in the way of their flight to God's arms. Hacked and lifeless, egotism was kicked aside as the saint flung herself with complete surrender into His embrace. Now asceticism has new purposes, Maloney explains: The saint has reached the peak of human freedom where, in joy and spontaneity, she wishes to "improvise" ways to return God's infinite love. Here self-denial becomes a lover's gift touching, says Maloney:

> the highest level of self-sacrifice out of a desire to return love by love, . . . in an act of self-denial that costs the individual a sacrifice and a pain. It is not the pain or sacrifice that is ennobling, but the motive to offer God something that is not seen as an obligation . . . or [even] a wish of God but sheerly as a free-gift return to God out of love.[20]

Or, like lovers who dress and style their hair alike, among Christians this level of asceticism-become-mysticism can express the profound desire to be like the adored Jesus. Thus former nineteenth-century businessman St. Anthony Claret after he became a priest not only tried to acquire a Christlike love and other virtues but also imitated Christ literally. For example, he insisted on walking from town to town carrying no provisions, he had only one change of clothes, and he refused to own a house even when he was archbishop of Cuba or, later, confessor to the queen of Spain, "because Jesus had no place to lay his head."[21] Becoming in everything like Jesus, the saint hoped, he said, to thereby "love God as Jesus does."[22]

Claret and all saints also practice self-discipline, asceticism, or mortification as some call it, for another reason: to help others, known and unknown. Granted no man is an island, still how can a saint's asceticism, however permeated by love, help someone else?

Remember the Hasidic insistence that the most mundane

act of a man could redeem the world if he were holy enough? All spiritualities, including shamanism, that I have ever studied practice this type of love, however differently they conceptualize it. My tradition speaks of the entire human family, including the dead (unless someone has definitively opted out of the human connection for the egotism called Hell), as joined psychically, mystically. In this situation one individual may spiritually carry another's burden of pain, illness, confusion, sin, or even a number of people's burdens until they are able to bear them themselves.

Saints living and dead, many great faiths believe, do a great deal of this interceding. I could give pertinent testimonies from Jewish, Hindu, and Moslem literature, as well as Christian. All speak of voluntary reparation during the saint's lifetime. For the Catholic this may take the form of offering to God, in mystical union with Christ's redemptive sacrifice through which it gets its power, both one's daily joys and all the ordinary sufferings of life from weather, other people, health, and one's own weaknesses, such as anxiety, as a form of intercessory prayer. Legitimate pleasures and needs may also be voluntarily forgone and "offered up" for others. If a spiritual director demurs over some sacrifice, the desire to have made it is also considered a prayer. (Conversely even the greatest sacrifice is worthless in God's eyes without proper motivation.)

This is truly saint's territory. Neophytes in the spiritual life are too lacking in love for God or others and must be warned away with the caution "Take on no sacrifice you can't do with joy." That willing joy precisely characterizes the sacrifices of the saint. Thus Anthony Claret can speak of "joyfully abstaining" from "the pleasure in question."[23] Stigmatist Theresa Neumann can say in exasperation, "Of course I don't like suffering. But I'm still willing gladly to bear it to help our Savior."[24] And holy rabbi Aaron Rokeach dares speak of the Holocaust death of his son as a "mercy of God" who has permitted the father "to offer a sacrifice."[25]

This type of love, which has nothing to do with masochism or guilt-induced actions, is so rarified it evokes suspicion. Each must find pertinent analogies for it. Personally I sometimes think of a dark night when I was five. Fingers pressed on my neck arteries as my father raced the car for a faraway hospital. There blood transfused directly from his big arm to my spindly one saved me as I was bleeding to death. My father hated giving blood but there was that night neither masochism nor guilt in his act: He was not only willing but eager to suffer to save his only living child. Saints see around them a hemorrhaging world. Moved by compassion and love, they forget themselves and run spontaneously to press on its arteries and offer their blood.

If the fasts, the vigils, and the sheer mountains of work to benefit others described in this set of chapters looks like folly, then remember it is the folly, not of self-hate or morbid fear of a harsh God, but the folly of love.

With this understanding, I present in the next chapters examples of that mystical energy which fuels saints. As with luminosity, there is a range from lesser to maximal degrees of what some call "supernatural energy." There are healthy saints whose work, day in, day out, over many years, is completely out of proportion to their rest and food intake; there are sickly saints who survive or even thrive under conditions, often including extreme food deprivation and almost total lack of rest, that ought to quickly kill them; and there are saints who work and do not eat at all, except, in the case of Catholics, for receiving daily one coin-size wafer of wheat and water which they believe is the body and blood of Christ. My examples from each of these categories must stand for hundreds of others that could be given if space permitted.

Again, I begin with the most subtle cases. These are the individuals who begin their lives with fine constitutions. If they work prodigiously, that seems understandable considering their robust health and ardent natures. That is, it seems

understandable until one examines closely the discrepancy between years of negligible food and rest input with tremendous,
sustained energy output. Up close, one finds people who have
reduced splendid bodies to rags but somehow continue to
work—often for years—when, physiologically speaking, there
is nothing left to work with. And instead of more food or rest,
they may need less. For instance, St. Anthony Claret in 1861
slept six hours a night. Seven or eight years later, after fasting
partially every day and completely three days a week, eating
no meat, wearing a hair shirt on alternate days, and endless
other austerities, all while carrying an inhuman workload, the
saint now needed to sleep three hours a night.[26] It is this type
of nineteenth- and twentieth-century saint I profile in the next
chapter.

notes

1. Paul Biver, *Père Lamy,* p. 20.

2. Charles Mortimer Carty, *Padre Pio: The Stigmatist,* p. 18.

3. C. Bernard Ruffin, *Padre Pio: The True Story,* p. 275.

4. C. Maxwell Cade and Nona Coxhead, *The Awakened Mind,* pp. 203–18.

5. William Johnston, *The Still Point,* pp. 2, 8.

6. William Johnston, *Silent Music: The Science of Meditation,* p. 37. Johnston took a researcher there, apparently from the Langley Porter Institute in San Francisco. No date is given. I infer the early 1970s.

7. Johnston, *The Still Point,* p. 10.

8. Herbert Weiner, *9 1/2 Mystics,* p. 335.

9. Ibid., p. 232.

10. Ibid.

11. Ibid., p. 158.

12. Yaffa Eliach, *Hasidic Tales of the Holocaust,* p. 41.

13. John G. Neihardt, *Black Elk Speaks,* pp. 169–70, 173–74.

14. Ibid., p. 152.

15. Oliver Statler, *Japanese Pilgrimage,* p. 129.

16. Johnston, *The Still Point,* p. 13.

17. Weiner, op. cit., pp. 243–49.

18. Bede Griffiths, *The Golden String,* p. 105.

19. See Bede Griffiths' *The Marriage of East and West.*

20. George Maloney, S. J., "Following Jesus in the Real World: Asceticism Today," p. 15.

21. Juan Maria Lozano, *Mystic and Man of Action,* pp. 124–27, 157–58.

22. Ibid., p. 130.

23. Ibid., p. 157.

24. Johannes Steiner, *Therese Neumann,* p. 186.

25. Eliach, op. cit., p. 188.

26. Lozano, loc. cit.

6 ▲

they
soar like
eagles

St. Jean Marie Vianney once confided to a friend, "Oh how hungry I felt during Mass! When the moment of Communion came, I said 'My God, feed my body as well as my soul!' and the pangs of hunger vanished at once."[1] If he was ravenous, it is no wonder. In his first eight or nine years as a pastor, living alone, he sometimes "let two, or even three, days go by without touching food. One Holy Week*—possibly that of 1818—he only ate twice."[2] When fresh bread was given him, he exchanged it for the old crusts of the poor. Certain periods he lived on potatoes cooked once a week and left in an iron basket attached to the wall so he could grab one in passing. Toward week's end, he ate them "covered with a musty down." To this diet he occasionally added an egg or pancake.[3]

* The week preceding Easter Sunday, a time when many saints take on special penances, such as fasting, to unite with Christ in his sufferings.

A woman he allowed to graze her cow in his yard surprised him gathering sorrel.

"So you eat grass," she chided.

Thrown off his guard, the notoriously wary French Curé admitted, "Yes, I've tried to eat nothing else, but I couldn't go on with it."[4]

Is this some kind of nut?

To speak of the Curé d'Ars (in French, the parish priest of Ars), as most people call Vianney, one must immediately mouth superlatives—from both ends of the spectrum. To begin with, he was so dumb intellectually that, although a model of piety, he flunked out of the seminary. Tutored privately by his confessor, who alone gauged his spiritual brilliance, he reappeared at the seminary three months later for another set of exams. This time he revealed himself hopelessly lacking in poise, for the mere sight of the imposing examiners reduced him to such a state he couldn't even grasp their questions.

Only by a fluke was he ordained. France had lost so many priests in the carnage of the French Revolution that the need was desperate. While the bishop was away, a vicar-general of the Lyons diocese took advantage of his momentary authority to erase the educational requirements and admit the intellectual dolt to the priesthood, hoping the grace of God would make up for the fact "that there was little hope he would ever acquire a knowledge of Latin." After serving under his beloved confessor until the former's death, the dolt was packed off to ecclesiastical Siberia, a remote village called Ars. In this backwater, it was hoped his piety would be admired and his intellectual stupidity overlooked.

Ironically the dolt's sanctity, which showed itself in ways much more reliable than asceticism—by itself no indicator at all—drew hordes of spiritual searchers to the remote area where his superiors had hoped to hide him. In his lifetime he became known all over the world—irony again—for such mental gifts of sanctity as the ability on occasion to read hearts, minds, and the future. Well-verified cures testify to his gift of healing, while other events, such as the multiplication of food for his beloved poor, are best described as miracles, literally wonder-inspiring acts. Not for miracles, but for the sanctity behind them, Vianney after death would become the only Catholic parish priest (i.e., committed to a diocese, not to a religious order) ever canonized.

In those days when he was living on potatoes and occasionally grass, he never spent more than three hours in bed (in the early years, the floor with a log pillow)[5] so he could go, might and main, twenty-one hours a day at turning Ars into a holy village. Later he was also inundated by the mobs of out-of-towners—usually several hundred a day—expecting individual counseling, shriving, healing, or other services from "the saint."

When his inhuman eating habits became known, his bishop ordered him to eat daily. To see that he did, from 1827 on Vianney's meal was prepared by the orphanage he somehow supported. During this era he continued to begin hearing confessions an hour after midnight. About six in the morning he left the confessional to say mass. Around eight, having worked seven hours, he breakfasted—out of obedience to bishop and doctor—on a little milk. If it was a fast day, however, he could in conscience take nothing. Infrequently, it is said, he also took "a tiny piece of bread." His one meal of the day, eaten standing around noon, was for years broth and vegetables.[6]

To a young priest he confided that curtailing one's sleep, drink, and food were powerful spiritual tools. He volunteered that during the years when he had gone days without eating, he obtained from God "both for myself and others, whatsoever I asked."[7]

Like all saints, he did not push such stringencies on others. Catherine Lasagne, who ran the orphanage, recalled he told her at the beginning of Lent not to fast.

"But you fast," she complained.

"True," he answered, "but I can do my work. You couldn't."[8]

Work he certainly did for a quarter century. Then, in 1843, he collapsed with pneumonia. Ordered from his bed (now a thin layer of straw on hard planks) onto a mattress, it was clear to the doctor that Vianney was dying. In a coma, the saint nevertheless heard the physician say, "He has only thirty to forty minutes to live." In the Curé's words:

> I thought to myself: "My God, I shall have to appear before you emptyhanded!" And I turned to the Bl. Virgin and St. Philomena saying "Ah if I can still be of use."[9]

Recovery began at that moment. After years of deprivation, strength returned to the emaciated body so quickly that puzzled doctors spoke of "marvels."

"Say 'miracles,' " corrected the saint.[10] Tossing out the mattress, he was on his way back to his 1 A.M. confessions.[11] But on food, he was forced to capitulate: Until complete recovery he was to eat two meals a day and to drink a quarter glass of old claret. Over those two tablespoons of wine, the chagrined saint groaned to friends, who tried not to smile, "I have become a glutton."[12]

A visiting missionary who himself had spent whole days hearing confessions, preaching, and catechizing, observed Vianney's still-penitential life-style (his main meal was over in less than ten minutes, most of the food invariably left in the dish)[13] and declared, "humanly speaking he couldn't live three months."[14] The observer only echoed doctors who insisted Vianney's survival depended on giving up the confessional for good and departing Ars for rest and a change of air. The saint ignored them. At periods (the Lents of 1849, 1850, and 1851, for instance) he even went back to one daily meal.[15] Yet he lived another sixteen years. And lived them with physical power: Until the end he had no diminution of hearing, eyesight, or memory, while his step, if heavy, remained rapid.[16] He even carried unaided a church banner so heavy others could barely lift it.[17]

Could he have been a secret eater? Hardly. There are plenty of witnesses that his stomach was so shrunken from years of fasting that he became ill if forced, as he once was by the bishop, to eat what others consider a normal meal.[18] Various priests familiar with his vacationless, seven-day-a-week, almost round the clock routine agreed only "supernatural assistance" could sustain this "crushing weight."[19] Let science have the last word in the person of a physician:

> Knowing as I do, his mode of life I look upon his existence
> as extraordinary and beyond the range of a natural expla-
> nation.[20]

▲

Another classic example is virile St. John Bosco of the warm heart and welcoming smile. His asceticism less tinged with Jansenism than the Curé's, Bosco still poured himself out serving impoverished children, only God knowing on any day whether the saint, who lost his own father at the age of two, was supporting several thousand wholly or partially. Stress should have killed him young, for bills were always pouring in and for forty years his only assured income was what he called "the Providence of God."

His days for years were a blur of cooking for boys, sewing suits for boys, giving haircuts to boys, even making their beds when they were too rushed or too lazy.[21] In addition, for a long time he was a one-man academic and technical school, with whatever help he could rustle from older boys or the community. And foremost a spiritual mentor, he spent hours counseling and guiding, in and out of the confessional. Saturdays he was often all night on a kneeler to hear a couple hundred boys who each wanted the saint's ear—no other would do—for his confession,[22] occasionally speeding the process by those gifts of the sanctified mind (shared with Vianney and many other saints) which at times let him read a heart and mind like a book.

There was no distance too far for him to walk in that pre-car and bus era to get a teenager a job or see how he was being treated there. To finance his schools, homes, and clubs for boys, he also covered miles on foot begging. He led unruly slum urchins on long hikes into the country, played every type of athletics with them and well past middle age, in spite of the terrible varicose veins[23] hidden under his long black cassock, regularly outran the fastest.

Burning the midnight oil, he wrote books for them and was on twenty-four-hour call to deal with their minor and serious illnesses. He was besieged by them and by outsiders, people "seeking advice in the sacristy, on the porticoes, in the playground or the refectory, on the stairs, and in his room. This went on morning, noon, and night.[24] Adults were drawn by his power of miracles, of healing† and the gifts of his sanctified mind, youngsters by his personality and genuine love for them.

For years he stayed up one entire night weekly to catch up and made it a rule never to sleep longer than five hours.[25] He also had a rule against napping—which he occasionally broke like the time he fell asleep against a store wall standing up. He vacationed on foot and with twenty to thirty boys in tow—a fitting "rest" for one who often laughed, "We'll rest in heaven."[26]

If you can't rest, it is standard advice to try to eat well. Bosco had a rule instead to never eat enough to be full.[27] He also was a great believer in not fussing over his food, although for his boys he willingly cooked the best he could afford[28] usually soup or the staple of the Piedmontese poor, the cornmeal

† See details of some cures in *Nothing Short of a Miracle*.

mush called polenta. When for a period his mother was his housekeeper, he insisted Mama Margaret cook for him no more than twice a week. In Turin's steamy summers, the un-refrigerated dish became rather rancid after a couple days.[29] Up by three in summer, by five-thirty in the coldest winter, he worked on only a cup of chicory coffee, adding a few drops of milk if he were not well, until about one, when he ate a little of his miserable dish. Fridays and Saturdays he fasted still more strenuously.[30]

In later years he had young priests living with him. For them he provided more substantial nourishment. But his own intake remained that of a peasant in a famine. And asked a moment after leaving the table, this brilliant man of photo-graphic memory could not recall what had been served.[31] Word of Bosco's asceticism got around. Scoffers countered that he was a charlatan who starved his boys while himself eating sumptuously. An argument broke out on the matter at a count's table one day. One Father Stellardi, chaplain to the king of Piedmont, said he could find out by dropping in, as a fellow priest, at this Bosco's at mealtime.

As expected, Mama Margaret invited the guest to join them but begged he give her time to prepare "something for com-pany."

"Nonsense," the court priest insisted, "I'll eat just what you do." Mama Margaret shrugged and served the meal.

> [It opened with] a piece of codfish moistened with olive oil. The smell alone of the oil was enough to force him to decline. Next . . . was a dish of cardoons [a vegetable related to the artichoke] boiled and salted, followed by a slice of cheese. Much to the secret amusement of the [stu-dent priests] . . . who ate with Don Bosco, Father Stel-lardi excused himself on every count.[32]

Selfless young men from time to time tried to duplicate their spiritual father's eating habits. In every case, they threw in the towel. None had reached the point in his spiritual life where he could eat so little or so lousily. When anyone commented on how little Don Bosco ate, however, he assured them with his irresistible smile that he had "a difficult stomach" and "became very miserable" if he overate. That appears to have been true but still one wonders how the "difficult stomach" handled the foods it did. For instance, staying at a country rectory the saint came into the kitchen late one night. Seeing only one pot on the stove, he assumed it was the dinner the housekeeper was supposed to have left him. He ate the gruel-like mess and went to bed. The next morning, breakfastless, he was back in the confessional when the housekeeper began complaining that her laundry starch had disappeared. The pastor was amazed: Don Bosco had said nothing about the miserable "dinner."[33]

With such inadequate food and rest, the saint maintained the look and drive of a powerful athlete—factors so appealing in his work with the young—for many years. And he did so in spite of pitifully swollen legs, near blindness, emphysema, and other infirmities. In 1884 a doctor compared Bosco's body to a once-fine coat reduced to an utter rag from overwork.[34] Yet the "rag" kept working almost until his death four years later at age seventy-three.

▲

France in the 1830s. The great era of the middle classes under the citizen king, Louis Philippe. The man known today as Bl. Jacques Laval (1803–64) was a stylish young physician. If he habitually "forgot" to bill the poor, such charities in no way crimped his indulgence in expensive clothes and furnishings, fine horses, and parties where he danced with the beauties of his class. Under that surface, however, were other stirrings.

Scolded for his worldliness by a sister, he surprised her by replying, "I'm resisting God."

In 1834 God won. Laval not only returned to the religious practices he had discarded, he soon abandoned medicine to become a priest.

At his first parish he found a dozen Sunday churchgoers. To draw grace to the lost flock, he spent every day from 4 A.M. to 10 or 11 P.M. praying in the empty church, with a few hours out for visits to the sick or study. Food he cut to the minimum: "a little dry bread" six hours after rising, soup and cold potatoes about midday, another "pitiful plate" in the evening. He slept on a "primitive," hay-stuffed mattress until he gave this to a poorer man, bedding down thereafter on "a sheepskin stretched on the floor." In case he had not done enough, under the former snappy dresser's shabby clothes there was also a hair shirt.[35]

Gradually people responded to his spiritual assault by letting him serve them. He assembled a good-size class of children for spiritual instruction, taking over their nonspiritual education as well when their schoolteacher quit. The river Eure overflowed and he housed and fed the flooded-out, searching them out on horseback. At his table regularly were an impoverished blind woman and a man so deformed his own parents found him repulsive. Soon there was also a steady stream of impoverished visitors, none of whom left unfed or empty-handed. When the sacristan protested that one was a con man, Laval only laughed. "He's not fooling me, only himself," he soothed.[36] Self-giving to all, in and for God, had become Laval's life. When he heard of Francis Libermann's (p. 55) new missionary society, he rushed to join, embarking in June 1841 for the island of Mauritius.

On this British possession of 14,000 people just taken over from the French, a new archbishop was busy sacking three of the island's eight priests for immorality. Three others he kept only because forced to. Of the white elite, six families were "slightly religious." As for the darker masses (Malaysians, Chinese, Indians, and—the majority—newly freed African slaves), the whites, including most clergy, used them as servants and sexually.

Into this pit of "corruption and riotous immorality,"[37] as he phrased it, the former bon vivant descended with his healing touch. Shunning the corrupt priests and ignoring the rich whites, he went at once to live among the blacks, learning their language, identifying with them culturally, giving himself to them totally. To Libermann he reported, "The whites are the big obstacle to the conversion of our black brothers."[38] Soon two policemen were guarding the troublemaking priest from men enraged by his cutting off their supply of nubile concubines.[39]

After three years on the island, he gave Libermann his daily and Sunday schedules. I quote the daily:

> Rising at 5 . . . visit to the jail for morning prayer with men and women prisoners; at a quarter to six I go to the church for a half hour meditation followed by half an hour [spiritual] preparation for Holy Mass, which is at seven . . . [with] half an hour thanksgiving. In the confessional until between half nine and ten; at half ten recital of Little Hours, a little scripture reading; a quarter of an hour for lunch and then the remainder of the day is . . . hearing confessions, marrying, baptising, visiting the sick; at five visit to the jail for evening prayer with men and women; in the confessional from half past five until seven; at seven the Rosary and [spiritual] instructions begin; at eight the main prayer followed by some hymns. . . . Instruction continues until nine in the evening; [when] . . . I shut the church door; then a little prayer, a little supper, to bed.[40]

He ends the letter that he is "sometimes a little tired but hobbling along none the less." This killing seven-day-a-week schedule included two light meals on weekdays. On Sunday the same letter shows he ate nothing until after three in the afternoon and no second meal. There was not even an occasional day off. As to sleep, I note that after fixing the hour precisely for every activity, he suddenly slips into generalities after he shuts the church door: "a little prayer" before bed. One wonders how much this saint considers "a little" even after a day which has been spent, if one looks at it closely, primarily in prayer.

Eventually an emissary from Libermann visited. He reported:

> All that I could say to you about Fr. Laval's mission would still be beneath reality. . . . I intended to spend only a month but . . . I could not without cruelty or inhumanity leave him. . . . He would have died. . . . I found his health considerably weakened; it is still clear that God sustains him in a supernatural way.[41]

They sent a permanent assistant, but by this time his holiness had drawn a flock so large it could have kept ten priests busy. In 1854 Laval writes to Libermann,

> We are like besieged soldiers, fighting desperately, looking daily to see if some relief is on its way. We are truly very tired.[42]

Libermann sent three more helpers. They were greeted with a cholera epidemic. Onlookers noted with amazement that "Laval, exhausted by years of prayer, fasting, [and] over work, found mysteriously a new self, capable of meeting every demand."[43]

After the tragic period, all the exhausted priests had to take a rest—except the saint. Exclaimed one witness of "the poor old man . . . , 'what a tough nut to crack!' "[44]

▲

Bl. Anna Maria Taigi (1769–1837), the pretty, somewhat vain young wife of a prince's porter, was called by God to become a mystic. Within a few years she was also being called by just about everyone else in Rome because of spiritual gifts that included healing, ability to read hearts, and knowledge of the future. Visit the sick, counsel warring marrieds, advise ordinary people, cardinals, and even the pope at times—here is a full-time apostolate. But it rests atop Anna's life as an impoverished housewife with seven children who ekes out her husband's pay by occasional sewing jobs between a nineteenth-century woman's time-consuming chores.

She was always still at them when her husband, Domenico, got home at two or three in the morning from his job, but she made him supper and listened with good humor to his talk of the day. Then at three or four o'clock, surrounded by sleeping children (the family usually lived in two rooms), Anna knelt for night prayers that, Domenico testified during the Beatification Process, were "sometimes lengthy."[45]

Grim determination at this hour? Her fiery-tempered, not overly devout husband did not think so. After mentioning all the groups from "evil-tongued people" to cardinals for whom Anna prayed, he reminisced, "It all seemed to me a Paradise."[46]

Then they went to bed. In an hour or two she was at a nearby church for 5 A.M. mass.[47]

What about diet?

"She ate like a sparrow" is the sworn testimony.[48] Specifically, after mass she took a cup of coffee; at noon a few drops of soup and a morsel of whatever she served the family sufficed. Her family were used to her never sitting down at the table. At times, though, the children made a face over the meat she set aside for herself for several days.

"Ooh Mom, that stinks!" She answered truthfully, "That's how I like it." Unsaid was the reason she liked it unpalatable: her hope, by such mortifications, to help balance the scales for all those who go through life crying "Me first." For the same reason three days a week she limited herself to morning coffee and midday soup, at various times made forty-day (not total) fasts, and in Rome's hot summers sometimes went as long as eight days without a drink to help some especially needy fellow human.[49]

After years with the hotheaded husband, rambunctious children, and cantankerous mother in two dark rooms off a garbage-laden alley, Anna's family got larger quarters just before the birth of her seventh child. These filled, too, with people she waited on and put up with. Both her daughters lived with her as adults, one with husband and six offspring. A son, his difficult wife, and their brood moved in for a time. And a temperamental priest was for twenty years a household member, stationed there by a bishop to record everything the "saint" said or did.[50] Only Anna's irascible father, whom she had to support financially, never lived with her. As he insisted on his own quarters, it required a daily trip to tend him and his repulsive skin disease. Domenico may have hit the nail on the head when he remarked during his Process testimony that his wife's whole life had been an exercise in patience.

Sans sleep, barely eating, a lamb in a household of lions, Anna outlived four of her children, dying in 1837 at 68.

▲

Eating stinky meat is frowned on in the twentieth century as an anti-body excess. In the rest of her asceticism aimed at helping others, Taigi is sister to a housewife mystic who died in 1936. Praxedes Fernandez lived her entire life in Asturias, the fiery mining region that played a bloody role in Spain's Civil War (1936–39). Born into a family of mine superintendents, Praxedes married "beneath her" into the working class.

Widowed six years later, she kept house for her four sons, aged mother, spoiled schoolteacher sister, and frequent guests, hauling water by bucket, raising a big garden, and sewing the boys' clothing to stretch her meager funds.* Besides unending toil, Praxedes faced the stresses of a woman raising four sons in violent and antispiritual times; family conflicts like that with her eldest son, who resented her position as unpaid servant to her younger sister (he was too immature to see this was a spiritual choice); the loss of one boy in a tragic accident; and finally the civil war, a source of danger to her sons and of spiritual anguish to her. Bearing all this, she somehow made time daily to feed, clean for, nurse, and spiritually sustain various elderly, ill, or poverty-stricken families.[51] For these quietly heroic charities, she was welcomed even by miners who hated Catholics. "Strong as a horse"[52] as she was, all this energy output would seem to eventually demand normal diet and sleep.

Instead, if work for others was her primary charity, another sacrifice was fasting. To help all those who needed her prayers, Praxedes fasted three days a week, Saturdays eating only bread and water, Fridays only a tablespoon of chickpeas. On her nonfasting days, "She hardly ever ate breakfast, . . . almost always gave her supper to some poor person [while] . . . lunch consisted only of one dish."[53] And working until late at night, she was up at four, attending three masses for years as the opening to her day. Passionate by temperament, Praxedes also regularly whipped herself as penance for the violence around her.

A morbid personality? Hardly. Praxedes was a cheerful per-

---

* Her well-to-do mother gave her no financial help beyond a place to live in her home.

son who loved to dance, at times sang for joy, and looked forward to eating good things, including candy, on Easter.[54]

In 1936 war came to the town of Oviedo where the family had taken refuge. People cowered in the basement from bombs —except fearless Praxedes.[55] Women hauling water with her also marveled that while they had to rest after the long, dangerous trek, the fifty-year-old went at once to her sewing machine. "Amazing strength," they told each other.[56]

The woman of "iron constitution" offered her life to God as a sacrifice for peace. She fell ill but neither her sister nor the one son at home would help. The day Praxedes finally went to bed, a doctor—told she had until that day done the housework —kept repeating, "Impossible!"[57]

To visitors Praxedes made light of her painful illness but sorrowed that "countrymen who should love each other as brothers were killing each other."[58] As always, she refrained from criticizing either side. At the hour she died, the carnage stopped; the ninety-day siege lifted eleven days later.

▲

Margaret Hallahan (1802–68) was a child of London's slums. Her Irish parents made their only offspring the focus of bitter quarrels. "Harassed by poverty, anxiety, and sickness," the mother took out her frustrations on Margaret, accusing the improvident alcoholic husband of "spoiling" the girl to whom he gave the affection withheld from her.[59] In the summer of Margaret's ninth year the drinker died, followed in December by his wife.

At ten she was employed. For the next twenty-seven years she would be a domestic in various homes. Hard work but she was equal to it. At sixteen, she is described as tall, strikingly good-looking, feisty (when an employer tried to seduce her, she grabbed a kitchen cleaver and ran him out the door), and strong as a horse.[60]

That strength was her downfall. When a manservant refused to carry a heavy iron stove up several flights of stairs, Margaret—who was as vain over her prowess as she was immune to vanity over her looks—boasted she could do it. She did but hurt her back badly. A couple years later, in 1820 when she was eighteen, a blow on the injured area resulted in the "first of terrible lumbar abscesses which were for the rest of her life an unending source of suffering." Her employer called in

> two famous surgeons who agreed that she would never walk again, and that in time her brain would probably be affected; a prognosis which used . . . to be smilingly recalled by Mother Margaret, when people wondered at her ceaseless activity of mind and body.[61]

In 1839 she had been maid to an English family, living in Bruges, Belgium, for fifteen years.[62] In financial difficulties, these pillars of respectability fired their other servants and piled all the work on Margaret. When she finally collapsed, they cast her off to a Catholic charity hospital which had only a mattress on the bare floor to give her.

When the news spread that the woman known all over the city "not only for her goodness and kindness to everybody" but for her power to free the scrupulous from their burdens was dying, it "occupied one person fully . . . to open the door" to her visitors.[63]

Odd as it seems, mystical theologians say it is not unusual that it was precisely when she had been cast off as useless, her splendid body wrecked, that Margaret heard the inner call that culminated in her founding the English Dominican Congregation of St. Catherine of Siena. Not that it was clear at first. When the forty-year-old domestic did not die, her spiritual director, who knew of the vow of chastity made when she was twenty, merely advised her to take up her apostolic activities full time.

She returned to England, working among the poor in the slums of industrial towns. Others joined her and a new religious order was born. Founding schools, orphanages, and a hospital, teaching, caring for the sick and evangelizing (in one year she made 365 converts to her faith) while recruiting, training, and administering the new order meant Mother Margaret worked harder than ever. Yet she was never free from the severe pain of her back, the terrible headaches this caused, and the excruciating abscesses that formed about three times a year. There was also a chronic skin disease, probably psoriasis. Her prayer life transcended this to the point that people remarked her unquenchable gaiety and the deep interest she took in everyone. No one dreamed she lived in chronic pain.[64] Her sleep and food intake patterns may be inferred from a spiritual guide's remark that he had always to hold her back in her desire for mortifications and self-giving lest she "exhaust her great strength."

One morning a nun who didn't feel well went to Margaret's room to ask permission to skip morning prayers.

> Entering unperceived, she found Mother Margaret standing erect, engaged in washing the [skin] wounds . . . [covering] her whole person, and praying aloud as she did so for the strength to carry out her daily duties.[65]

The prayer heard by the suddenly shamed nun seems to have been abundantly answered, for Mother Margaret Hallahan even survived typhus, caught in 1846 from one of the slum families she nursed. She lived to be sixty-six.

▲

I reported Père Lamy's sister's avowal that she never saw him asleep during their youth. There are no witnesses as to whether he continued his all-night prayer vigils during the years he was consumed by his parish duties and special apostolate to the young and the very poor—he was called "the priest of the hooligans" and "the priest of the ragpickers." But his workload alone, says philosopher Jacques Maritain who knew Lamy well, proves the priest "possessed a supernatural energy."[66]

He certainly didn't get his power from food. From his childhood as the only son of hard-working farmers, his diet reveals the self-denial associated with holiness, including refusing to drink the table wine his family made. As a youth, he distilled many a liter of grape and plum brandy but never tasted either until it was ordered for his heart condition at age seventy-five.[67]

At Troyes, when he was thirty, Lamy lived "in great poverty," eating primarily beans, potatoes, peas, and other vegetables, according to a letter from Père Andre Stoecklin of the Servants of Jesus and Mary, the order founded by Lamy in his last years. Stoecklin writes me that this same diet was lifelong. "He had extremely simple habits in this area," my informant sums up; "above all [when I think of his diet] I think of vegetables."[68]

By seventy, suffering from heart disease, Lamy moved slowly with the aid of a cane. Yet on occasion witnesses testify that sans cane he could move at the speed of a young man running. (See other evidences of Lamy's unusual energy, p. 302). The old scallywag, as Lamy called himself, lived to age seventy-six.

▲

Looking at these representative saints of the many born healthy who are yet so discrepant in energy input and outgo, I ruminate on what, besides tapping into an outside energy source through prayer, might empower these people. Diet? A low-fat, low-sugar diet can be cited as a plus in the case of most—not all—saints' *longevity*. But even then it is not an adequate explanation for their *unfailing daily energy* in spite of minuscule rest and nutrition. Vegetarianism is cited—especially by vegetarians—as energizing. But not all these saints are vegetarians. In the case of Père Lamy, who rarely ate meat, besides failing to explain how he may have worked without normal sleep, a vegetable diet did not even keep him from developing heart disease.

Some researchers claim that the underfed are healthier and longer lived. This is only true, however, to a degree, beyond which lie malnutrition and starvation. Moreover lab animals may be strong and long-lived on a tiny, high-quality diet, but millions of underfed people on inferior food like that eaten by most saints are beset by malnutrition-related diseases these saints escaped. Don Bosco's seminarians, for instance, who ate somewhat better than he did, sometimes died of tuberculosis, while he remained TB-free. Moreover, other research claims that being underfed increases risk of illness or death as much as overfeeding.

With each saint there are factors from a specific ethnic group and era that affect health, longevity, and energy. Italians from the Piedmont province where Don Bosco lived, for instance, are noted workers. But Bosco's energy, considering his rest and diet, exceeds even the standards of Piedmont.

I asked myself, could the group of this chapter represent, not a subtle psychology of holiness but spectacular heredity? Would I find parents or several siblings who lived to a ripe old age under very hard circumstances, showing a genetic inheritance of exceptional sturdiness? As would be expected of healthy people with good life-spans (I ignore Praxedes, as she *willed* to die at fifty), *most* had at least one parent who lived long enough, say into the seventies, to be considered old. Still not a single one appears to have come from a family of unusually long life-spans from the available information. Not all even had one parent who made it to old age. Some like Margaret Hallahan, lost *both* parents when they were still young. And this lack of spectacular heredity was true of many others who could be profiled if space permitted.

Generally the saints, in spite of less adequate rest and nutrition, had *longer* life-spans than their parents. I found only one of this group, Bl. Anna Maria Taigi, who had a parent (among those whose life-spans are available) with a longer life than the child. Anna's mother, who bore only the one child, outlived by five years her daughter, who bore seven. The real point of comparison is not the obvious one of the demands of carrying, nursing, and rearing children; it is that Anna Maria's mother ate and slept normally while expending a modicum of energy, whereas her daughter carried a prodigious workload with almost no sleep or food. St. John Bosco's father died young of pneumonia. John outlived a "fatal" pneumonia attack, and his life-span was five years greater than his mother's. Her life as a widowed Piedmontese peasant had been tough. But his was tougher. The Curé d'Ars' life outspanned his mother's by a year (I have no death date for the father). Compared to the son's life, the mother's was one of ease and luxury.

Next I wondered if these could be predominantly first children, who are theorized stronger than their siblings? Or could these saints be energized by the psychological nurturing and superior care patterns associated with a family's most favored child? I found that placement among siblings and psychological position vis-à-vis the parents also fail to provide the answer to saints' inexplicable energy. Anna Maria and Margaret, for instance, were only children, which can lead to superior care and psychological sturdiness. But Margaret's parents made her the object of their quarrels; and Anna Maria's parents, far from doting on her, were demanding, difficult personalities who caused her endless trouble. John Bosco was the oldest child of his mother, the middle of three sons of his father, who had been a widower. Since John's mother raised the half-brother as her oldest, John occupied the middle-child position.

Saintly Margaret Bosco so far avoided favoring her flesh and blood children that, in a conflict between John and the older boy, it was John she turned out of the house because she felt he had more resources than sullen Anthony. Resources John had, but he still felt, he said himself, lonely, rejected, and frightened as he wandered looking for farm work. The Curé d'Ars was the youngest of six and perhaps the favorite. He outlived four siblings (a soldier brother disappeared), but the sixth outlived him by thirty years. Père Lamy was the oldest, but he was more hardworked than catered to by his peasant parents. For instance, the mother knew something of his night vigils after days of heavy labor but merely remarked, "That isn't really necessary." Praxedes was the favorite of her father but not of her mother.

As for being born in some optimal time of year, the saints represent a spectrum of birthdays. In the end, I find these representative figures have only one thing in common, besides inborn vigor. Born in an era when a child had a life expectancy of thirty to thirty-five years (in the case of Père Lamy, forty to forty-five years), they worked inhumanly, including carrying on for years *after* the deterioration of their splendid bodies, while living well past the average life-span of their generation. And they did this on rations of food and rest that force consideration of mystics' claims that prayer at certain levels is as energizing as good food and sleep.

To close this chapter, let us look briefly at a man and a woman for whom there are as yet no death dates.

▲

He came from rather a poor family and early lost them all— mother, father, sister, brother—to various illnesses, indicating poor heredity. Due to war of the cruelest sort, he was forced to study for the priesthood clandestinely while supporting himself for a time by the heaviest kind of labor, quarrying stone.

He had several close brushes with death: a streetcar knocked him down, fracturing his skull; a truck nearly crushed him, causing a permanent slight stoop from one shoulder's being higher than the other; a gunman's bullets seriously wounded him.

He has always been admired for his vigor; yet at his first assignment as a priest the housekeeper whispered that his bed was never slept in. Did he sleep on the floor, people wondered, or pray all night? They clucked, too, over his poverty of dress. The faded, threadbare cassock was covered with huge patches, which grew in number as time passed. Fearing he would freeze to death as he sat hour after hour in the chilly confessional during the icy winter of the area, they presented him with a new cassock, which he wore, and an overcoat, which he promptly gave away. When he served for a time in a country parish, he refused to use a horse and cart, walking everywhere in order to identify with the people's poverty. He also offered to replace in the fields anyone who was ill. Later as a high churchman his "battered hat and shabby cassock" were the first things Cardinal Franz Koenig of Vienna noticed when they met.

He has always eaten simply, favoring the sausages, potatoes, and cabbages of his forebears. From these few facts, which leave us tantalized by all that is still unknown about Pope John Paul II, we can infer what his pattern of energy intake and output may be. Asked to comment on the pope's unusual stamina, Los Angeles-born bishop Justin Rigali, who works in Rome, says:

> He has an immense amount of spiritual energy. [This] . . . channels all his psychic energy.
>
> Somehow or other in some mysterious way it just gives him physical stamina. I don't know how it works because it's mysterious. I know the fact is there and I'm convinced

that his real secret is in his prayer life, his spiritual communion with God.[69]

This is a churchman's estimate. It is seconded by *Los Angeles Times* reporter Don A. Schanche, whose 1982 article on the then sixty-one-year-old pope's unusual energy I can only quote in part:

> When Pope John Paul II slowly mounted the steps of a tall, makeshift altar in . . . northern Nigeria, last Sunday . . . his perspiring face, . . . drawn and pallid since [serious wounds from] the attempt on his life nine months ago, was flushed. . . . Only three days into the arduous schedule that would require him to preside over eight Masses, deliver more than 30 speeches and stand for hours in heavy vestments in relentlessly humid tropical heat, the Pope's vitality appeared to have drained away.
>
> But a few minutes later, after taking his place on a canopy-shaded throne, John Paul's color returned. . . . If any thing, he appeared healthier than he had when the papal plane left Rome. . . .
>
> The pontiff . . . conduct[ed] a sweltering outdoor Mass, including the ordination of 92 Nigerian priests, that lasted more than three hours. While many . . . slipped away from the ceremony to the restorative air conditioning of a nearby hotel, . . . [he] seemed to gain strength.
>
> From that day on, until the end of the journey on Friday, John Paul kept a pace that exhausted men half his age, yet never seemed to flag.[70]

Four years later Schanche covered a two-week trip in which the sixty-five-year-old pope gave over fifty speeches in seventeen cities of six countries, was always up at 5 A.M., and rarely to bed before midnight. Schanche says that by the eleventh day most of the seventy-three journalists and thirty-one Vatican officials on the trip "were on the verge of collapse but John Paul appeared fresh and energetic." Then Schanche quotes Dr. Edmond Chiu, an Australian physician who said regarding the pontiff's inexplicable energy, "He has spiritual resources. . . ."[71]

▲

Those who know one living foundress of religious orders say hers is a life of tedious waits and tiring travel crisscrossing the planet in crowded buses, planes, and trains. Sitting up whole nights in cheap railway compartments, her destination as often as not is some unfurnished dwelling where she will squat on the floor with the poorest of the poor.

Her diet is meager and ascetic, consisting mostly of a kind of third-world pancake. Always up at 4:30 A.M., she works habitually till midnight or 1, sometimes 2 A.M. A priest friend, Father Edward Le Joly, speaks of one mortification he notices: Even when sick or dog-tired, she always sits on the edge of a chair, her back erect.

Although she says she was born with good health, Le Joly notes she appears increasingly frail. Yet to describe her he chooses the phrase "bundle of energy," while other onlookers characterize Mother Teresa of Calcutta as a "dynamo," "energizer," and "indefatigable."

Prefacing his remarks with the scripture passage (Isaiah 40:31) "Those who trust in the Lord will renew their strength; they will soar like eagles," Le Joly says Teresa's spiritual strength increases with the years, while, notwithstanding her hard life, her physical forces are "renewed in a remarkable manner." To the priest the explanation for this vitality is simple: "Her power comes from above."[72]

notes

1. Francis Trochu, *The Curé d'Ars,* p. 527. Based on the Process, this work is scrupulously documented.

2. Comtesse Des Garets, *Procès de l'Ordinaire,* p. 911, quoted by Trochu, op. cit., p. 122.

3. Trochu, op. cit., p. 123.

4. Ibid., p. 124.

5. Ibid., p. 120.

6. Ibid., p. 479.

7. Ibid., p. 125.

8. *Procès de l'Ordinaire,* p. 498, quoted by Trochu, op. cit., p. 311.

9. Trochu, op. cit., p. 349.

10. Comtesse des Garets, letter of May 17, 1843; *Procès de l'Ordinaire,* p. 900, quoted by Trochu, op. cit., p. 350.

11. Trochu, loc. cit.

12. Ibid., p. 352.

13. *Procès de l'Ordinaire,* p. 1208, quoted by Trochu, op. cit., p. 479.

14. Ibid., p. 1495, quoted by Trochu, op. cit., p. 352.

15. Trochu, op. cit., p. 479.

16. Ibid., pp. 415–16.

17. *Procès apostolique continuatif,* p. 157, quoted by Trochu, op. cit., p. 416.

18. Trochu, op. cit., p. 480.

19. Ibid., pp. 352, 475, 525, quoting various Process witnesses and documents.

20. Ibid., p. 525, quoting one Dr. Michel of Coligny.

21. John Baptist Lemoyne, *Memorie biografiche di San Giovanni Bosco,* Vol. 3, pp. 254–55.

22. Ibid., Vol. 3, pp. 106–8. See also p. 154.

23. A. Auffray, *Saint John Bosco,* p. 282. By a Salesian, this life is taken from the twenty-volume *Memorie biografiche* and other authentic sources.

24. Lemoyne, op. cit., Vol. 5, p. 487.

25. Ibid., Vol. 4, p. 131.

26. Ibid., Vol. 5, p. 482, describes one of these trips.

27. Ibid., Vol. 3, p. 20.

28. Ibid., Vol. 3, p. 255.

29. Ibid., Vol. 3, p. 20.

30. Ibid., Vol. 4, pp. 131–32.

31. Ibid., Vol. 4, pp. 133–34, 139.

32. Peter Lappin, *Sunshine in the Shadow,* p. 173. This life of Don Bosco's mother by a Salesian is from authenticated sources, including the *Memorie biografiche,* which reports the same incident in Lemoyne's Vol. 4, pp. 135–36.

33. Lemoyne, op. cit., Vol. 4, p. 139.

34. Dr. Combal, professor of medicine in Marseilles. See Peter Lappin, *The Wine in the Chalice,* p. 135.

35. Michael O'Carroll, *Blessed Jacques Désiré Laval,* pp. 8–9. Written by a member of the saint's religious order, this work was supplied by another member, Fr. Farrell Sheridan.

36. Ibid., pp. 9–10.

37. Ibid., p. 19, quoting a letter from Laval to Libermann. While no date is given, it is likely late 1841 or 1842.

38. Ibid.

39. Ibid., pp. 27–28.

40. Ibid., p. 25, quoting a letter dated 1844.

41. Ibid., p. 33.

42. Ibid., p. 56.

43. Ibid.

44. Ibid., p. 57.

45. His sworn deposition was given when he was ninety-one. Its details, reported here, are all corroborated by others who lived in

their home, most significantly the priest stationed there as the saint's "observer."

46. Her husband's testimony.

47. Testimonies of her daughter and husband.

48. Testimony by her husband.

49. Testimonies of daughters and husband.

50. Don Rafaele Natali, stationed by now Bl. (then Bishop) Vincent Strambi.

51. Martin-Maria Olive, *Práxedes,* pp. 128–38, report many sworn testimonies to her charities. See also p. 99.

52. Ibid., p. 180. Her strength was general knowledge.

53. Ibid., p. 113. Her son's testimony.

54. Ibid., pp. 79, 22, 123, 157, and 113, reporting various firsthand testimonies.

55. Ibid., p. 168, testimony of her son.

56. Ibid., testimony of Lucrecia Garcia, Sept. 12, 1966.

57. Ibid., p. 172, testimony of her sister.

58. Ibid., p. 174, quoting sworn statement of Carmen Martinez, who visited the dying woman.

59. S. M. C., *Steward of Souls,* pp. 11–12. This biography is based on letters of her associates and the unpublished *The Inner Life of*

Mother Margaret by Bishop Ullathorne, her close collaborator. This manuscript is in the Dominican sisters' archives in Stone, England.

60. Ibid., p. 26.

61. Ibid., p. 27.

62. The Thompsons were unfeeling, but their children adored Margaret, who loved them dearly.

63. S. M. C., op. cit., p. 40.

64. Ibid., pp. 164–65. Also p. 46, quoting Bishop Ullathorne's unpublished manuscript.

65. Ibid., p. 165.

66. Jacques Maritain's preface to Paul Biver's *Père Lamy,* p. 8.

67. Biver, op. cit., p. 20.

68. Dated May 20, 1980, Stoecklin writes: *"Au point de vue alimentation le Père Lamy durant son enfance avait celle des paysans de France de son époque: assez frugale et à base de produits cultivés sur place: légumes, oeufs, sans doute plus rarement de la viande. A Troyes, comme jeune homme de 30 ans, il vivait une grande pauvreté et ne mangeait sans doute pas tous les jours à sa faim. La nourriture était à base de féculents: haricots, pommes de terre, poirreau, salades. Il en était de meme à La Courneuve et durant ses années de retraite: surtout je pense des légumes. Mais nous n'avons pas de renseignements très précis sur la matière. Il était très simple en ce domaine."* I note that a seminarian quoted by Biver (op. cit., p. 167), after saying "the fare was very simple," reports meat was served. This may have been company fare, however.

69. *The Tidings,* Sept. 13, 1985, pp. 1, 13.

70. *Los Angeles Times,* Feb. 21, 1982, Part 4, p. 2.

71. *Los Angeles Times,* Nov. 29, 1986, Part 1, p. 22.

72. As Edward Le Joly has been associated with Mother Teresa for a long time, his book *Mother Teresa and her Missionaries of Charity* is my source for details of her rest and food.

7

"i just knew
he couldn't last
—but he did"

We come next to a group where established facts of physiology and medicine are suddenly laughable. To represent them, nine chronically frail or terminally ill men* who survive, even thrive, deprived of normal food and rest in situations that ought to quickly prove fatal.

▲

Born in 1887 in southern Italy, where poverty is as much a part of the landscape as the rocky soil, Padre Pio (Francis Forgione) lived to be eighty-one, dying in 1968, in spite of an early "terminal" illness, unparalleled labor, fifty years of daily

---

* Due to space limitations, I have dropped a chapter on women of this type, featuring Edel Quinn and Maria Troncatti from the twentieth century; St. Frances Cabrini, who died in 1917; and St. Julie Billiart and St. Jeanne Thouret, who died in the nineteenth century.

blood loss, and the rest and food patterns so often associated in all faiths with sanctity.

As a child he had digestive problems. Entering the Capuchin order (one of three branches of the Franciscans), his health worsened. At periods he vomited uncontrollably, not always all at once, he had migraine-type headaches, a tubercular-like cough, and severe fevers. In 1917 the thermometer in his mouth cracked after passing 108 degrees Fahrenheit. Substituting a bathhouse thermometer, in Pio's armpit it climbed at once to 125.5 degrees. Not only did such fevers not prove fatal, the young mystic had none of the delirium or other mental disturbances associated with very high temperatures. Nor did he become emaciated when he once had to live six months on milk alone.[1]

One authority speculates that odd illnesses occur in mystics from "the immense strain which the exalted spirit puts upon a body." In *Nothing Short of a Miracle* I have told how between 1903–18 various doctors diagnosed tuberculosis or chronic bronchitis, while one physician sensed Pio's physical illness had a spiritual base.[2] In 1911 specialists in Naples simply declared him terminally ill.[3] During those years his superiors sent him to various friaries, hoping to find a climate that might prove healing. Every time he had to return to his parents because of his terrible health.

Drafted, Pio spent World War I on health leaves except for a brief period when he was ordered to noncombatant duty and immediately hospitalized. In early 1918 he was invalided out of the military.

Since 1910, unknown to all but a handful, he was at times a stigmatist, that is, one with wounds duplicating some or all of those suffered by Christ in crucifixion. Sent to the inaccessible Our Lady of Grace friary in San Giovanni Rotondo in December 1917, Pio appeared to have only a short time to live. Then

in September 1918 the failing monk was suddenly visibly†
restigmatized, his hands and feet pierced and a lance-like
wound in his side.

Seeing his sanctity, people had already run after the young
friar. After he became—to his intense embarrassment—the
first known stigmatized priest,‡ Pio simply never again knew a
moment's peace. By two o'clock each morning phalanxes of
jostling pilgrims positioned themselves for the moment when
the bolted church doors would swing open for the mystic's five
o'clock mass. To get in his confessional took a week to ten
days.

The Franciscans who lived with Padre Pio say that in his
prime, when he was forty to fifty, he was eating three and a
half ounces, primarily vegetables, every twenty-four hours.
With his digestive problems there were also times (see p. 87)
he didn't eat at all. He slept about two hours a night, napping
two to three hours in the afternoon.[4]

Year after year his workday was about nineteen intense
hours. Besides the crowds come to see "the saint," postmen
left Pio six to eight hundred letters and up to eighty telegrams
a day. For a healthy priest such as the Curé d'Ars or Don
Bosco to carry this kind of load with similar food and rest was
thought explicable only "supernaturally."

In the case of Pio, whatever you think of them, the stigmata
added ongoing blood loss for fifty years. None of the physicians who made studies of the stigmatic pinpointed how much
blood trickled from the wounds in a given period, but it was
considerable. Pio felt the heart wound lost a cup a day. Even if
this estimate were too high, it is still remarkable he never
became anemic on a meager diet that rarely included meat.

† Among Christian mystics, there are stigmatics whose painful wounds usually remain
invisible, something Pio, after 1918, prayed for unsuccessfully, writing a spiritual
director that "these visible signs . . . are an embarrassment and an indescribable
humiliation."

‡ St. Francis of Assisi, the best-known stigmatic, was not a priest.

Certainly his estimated daily intake of 300 to 400 calories[5] (concentration camp inmates starved laboring on 1,300 to 1,700; a sedentary male worker is estimated to need 2,900, a carpenter 3,700) was insufficient for arduous days. Add blood loss year after year and the death bell ought to soon toll, especially for one at his end in 1917. Yet Padre Pio not only lived on year after year but his tuberculosis or whatever was killing him simply went away. Photos of the doomed, pale young priest of 1917–18 bear little resemblance to the stocky, robust-looking friar of later years.[6]

▲

The theater in Phenix City, Alabama, was hot and crowded. Murmurs of discontent filled the darkness because malfunctioning lights would not let the play begin. A man nudged his companion.

"Ask me to say a few words."

Dubiously, the request was made and in the darkness a form bounced up. A vibrant, happy voice rang out, "Friends, I've just been asked to say a few words . . ." No matter to Father Thomas Judge that this was not a church service. No matter that not twenty of the three or four hundred impatient souls squirming in their seats were Catholic. No thought that Catholicism, in fact, was anathema in the South in this early part of the twentieth century. For half an hour he preached to his captive audience. Nor did they hoot him down. Like many before and after them, they were captivated by the joyful dynamo.[7]

That was Tom Judge. Intensely, tirelessly using every minute to entice others toward God, although he was a dying man.

Ordained a member of the Vincentian Fathers* in May

* Also known as the Lazarists sometimes for the college where they were founded in 1625 by St. Vincent de Paul. The group's formal title is the Congregation, or Priests, of the Mission.

1899, he had been tubercular then for over a year and his superiors believed "he would die soon."[8] Sent home in hopes of a cure through complete rest, by September of that year, still tubercular, he was working among the Italian poor in Philadelphia the only way he ever worked—heart and soul. Until his death, he simply ignored the nausea, the pain in his lungs, fevers, and other symptoms to bring something of his own joy in God to others. Inspiring two lay groups and founding two religious congregations, just answering letters kept him up until one in the morning. But four hours later, at five A.M., he was in the confessional without fail. When he was stationed in New York, he took his allotted daily rest time to rush out to organize lay groups in Manhattan or Brooklyn, hurrying back to his three o'clock session in the confessional.

Someone who gave a spiritual conference with him said, "He worked harder . . . than any of us" and noted that at the same time Judge was carrying on other work "that was far more exhausting—and all with but four hours sleep a night. I just knew he couldn't last—but he did."[9]

When Tom Judge died on November 23, 1933, doctors said they had never seen a human body so completely worn out.

No wonder. A dying tubercular in 1899, in his passion for God this mystic had stretched his last days into thirty-four years of ceaseless toil.

▲

In the case of Blessed Miguel Pro (1891–1927) the exterior of an exuberant, guitar-strumming prankster hid both mystic depths and chronic ill health.

Three years into his Jesuit training, seminarians had to run for their lives in his native Mexico. After studies in California and Spain, Pro was ordained a priest in Belgium in spite of a life-threatening stomach ailment.

He rushed off to tour Belgium's humanely run coal mines.

As a mischievous but tenderhearted middle-class teen whose father worked for the Bureau of Mines, his heart had gone out to Mexico's miserable miners. He had learned their dialect, brought them food and clothes; now he hoped to do much more. Instead he spent the next six months undergoing three painful surgeries, causing comment among medical personnel because he never complained.

That he would ever recover was still in doubt when he was permitted to return to Mexico. In that country where the church had been outlawed, Father Miguel became an underground priest, working fourteen to fifteen hours a day. For the next sixteen months, he spent himself housing and feeding orphans and other needy, preaching secret conferences, and clandestinely administering sacraments to Catholics who suddenly appreciated what had become dangerous to get. Humorously he told a friend, "From the first day my confessional was a riot. . . . I kept it warm from five to eleven in the morning and three-thirty to eight in the evening."[10] He barely mentioned that he had fainted twice in the process.

This vibrant man would always refer to his rotten health in ways that evoke laughter, like the time he said that hearing confessions with a terrible toothache, he had strong urges to hit long-winded, scrupulous penitents over the head.

He wrote his worried Jesuit superiors that after years of daily attacks, his health was "vastly improved."[11] Certainly he never acted ill. To all, Pro appeared a virile man of great charm, gaiety, and wit, completely equal to the disguises and impersonations necessary to outwit those seeking to collect the bounty placed on his head. He looks healthy in photographs,[12] disguised in dapper suits or the workman's garb in which he made cheeky remarks to the police as he passed, using the laborer's dialect learned long ago from his miner friends.

Consumed by the fire of his love for God, Pro—like Praxedes Fernandez in the Spanish Civil War—wanted to offer his very life as a holocaust.[13] He confided this to some nuns[14] and said, "I believe God has accepted my desire." Shortly afterward he was betrayed and condemned without trial (to try to smear his name, he was linked to an assassination plot by the tenuous thread that his brother had formerly owned a car used in the crime).

The international press were invited by Mexico's President Calles to witness the November 23, 1927, execution. So we have on film the perfect calm of Pro's last moments as he not only forgave but thanked the man who arrested him, refused a blindfold, and spread his arms wide in a gesture that is both acceptance and a cross. In the serene face and erect figure that faced the firing squad with the words *"Viva Cristo Rey,"* there is no sign of ill health.

▲

Maximilian Kolbe became seriously ill with tuberculosis as a brilliant young Polish seminarian doing dual doctoral studies in Rome during the closing days of World War I. The Conventual Franciscan got his degrees but spent parts of 1921–22 and 1926–27 in Polish sanitariums for the tuberculosis. Yet he was always at work, forming an international spiritual army and seeding multimedia centers he envisioned worldwide as sources of publications, radio, television and films that would counter materialistic values with spiritual ones.

In 1927, fresh from a TB hospital, the communications genius was constructing a media friary on former Polish potato fields. A co-worker says:

> Father Maximilian was the first at work and did not spare himself. It was . . . October, and every morning the surrounding fields were white with frost. He often had to sleep in the open air or in the barracks with its gaping holes for windows. He went to Warsaw every day and came back loaded with packages. Only a year previous,

the doctors had prescribed for him, "a very calm and regular life, most nourishing food, much rest and sleep, and above all no carrying of heavy loads."[15]

Disobeying on most counts (he tried to eat nourishing if very simple food), he somehow got by. In 1930 he was building a media center in Japan. There, sometimes he was spitting blood so badly, he had to give conferences from his bed. But in spite of overtiring work, overlong hours, Nagasaki's harsh climate, and an extremely impoverished diet for the first several years, Kolbe never again spent time in a sanatorium. One can only link this to the great mystical experiences of his six years in Japan, a period when Buddhist bonzes and other non-Christians recognized in him universal signs of great sanctity.

In 1939, medically certified as no longer tubercular at all, he was back in the Polish friary, now the world's largest with nearly eight hundred men and seminarians. Under Kolbe, the friars were putting out eleven publications† when Germany invaded Poland and he was arrested. Housed in unheated tents, prisoners who awoke at night were apt to find Fr. Maximilian kneeling in prayer on the lice-infested straw or covering someone shivering in his sleep. The priest also gave away much of his meager ration to a young friar who suffered greatly from hunger.

Released, he was rearrested by the Gestapo in 1941 for refusing to collaborate. Shipped to Auschwitz, there the forty-seven-year-old mystic experienced the special viciousness re-

---

† In 1982 when Kolbe was canonized, charges were made that he wrote anti-Semitic material. A joint Jewish-Christian investigation by the Director of the St. Louis Holocaust Center, Warren Green, and historian Daniel Schafly, Jr., of St. Louis University, discovered that the material in question was written by a Polish priest totally unconnected to Kolbe. The saint insisted to all his writers and editors, "It is never permissible to publish anything to foment hatred," and lived out his personal motto: "to do good to all people."

served for priests and Jews.‡ Henry Sienkiewicz, an Auschwitz survivor, recalls:

> Priests and Jews were . . . building . . . the crematorium. . . . I saw how Fr. Kolbe was pushing a wheelbarrow filled with sand, . . . driven and beaten. . . . I approached . . . and begged him "Father, I'll take the load for you a few times. . . ." [For this] we both received 25 lashes; and as a punishment we had to carry each other. . . . He drove me when the wheelbarrow was filled with gravel and I in return when the wheelbarrow was empty.[16]

Above all, no carrying of heavy loads, physicians had warned. Yet Kolbe did not collapse pushing a sand-filled wheelbarrow with a man atop. He also cut and carried tree trunks until "beaten to death" by Krott the Bloody, who had killed enough men to know how many lashes it took. Left for dead, he was somehow alive when friends dared approach at day's end. Carried to the camp hospital, he insisted on the bed by the door where rain or snow fell with every entry or exit— in spite of the fact that he had pneumonia atop his injuries. "This way I can pray for the dying as they're carried out," he explained. Hearing confessions meant instant execution but each night men crawled to Kolbe's bed, and he had the strength to hold them in his emaciated arms, listening to their terror and rage, gently urging them to fight evil with "love— the only creative response."[17]

A survivor has told how he managed to get a cup of tea to Kolbe so "he might moisten his feverish lips for I could see how parched they were." Kolbe was grateful but refused to so much as wet his lips, as the others had none.[18] Survivors have also sworn under oath about times when Kolbe gave them or

‡ To be a Jew was the worst possible crime; to be a priest, the second.

others part of the pitiful food ration on which 500,000 prisoners starved to death.

This strange attitude toward self-preservation was noticed by the camp physician, who was not a believer in any "divine power." Dr. Diem was fascinated, he says, that where "there was in every other prisoner the desire to survive at any cost, even at the expense of another," Kolbe "was so different." The physician's long testimony, given in full in my book *A Man For Others,*[19] tells how he tried several times to rescue Kolbe, only to have the priest urge him to help some other prisoner. When Diem snapped, "If you don't go to bed, you'll die," Kolbe answered mildly, "Oh I think I'll hold out." The saint proved the better diagnostician. He was still alive and, according to another doctor-prisoner, "in good condition" at the time an inmate escaped.

When ten men were condemned to the camp's most feared death, that of hunger and dehydration in an underground bunker, Kolbe volunteered to replace a prisoner wailing for his wife and children. After two weeks, having awed the Nazis by transforming the dark cell, where crazed men sometimes bit one another to death, into an oasis of peace, Kolbe was one of four still alive and the only one still conscious. Murmuring a prayer, he had the strength to hold out his arm for the fatal injection.[20]

▲

Another "weak" individual who proved stronger than concentration camp brutalities is Blessed Titus Brandsma (1881–1942). A Dutch Carmelite priest, Brandsma became an enemy of the Third Reich by rallying the Dutch Catholic press against Nazism.

The son of dour Frisian farmers, the exuberant extrovert thought of becoming a Franciscan, but "he simply wasn't strong enough . . . [for their] busy pastoral life."[21] So he

joined the more contemplative Carmelites—"an ironic decision," notes a biographer, "in view of the whirlwind energy
which later marked his career."[22]

As a seminarian he was in bed for several weeks after
hemorrhaging, apparently from the stomach disorder from
which he suffered all his life. Later, like Maximilian, he was
sent to Rome for advanced studies because of his intellectual
brilliance. There he hemorrhaged again, so severely his life
was endangered. This time recovery took several months.[23]

Yet even in these early years, others noticed that for someone weak, Brandsma was extremely vital. In chapel, for example, "he made such a joyful noise unto the Lord that his brethren sometimes asked him to tone it down a little." They
observed that his prayer seemed to provide "the energy which
he needed for his dynamic activity."[24]

After gaining a doctorate in Rome, the "whirlwind" was
busy as a priest known for his holiness, an ecumenist in an era
of separation with close ties to people of many faiths, a greatly
loved seminary and university professor and administrator,
founder of a newspaper, spiritual advisor to the Dutch Catholic press, and a scholar who achieved recognition of his native
Frisian as an official language in Holland. The leading member
of the four-man team that translated Teresa of Avila's mystical
masterpieces into Dutch, others felt he understood Teresa
from experience as well as study.

If his holiness let him do the work of a strong man, it did
not give him the body of one. A fellow Carmelite has said you
can see Titus' life in a nutshell if you picture a sick man working feverishly in bed to finish a book.[25] Besides his chronic
stomach disorder and recurring urinary infection, before his
1942 arrest by the Nazis he had a disease "of the spinal mar-
row," symptoms of which included giddiness, headaches, and
memory failure.[26] An ordinary man of his intellectual occupa-
tions might have succumbed to depression. Brandsma remained cheerful.

From prison he was sent to a concentration camp where the sick, aging scholar for a short time worked with pickax and spade in below-freezing temperatures, in spite of suffering somewhat from dysentery. Still "Uncle Titus"* had the strength to help others in so many ways that he was soon known and loved by Catholics, Protestants, Jews,[27] and non-believers. Because of his remarkable influence on other prisoners and even guards, the Nazis found Titus "a dangerous man" even in a concentration camp. They returned him to a conventional prison where he could be safely isolated in a cell. But eventually he was sent to a second concentration camp.

In Dachau he was beaten again and again by one sadist,[28] which did not keep him from trying to reach out to the guards† the same way he did to others. Like Betsie ten Boom (p. 12), he sorrowed over his persecutors' spiritual state rather than his own fate. In this camp "Nazi doctors made cruel and degrading experiments on the defenseless" inmates. Titus was one of the "guinea pigs." But his spirit remained free. "We are in a dark tunnel here," he comforted those despairing around him. "We must pass through it but somewhere, at the end, shines eternal light."[29]

In concentration camps strong, healthy young men often quickly perished from disease, injury, malnutrition, or violence. To live two weeks was considered an accomplishment. The weak, sick, often brutally beaten sixty-one-year-old saint lasted five before a lethal injection ended his life.

▲

St. Gaspar del Bufalo (1786–1837), nineteenth-century founder of an order of priests, began life in the era tinged with Jansenistic (p. 101) austerities. Extreme bodily asceticism was

* Religious titles were forbidden.
† I have told (p. 12) of his compassion toward the "nurse" who killed—but couldn't forget—him.

common in those seeking mystical union with God. In spite of physical frailty—he almost died twice as a child from illnesses[30]—and a nervous temperament, Gaspar began such practices early. When only eleven or twelve, "on Fridays, Saturdays and in Lent he ate extremely little." He put stones in his bed to deprive himself of a decent rest. Once a week he probably slept better—that night he slept on the floor. Overdone as it may have been, that his asceticism reflected an authentic passion for God[31] can be seen in other aspects of his life.

Studying for the priesthood, he is already what Buddhism calls a bodhisattva, one who has received so much from God that he turns from ecstasy to serve others. The young man's service included care of a hospital for aged, infirm priests, work at a hospice for foreign clergy, spiritual classes for the poor, and "adopting" a large number of children ostracized because of some repulsive skin disease.

At the age of twenty-four he refused to swear allegiance to Napoleon, who had imprisoned the pope, and was exiled with other "intractable priests" to a remote part of the Italian peninsula. After the arduous trip on foot or jolted in wagons, Gaspar's weak body, no longer buoyed by working itself to death, collapsed. "Hopeless" was the medical verdict but as he lay dying a spiritual mentor ordered him to pray to live.[32] He did and was soon up, but he would be "weak for the rest of his days."[33] His nerves, always bad, seemed shattered as well—even before he received word that his mother, to whom he was closer than anyone in the world, had died in his absence.

After four years of exile, part of it in prison, all in terrible hardship, Gaspar was a survivor where many stronger had died. At last able to return to his native Rome, he founded a religious order to work in the area of his exile where spiritual life was almost nonexistent. No one cheered. In Rome he was accused of the egotistical urge to power. And in the area he was headed for, controlled by *banditi* much as Sicily is strangled by the Mafia today, there were vows to assassinate him if he preached any of that love and nonviolence stuff. A bomb discovered in his pulpit just in time evidenced the banditi meant business.

Between the mental stress of being considered by various groups a charlatan or a fool who should be knocked off and the dangers of horse-drawn or foot travel in almost roadless areas (he survived several serious accidents), Gaspar was considered "prematurely old" by his mid-forties. Actually he was miraculously old. As a biographer says, "He had always been frail and sick, suffering from disorders of the stomach, tuberculosis had threatened him. . . . He was so nervous and sensitive that the sight of a mouse . . . set him trembling."[34] Yet here he was carrying on work demanding the stamina of a foot soldier and nerves of steel.

And in fact timid Gaspar had *become* such a man, a spiritual giant who healed or worked other miracles with casual ease and who, face to face with an assassin, ignored the raised knife and asked, "My son, wouldn't you like to go to confession?" with such tender lack of self-concern that the unnerved killer fled. Warned another time that the tough-looking bird waiting to talk to him was in reality there to kill him, the saint greeted the hit man like a long-lost friend, took him by the arm, and led him into an empty room, closing the door behind them. When they reappeared, it was the other man who had "died"—to his old way of life.[35]

The mystical transformation affected Gaspar's body as well. In July 1818 he was at Meldola, a banditi stronghold where several attempts had previously been made on his life. As a result of the saint's work, many were turning in their weapons and beginning new lives. This inflamed the banditi leaders "to a fever pitch." Even quartets of hit men having been unnerved by the saint, this time poison was put in the cup of barley water he always drank before preaching.

At the last second, a young conspirator had a change of

heart. He rushed to two of Gaspar's companions and confessed. These Fathers Muccioli and Valentini burst into the saint's room just as he picked up the deadly cup.

"Stop!" they screamed, warning him of the plot. Their testimony, which I am translating from an Italian account, says that Gaspar did stop. He did listen. But then he considered the dishonor that would come upon the family who were his hosts (apparently one of them or a relative had doctored the cup):

> And moved by one of those wondrous "divine impulses" of the saints . . . repeating the words "they shall drink poison and it will do them no harm" (Mark 16:18), he swallowed every drop.[36]

Muccioli and Valentini, the latter considered a saint himself, "were so shocked they fell trembling to their knees." It was the saint who helped them up. He quoted Jesus: "Oh men of little faith, why do you doubt?" Then he was off to preach.

The incident was sworn to by its two witnesses when testimonies were collected for the Process.

▲

The year that St. Gaspar del Bufalo died in ecstasy (p. 58), another weak, scrawny infant took his first look at the world. Bl. Michael Rua (1837–1910) inherited a slight build and poor health from his father, five of whose nine children (by two wives) were already dead at Michael's birth.[37] Of the four children of Michael's mother, only he and a brother, Anthony, were alive when she died in 1876.[38] And Anthony died in 1889, eleven years before Father Michael.

Was his survival due to an easier life? Hardly. Rua's is one of those cases inexplicable by either heredity or life-style. The first to join St. John Bosco's new religious order, Michael was worked to the bone by the saint, whose prophetic gifts included knowing his helper's life-span.

In 1853, for instance, studying at the archdiocesan seminary, between classes Rua was learning Greek, in charge of a dormitory full of Bosco's boys, and keeping order on the playground, in the study hall, in the dining room, and in church for the whole institution. In addition he was helping Bosco prepare a magazine and a book, *The History of Italy.* Bosco also put him in charge of a satellite boys' club a twenty-minute walk away. Rua not only was responsible for sports, classes, a helping hand in getting employment, and spiritual instruction for this group of boys, but he had to walk over and back twice each Sunday and holiday to do it. Later that same year he found time to add Hebrew to his studies by rising at four, and Bosco made him teacher for a group of students his own age.[39] That heavy a workload would be characteristic of Rua all his life.

In fact, by the school year 1859–60, Rua regularly got up at 2:30 A.M.[40] He was also a survivor of voluntarily nursing townspeople alongside the much-stronger Bosco during a rabidly contagious cholera epidemic.

The young man's mattress stood in a corner of his room.[41] He claimed he slept just as well without one. As for food, he was one of those who tried to imitate Bosco. While he failed in those early years, a glance at the prisoner-of-war-like face of his maturity makes further details superfluous.

By 1885 when Rua was forty-eight, having lived over twice as long as all his siblings with an impossible workload and dreadful care, physician Dr. John Albertotti said his body was "worn out."[42] He kept working. About a year later he was in Rome with Bosco spending all day and most of the night on the older saint's correspondence while dealing with the horde of people, from cardinals on down, who wanted to see "the living saint" or invite him somewhere. One morning Rua:

> passed out completely. . . . Finally revived . . . by applying strong vinegar to his forehead and wrists, when he came to he rose and thanked his helpers.

Always known for his wry humor, he said, "It must have been that coffee I had yesterday." And went on with his day.[43] Bosco found rest in 1888 while responsibility for feeding several thousand mouths and maintaining over one hundred schools and other institutions descended on the bony shoulders of the exhausted fifty-one-year-old Rua. He kept it all going by the method he had learned from Don Bosco, according to a Salesian who asked Rua for permission to enlarge a school.

"Fine," agreed Rua, "so long as you have no objection to adding fifty new penniless boys to your rolls. That way, we know Divine Providence won't fail us."[44]

As the new man in charge, Don Rua had to move into Don Bosco's room, but he put in a couch, refusing to use the saint's bed. Brother Balestra, who took care of his room, often found . . . the couch had not been touched the night before.[45] After twenty-two years of the retiring (Rua worked miracles on occasions but hated notoriety) mystic's management, the men's branch of the order alone had burgeoned to 350 schools and other institutions for poor youth staffed by four thousand Salesians in over thirty nations. In spite of a workload that at one time had him building twenty-five churches around the globe in addition to supporting and guiding the entire Salesian edifice, frail Michael Rua was rarely ill and lived to seventy-three.

▲

Never robust, St. Peter Eymard got the first of a lifetime of migraine headaches as an overage novice with a religious order. The young Frenchman next evidenced digestive disorders, then lung troubles that would be with him all his life. When a physician decided to bleed a patient already half dead, the near corpse was soon "sent home to die with his family."[46]

It took two years before he could try again. At the diocesan seminary in Grenoble, his "delicate health" often put him on the sick list, but he was finally ordained in 1834. A religious order rejected him, however, citing his "precarious health."[47] So the new priest became assistant in a parish, putting in long hours and praying so much that people said he lived in the church.

The housekeeper sniffed she was sure he was tubercular.[48] He certainly took no care of himself, giving away the salary supposed to feed him with such regularity that the parishioners affectionately dubbed him "the spendthrift."[49] Sent next where there had been no resident priest for years, he prayed, fasted, and worked so ardently that within a year the place was spiritually revitalized. His two sisters attempted keeping house for him there. It was uphill work. Marie Anne Eymard would look for the soup makings and find her brother had given them away again.

"But what will we eat?"

"Oh, there's a bit of cheese, isn't there?" he would smile, sorry to have put her out but unrepentant.[50]

In 1839 he finally found a religious order that would take someone so frail. As if someone figured he wouldn't live long anyway, so why spare him, Eymard soon had enough jobs at a junior seminary for two men. Because of his joyful amiability, sheer goodness, and spiritual power (like Rua and others of this chapter, he worked miracles, healed, and at times read hearts or saw the future), everyone from the soberest town person to the rowdiest student went to him confidently—and at any hour. Told he should set hours, he replied that God was always available, so who was he, only God's servant, to keep others waiting.[51]

In 1846 with even heavier responsibilities as a leader in his order, he wrote someone he had no time either to know the hour or to eat.

A decade later he was barely alive. A friend said he looked like a skeleton and when Eymard's physician warned he had only a short time to live, the saint believed him. Ready "to die on the battlefield," as he put it in a letter, the forty-five-year-old priest took no precautions. In Paris he promised a young couple who loved him to marry them. Pale, fevered, coughing, he refused to send a substitute in spite of pouring rain. When he returned from the far-out suburbs, he was scolded.

"Oh, you're right," he smiled, "but those poor youngsters were so happy I came."

So much for attention to rest. As for food, one glance at the cadaverous but happy face in photographs tells all.

Facing his life's end, suddenly visions told the saint he must start a new religious order. Wisely he distrusted his visions, but his spiritual advisors believed God was speaking to "the living skeleton."

In great hardship and experiencing all the persecution holiness can evoke, Eymard went ahead. He had enormous stresses: handbinding poverty coupled with heavy financial obligations, attempts to blackmail him, plots to make him appear a scoundrel, and betrayal by his closest associate. Yet in these years a life-threatening heart problem was instantaneously and permanently healed at a shrine.[52] Refusing to defend himself and waiting for God, not men, to help him, the saint lived until the new organization had its start. Fifty-seven at his death, how he lived even that long can only be explained by his sanctity.

▲

Striking, sublime, and downright comical at times is the life of Alfred Bessette, a French-Canadian from the backwoods near Quebec, known today as Blessed Andre Bessette. The sixth of eight children, Alfred at birth was so frail the experienced midwife warned he would live only an hour or so.

Perhaps mother love saved him.[53] Through a sickly, desperately impoverished childhood, Alfred never recalled his early-widowed mother without a smile on her face.[54] Although hardships had killed her by the time he was twelve, she had formed her frail, five-foot-three, featherweight son into a happy person who loved to laugh.[55] But she could not make him less frail.

Apprenticed to a shoemaker in hopes he could do sit-down work, Alfred proved too feeble for shoemaking[56]—or for baking, working in a Connecticut cotton mill, or grooming horses. Then at twenty-five he had a numinous dream about St. Joseph and decided to join a religious order. He had going for him a spirituality so extraordinary that his parish priest wrote, "I am sending you a saint"[57] to the Holy Cross Brothers.

On the other hand, this candidate for an order of educators could neither teach—he was practically illiterate—nor join in the hard physical labor of the lay Brothers who did maintenance work. Hardly a great prospect but they gave him a try.

Renamed Andre,† the novice scrubbed floors, washed dishes, and worked at the other physically demanding tasks that keep large institutions running. He had assured the Brothers that St. Joseph would obtain better health for him if he entered God's service. But he remained the same semi-invalid, causing the Brothers to ponder if one apt to end up a drain on the rest of them should be permitted to make final vows. Prudence dictated dismissal but because of his exceptional spiritual qualities, they kept him.

A wise decision, it turned out, for far from becoming an invalid, Brother Andre somehow always did his heavy maintenance work in spite of his frailty *and* in spite of sometimes

---

† In a number of religious traditions a new name is given at a point of spiritual initiation. Here, it symbolizes a new life "for God instead of self." The name "Andre" honored his former pastor, himself widely believed a saint.

staying up all night in prayer and frequent forays to visit the city's sick.

Working seventeen- or eighteen-hour days, "he ate hardly anything; a piece of bread dipped in milk and water was his idea of a square meal."[58]

Never healed himself, at some point it became obvious he had a remarkable gift for healing others.

"St. Joseph‡ does it,"[59] Br. Andre insisted when publications began dubbing him "the miracle man."[60] This humility never faltered: Years later he told another Brother how he had arrived in Jersey City in the states just as there was a big parade. "Must have been some local feast," he mused. He had totally failed to grasp that the parade was in his honor.[61]

Some of those who interrupted his chores demanded healing. "God owes you something?" Andre would scowl. "I suggest you take the matter up with him directly." His favorites were perhaps injured working men with families to support, people with painful illnesses, or individuals who were all screwed up and who couldn't fathom why God would want to do anything for them. For such as these, he had an endless tenderness. But where did he get the energy? Between visitors —and some ill men he personally nursed for days in his tiny room, including cooking them the nourishing meals he rarely ate—his duties as a maintenance man, and his long hours of prayer, he never had more than a snatch of sleep and lived "chiefly on dry bread and strong coffee."

That was not pure asceticism. He was apparently born with abnormal digestion. He had ulcers most of his life, from which he often coughed blood. Digestive difficulties impaired his liver. Frequent symptoms included headaches, vertigo, and a distended, miserable stomach and intestines. For considerable periods he could digest nothing but liquids.[62] Other times, he

‡ This has, at times, obscured that Christ was the saint's primary passion (Catla, *Le Frère André*, pp. 516, 534–35).

carried on eating only flour stirred into warm water. His last years he had atrocious angina spasms to wear him down as well.[63]

When he was sixty, he was released from his maintenance duties. Without any improvement in his health, diet, or rest, he went into his healing ministry full-time. For five to six and a half hours a day, *always standing,* the frail little man received a steady stream—about forty an hour—of petitioners.* The rest of his days and nights, he prayed for them or called on the sick who were too ill to come to him. Actually, his friends say, he was often in worse shape than those he visited.[64] It is downright comical but, keeping up this killing lifestyle for the next thirty years, the man who should have died the day he was born lived to be ninety-one.

And he was rarely incapacitated in his sixty-five years as a Brother. In 1918 he joined an estimated billion laid low by the worldwide influenza epidemic; unlike millions far more robust, he recovered. At eighty-five, in 1931 he survived gastritis. When he was hospitalized in 1932, a nurse found the pious old man patient and uncomplaining, but his wanting to eat only flour with a dash of salt in hot water maddened her. Exasperated, she snapped, "So it's glue you want to eat, is it?"

"That's right," he nodded serenely with his habitual little smile. She had to give in. And on that absurd diet, without any antibiotics, the eighty-six-year-old recovered from double pneumonia.[65]

Which only goes to show that a man too weak for even the sedentary life of a shoemaker can become a mystical powerhouse.

---

* One day he saw seven hundred.

notes

1. I have verified with Father Joseph Pius Martin, a close associate of Padre Pio's, these facts from the Capuchin-recommended biography *Padre Pio* by Lutheran minister C. Bernard Ruffin (pp. 62–65, 72, 84, 121–22) quoting firsthand sources.

2. Ibid., p. 83.

3. Ibid., p. 74.

4. Ibid., p. 215.

5. Fr. Martin (see endnote 1) verifies this estimate from *Padre Pio: The Stigmatist* by Charles Mortimer Carty, p. 17.

6. See those in Carty's book, for example.

7. Joachim Benson, *Father Judge: Man on Fire,* pp. 15–16. This work by one of their members furnished me by the Missionary Servants of the Most Holy Trinity, founded by Fr. Judge.

8. Ibid., p. 12.

9. Ibid., p. 19.

10. John V. Sheridan, *Saints in Times of Turmoil,* p. 128, quoting Pro's communication with a fellow Jesuit.

11. Boniface Hanley, *No Strangers to Violence, No Strangers to Love,* p. 216, quoting Pro's letter.

12. Ibid., see examples pp. 201, 217–18.

13. Ibid., quoting Pro's asking a fellow priest to pray for this.

14. Sheridan, loc. cit., quoting Pro's prayer request of a group of nuns on Sept. 21, 1927.

15. Maria Winowska, *The Death Camp Proved Him Real,* p. 104. See also Patricia Treece, *A Man for Others,* pp. 33–34.

16. Treece, op. cit., p. 156, gives this witness's full testimony, which I have had to greatly condense here.

17. Ibid., p. 147, quoting survivor Joseph Stemler.

18. Ibid., pp. 141–42, quoting survivor Fr. Conrad Szweda.

19. Ibid., pp. 150–52.

20. Ibid., p. 176, testimony of Bruno Borgowiec, who was present as penal block interpreter.

21. Joseph Rees, *Titus Brandsma,* p. 22. This authenticated English-language biography furnished me by the Dutch Carmelites.

22. Leo Knowles, *Candidates for Sainthood,* p. 98.

23. Rees, op. cit., pp. 29, 39–40.

24. Ibid., p. 84.

25. Fr. Albert Groeneveld, *A Heart on Fire,* p. 15. Supplied by the saint's order.

26. Rees, op. cit., pp. 94–95.

27. Dutch rabbi J. Soetendorp found Jewish survivors constantly mentioning stories and recollections of Titus.

28. Rees, op. cit., pp. 171–72, 174.

29. Ibid., p. 175.

30. Amilcare Rey, *Gaspare del Bufalo,* Vol. 1, p. 34. The authoritative Italian-language biography from primary sources supplied me by the saint's order, The Congregation of the Most Precious Blood, Rome. Also supplied by their Rome headquarters is the Italian-language, one-volume biography *S. Gaspare del Bufalo* of Giusepe De Libero. See p. 26.

31. Ibid., pp. 81–83.

32. Rey, op. cit., p. 172.

33. Vincent Sardi, *Gaspar del Bufalo,* freely adapted from the Italian by Edwin G. Kaiser, p. 45. This short English-language life also furnished by the saint's order.

34. Ibid., p. 111.

35. De Libero, op. cit., pp. 165–66.

36. Ibid., p. 167, from the Beatification Process testimonies.

37. Peter Lappin, *The Wine in the Chalice,* p. 16. This Salesian-authored biography is from the official sources, including interviews with those who knew the saint.

38. Ibid., pp. 128 and 267.

39. Ibid., pp. 58–59.

40. Ibid., p. 79.

41. Ibid., p. 71.

42. Ibid., p. 135.

43. Ibid., p. 142.

44. Ibid., p. 165.

45. Ibid., pp. 161–62.

46. Un Religieux du Très Saint Sacrement, *Le Bienheureux Pierre-Julien Eymard,* Vol. 1, pp. 45–46. This authenticated French-language work is based on the Beatification Process and other original materials furnished by the saint's order, the Congregation of the Blessed Sacrament.

47. Ibid., p. 62.

48. Ibid., pp. 78–79.

49. Ibid., p. 68.

50. Ibid., p. 90, testimony of his sister.

51. As he aged, this remained true. See, for instance, Ibid., Vol. 2, p. 237.

52. Ibid., p. 17.

53. Étienne Catta, *Le Frère André* (1845–1937) *et l'Oratoire Saint-Joseph du Mont Royal,* p. 107. This definitive work was loaned to me by the Holy Cross Brothers of Montreal.

54. Ibid., p. 108.

55. Ibid., pp. 487–88, 415–16, 492–94.

56. Ibid., p. 119.

57. Ibid., p. 148 footnote.

58. Leo Knowles, *Candidates for Sainthood,* p. 52.

59. Catta, op. cit., pp. 506, 515.

60. Ibid., p. 415.

61. Ibid., p. 464.

62. *Summarium,* p. 516. See also Henri-Paul Bergeron, *Brother An-dré, C.S.C.: The Wonder Man of Mount Royal,* p. 31.

63. Catta, op. cit., pp. 863–64.

64. Catta, op. cit., pp. 573–77.

65. Ibid., p. 804. See also p. 863, which gives dates of his illnesses.

8

everything you always wanted to know about inedia

In May 1876 a young visionary took to her bed—thereafter an invalid. Two years later, when she believed she lay dying, a priest interrogated her: "Is it really true that you have not eaten or drunk anything for seven years?"

"As God is my judge," the pious peasant swore, "I have taken nothing to eat or drink in that time."

For the first five of those years, five days a week Louise Lateau (1850–83) did the hard manual labor of farm life. Saints with healthy bodies whose energy input and outgo still don't tally and feeble saints who are prodigious workers give way in this final category to individuals like Louise—few in number but well documented—who live without either eating or drinking at all.

▲

Some are bedridden invalids, some are normal-appearing individuals with healthy workloads. "How do you live on nothing?" people who managed* to meet her used to ask a sturdy-looking twentieth-century Bavarian as she bustled about the church decorating for the next service or worked in her garden.

"I don't live on nothing," Theresa Neumann always corrected. "I live on the Savior." In saying she lived on Jesus Christ, Theresa referred to her once-daily reception of what Catholics call Communion or the Eucharist, a wheat wafer the size and usually half the thickness of a quarter coin which somehow becomes the body of Christ upon consecration, Catholics believe.

Bizarre as the idea of "living on God" sounds, examples from other traditions show this rare phenomenon is a universal bodily potential of mysticism.

In his English-language *Autobiography,* Paramahansa Yogananda (p. 34–35) writes of Giri Bala, a Bengal yogini† he met on a 1936 visit to his native India. Giri Bala reportedly had neither eaten nor taken liquids for fifty-six years. Yogananda was told a Bengal Maharaja, Sir Bijay Chand Mahtab, conducted three tests, having Giri Bala observed in his palace, first for two months, then for twenty days, and a third time for fifteen days, during which he established to his satisfaction that she neither ate nor drank. Although the maharajah was dead, Yogananda believed his informant was reliable.

"Are you never tempted to eat?" Yogananda reports he asked Giri Bala.

"If I felt a craving for food, I would have to eat," she replied.

"But you do eat something!"

---

* She preferred to avoid strangers but felt it a duty to meet people if her pastor or bishop seconded their request.

† Woman yogi.

Giri Bala smiled at his insight, Yogananda says, as he theorized she was nourished "on the finer energies of air and sunlight and from cosmic power that recharged her body." She volunteered she also used a certain mantra and a breathing exercise "too difficult for the average person." These were taught her, she said, in a vision she experienced as a twelve-year-old after her mother-in-law taunted her for her gluttony and she resolved to learn to live without food entirely. Giri Bala reported the "master" who appeared to her said she would live "by the astral light, (her) . . . bodily atoms . . . recharged by the infinite current." She had been singled out to live without eating, the Hindu woman revered as holy concluded, "to prove that man is spirit" and "to demonstrate that by divine advancement he can gradually learn to live by the Eternal Light and not by food."[1]

The Torah of Judaism makes a similar statement in regard to manna‡ given every morning as nourishment to the Jews fleeing Egypt "to show you that not by bread alone does man live, but by every word that comes forth from the mouth of the Lord."[2]* In literal living out of that statement, the book of Exodus reports Moses stayed on Mount Sinai "with the Lord forty days and forty nights eating and drinking nothing."

Jewish scholar and author of *Hasidic Tales of the Holocaust* Yaffa Eliach tells me that around the time of Christ, a Jewish rabbi-mystic named Zaddok for forty years had only the physical nourishment from dates which he sucked and then spit out. This saintly Talmudic scholar led a very active life. Others, up to the seventh century, who lived on such "impossible" intakes are also detailed in the Talmud, Dr. Eliach says.

---

‡ Found on the desert floor each morning when the dew evaporated, these "fine flakes like hoarfrost" saved the Jews from starvation. This food is today felt something natural, which need not make the occurrence less "miraculous."

* In somewhat the same vein Elijah was brought a loaf of bread and jar of water by an angel (1 Kings 19:5–8), a repast, scripture says, which so energized the demoralized prophet that he walked forty days to refuge on Sinai.

Besides showing the phenomenon is also found in Islam, the reaction of Sufi mystic Muhyi'd Din Ibn 'Arabi (d. 1240) to visions of the angel Gabriel shows *how* mystical fasters may escape the normal exigencies of hunger. He says:

> These apparitions [of the angel] left me in such a state that for many days I could not take any nourishment. Each time I went to the table, the figure was standing at the table's end, looking at me and saying . . . "Will you eat while contemplating me?" It was impossible for me to eat, but I did not feel hunger! I was so full of my vision that I stuffed myself and became drunken in contemplating the figure to the point that this contemplation took the place of all nourishment. My good appearance astonished my friends who knew of my total abstinence. The fact is that I continued for a long time without tasting a bit of food, not experiencing either hunger or thirst [so long as] this figure was never out of my sight. . . .[3]

Rooted in Judaism, the Christian tradition of fasting begins with Jesus whose fasts included a forty-day one as preparation for beginning his ministry. Among the small group who have successfully imitated him is extreme ascetic St. Simeon Stylites (d. 459).† Simeon's case shows how the most phenomenal ascetic fast has totally different characteristics from the fast classed as a mystical phenomenon.

Simeon *chose* to abstain totally from food and drink for the forty days of Lent as a spiritual exercise. He began his fast standing, praising God; days later, too weak to stand, he prayed sitting down; by the end of the forty days, he was stretched on the ground more dead than alive. A man of great bodily vigor—and perhaps less sense—the following Lent he

† He should not be confused with St. Simeon the Younger (d. 592), a mystical faster and near-inedic.

repeated the fast. At the time one Theodoret wrote of it, Simeon had done this every Lent for twenty-eight years (one source says he did so for forty years).[4] Apparently his body even gradually acclimated itself to the ordeal to a degree; he always ended flat on the ground, but only appears to have come close to death the first time. Some may find this edifying but no one can cite the emaciated man, in a half-dead stupor every Easter, as an example of the mystical faster, for Simeon obviously suffered the normal consequences of dehydration and starvation.

Had he fasted much longer, he would have lost not only his footing, but his life as pain wracked the starved organism, its water-denied flesh wizened and cracked, sight and organs failed, and at last coma and death brought relief to horrendous suffering. I take this description from accounts of the final days of Irish hunger strikers, famine victims, and the attending physician's account of a less-than-perfect baby "permitted" to die of dehydration and starvation. Let me sum up what folly poor old St. Simeon and all total fasters‡ court by saying, far from the peaceful, painless death it may appear, the prolonged tortures of starvation and dehydration—thirst being perhaps most maddening—led the Nazis in Auschwitz, with hanging, shooting, beating, torture, and mass gassing at their disposal, to design the "hunger bunker" as perhaps the ultimate in horrific death.

Considering the normal consequences of prolonged food and liquid deprivation, even in fasting saints like Simeon, that some individuals have been proven under medical surveillance to live without any food—the phenomenon is called inedia—

‡ An article on Simeon in *Butler's Lives of the Saints* mentions a Benedictine monk of Saint-Maur, France, attested in writing by his Abbot and fellow monks to have fasted forty days in 1731. Sister Marie della Passione, a current candidate for canonization, was permitted in 1912 to fast from Easter to Pentecost (about seven weeks). Besides the Eucharistic wafer, she had a little coffee each evening. More details on Maria, whose fast appears mystical, appear in Herbert Thurston's *The Physical Phenomena of Mysticism*.

and, in some cases, even no water without showing any evidence of malnourishment or dehydration is astounding, whether supernatural, as some claim, or not.

We know, of course, from hunger strikers that the human body, kept warm and quiet, can go many days before coma and death. Indian fakirs* are said to have allowed themselves to be buried as long as four months without air or food, quasi-hibernating through self-hypnosis. In *The Physical Phenomena of Mysticism*, Herbert Thurston describes rare invalids—he judges them complex neurotics—who seem to involuntarily live without food or drink, without any spiritual connotations or religious motivations, for periods that far outdo any fakir. He mentions Scottish epileptic Janet McLeod (c. 1763) and Swiss paralytic Josephine Durand, both believed total inedics for several years and Bavarian Marie Furtner (d. 1884), thought to have taken only water for forty years following several illnesses. Another case Thurston examines that illustrates how little we understand the outer limits of body potential is that of American Protestant Mollie Fancher, who lived in Brooklyn near the end of the nineteenth century. Invalided after two accidents, she, too, seems to have lived years without nourishment without being a mystical inedic. Mollie had convulsive seizures and at times went into trances, some with spiritual content, others revealing multiple personalities, all fairly benign. Because of inedics like these individuals, inedia must be considered as also having other causes than sanctity, at least in invalids.

Prospero Lambertini whose *De servorum Dei beatificatione et beatorum canonizatione* provides insightful guidelines for evaluating mystical phenomena cautioned this. He writes:

---

* Unlike the yogi seeking spiritual development, the fakir (which does not mean "fake") strives to master various unusual feats of magic and endurance. Many of his spectacular feats demonstrate remarkable mastery of the body's capabilities. Others definitely involve illusion and other techniques of the magician.

> [If] long abstinences from food have their origin in a dis-
> eased condition of the organism [or] if they are attended
> with a prevalent state of ecstasy and a suspension of the
> normal activities of life, we cannot safely conclude that we
> are dealing with a condition of things which is of super-
> natural origin.

In other words, if a holy body is diseased or immobilized by
frequent ecstasies *and* lives without food, who dares pinpoint
the cause? He does not dismiss the supernatural factor however, writing:

> If . . . it can be proved that this entire absence of nour-
> ishment . . . is maintained concomitantly with the con-
> tinued discharge of ordinary duties, then natural causes
> supply no explanation.[5]

When Lambertini warns we can't jump to the conclusion
inedia is a mystical phenomenon in invalids or people whose
long, frequent ecstasies make them unable to lead a normal
life, he is careful not to deny there could be a mystical basis
even here. But his guidelines have been carelessly interpreted
and extended to dismiss inedia in all invalids, especially those
who have visions in ecstasy, labeling them "complex neurotics," while applauding as "genuine mystics" whose inedia is
"supernatural" individuals who are normally active.

This division proves artificial. Did ecstatic visionary Louise
Lateau evidence genuine mysticism and supernatural inedia
for the five years she did farm labor without food or drink,
then become neurotic, her inedia no longer supernatural, the
last years of her life when she was an invalid? This no more
makes sense than suggesting Padre Pio was a nut when on
invalid leave, a true mystic later.

When Lambertini cautioned that inedia may be other than
supernatural in some circumstances, his careful wording

shows no intent *on that basis* to impugn the integrity, psychological health, or sanctity of any inedic. Because there are nonmystic inedics like those profiled by Thurston, we must posit that every century or so an invalid has a suspension of the normal need for physical nourishment. This *could* be part of a "complex neurosis." Or the interplay of psychological, physiological, and spiritual factors may, at least in some cases, involve nothing neurotic whatsoever. We can no more hastily generalize every bedridden inedic is a "complex neurotic" than we can insist every walking inedic a "supernatural sign."

The truth is the majority of inedics are plagued with illnesses, bedridden for periods, or permanent invalids. To understand even slightly this group of people, some of whom appear to be holy, it is necessary to look at some of the roles illness can play in the process of human growth toward wholeness and holiness.

In the area of mental breakdown, clinicians and researchers now recognize types of nonpermanent psychosis or other illness they term "positive disintegration," "creative illness," "problem-solving schizophrenia," or "spiritual emergency" because, rather than destructive, such illnesses "result in improvement in the individual's functioning."[6]

Without denying that physical illness is often an unhealthy response to life, here, too, there prove exceptions. Jungian therapist-Episcopal priest John Sanford observes in *Healing and Wholeness,* "To become whole, certain people may have to become ill." Says Sanford:

> Illness can have the effect of dissolving (dismembering) our conscious personality in such a way that an entirely new state of consciousness is allowed to emerge. . . . In this state of dissolution, which is certainly experienced in a painful way, a new personality develops . . . from . . . the deepest inner Center.[7]

A number of future inedics such as Theresa Neumann (along with others† who became holy but not inedic) set out on the road to sanctity after this sort of nonpermanent, breakthrough illness. And I can think of no holy inedic whose early progress toward sanctity did not involve illness. One has a sense of an "initiation period" similar to the period of physical-psychological disintegration that often immediately precedes entry into the shaman's vocation.‡ It is "at the climax of a serious illness" that often a future shaman, whether a Siberian or a South or North American Indian, has the first very deep altered state of consciousness.[8] I find this pattern typical of inedics. Energized by new powers after Sioux visionary Black Elk's strange illness*[9] or African shamaness Dorcas'[10] three bedridden years when she could neither eat nor drink** full health returns. This is also true of some inedics, such as Theresa Neumann. For others, however, we need different models.

Speaking specifically of mystics and mentioning as examples the two Sufis Jami and Jalalu'ddin, Plotinus, St. Bernard, St. Teresa, and St. John of the Cross, mystical authority Evelyn Underhill notes many "great contemplatives though almost always persons of robust intelligence and marked practical or intellectual ability" suffer "bad physical health," not just during a breakthrough period but "often." Quoting the mystic Tauler's insistence that "one who would know much about these high [spiritual] matters would often have to keep his bed, for his bodily frame would not support it," Underhill says in her monumental *Mysticism:*

† St. Francis of Assisi is one of the best known.
‡ For those who will become shamans, sickness—like dreams and ecstasies—usually by itself can "constitute an initiation," according to Mircea Eliade *(Shamanism,* p. 33).
* Physically near death for twelve days, the nine-year-old boy had a vision which shaped his life.
** Whether this was a total fast is unclear to me.

> If we see in the mystics . . . the sporadic beginning of
> . . . a higher consciousness, towards which the race
> slowly tends; then it seems likely enough that where it
> appears nerves and organs should suffer under a stress to
> which they have not yet become adapted. . . . [One may]
> look upon the strange "psycho-physical" state common
> amongst the mystics as just such a rebellion on the part of
> a normal nervous and vascular system.[11]

Not all saints suffer frequent "mystical ill-health." But most
holy inedics and near-inedics like Padre Pio do,† suggesting
that the holy invalid inedic *could* be the class of mystics with
the least psychophysical resistance to the mystical life.

Underhill finds a number of mystics with "a particular kind
of illness . . . accompanied by pains and functional disturbances for which no organic cause" is found. Illness without
organic cause is the classic description of neurotic illness. But
in genuine mystics like Padre Pio (Ch. 7), Underhill says such
illnesses are caused by "the immense strain which exalted
spirit puts upon a body."‡[12] In other words, if their root isn't
organic, it is still the identifiable, often non-neurotic one of
extreme, prolonged spiritual stress.

Since even those invalid inedics who seem undeniably holy
are so often accused of "hysterical," that is non-organic, neurotic illness, you might want to consider "spiritual stress" in
your own evaluations. My own assessment is that most invalid
inedics were felled by organic causes such as spinal injury or
polio.

That a number of inedics were healed of serious conditions

---

† Oddly enough, while total inedia remains a mystery there is much greater acceptance that near-inedia and near-sleeplessness, such as that of a Pio or Brother Andre
Bessette, are the result of an intense spiritual life in which prayer states refresh and
nourish the entire person, body included.

‡ She writes, "Our bodies are animal things, made for animal activities. When a spirit
of unusual ardour insists on using its nerve cells for other activities they [rebel]"
(*Mysticism*, p. 61).

"miraculously"—i.e. in non-medically explicable ways—was held some years ago to prove they suffered "hysterical" illness or injury. Since then the reality of non-medical healing of even the most serious organic conditions is beyond dispute.

One last thing relating to illness has also made it difficult to save inedics, above all the invalids, from being consigned to the discredited fringes of mysticism. This is the vocation of many inedics (along with more non-inedics) to reparatory suffering—that is, psychically, spiritually, and sometimes literally taking on the burdens of others, including at times physical illnesses. The concept is a universal one. Writer and Lutheran minister C. Bernard Ruffin has told me of Methodist Frances (Fanny) Crosby (1820–1915), Presbyterian John Nelson Hyde (1865–1912), and less well-known figures who felt called to reparatory suffering.[13] Hinduism also speaks of holy ones who spare those of lower spiritual stature by mystically taking on their physical sufferings and working them out in their own bodies. Judaism is rich with heroic tales of the *just man* who suffers for others.

Certainly this is an area that draws the weird, from masochists to those with spiritual delusions of grandeur. I think of the contemporary photo of an Italian "stigmatic." Wearing long dangling earrings and a tight-fitting smock, she gives the tabloid photographer a beauty pageant smile as she holds up her "wounded" hands to his camera. Most likely she is a fraud. Certainly "reparatory sufferers" like her have nothing to do with genuine mysticism or sanctity.

With masochism such a possibility, it is good to note that many who become inedic reparatory sufferers have no initial interest in "suffering nobly for God and humanity." Inedics like Alexandrina da Costa and controversial American Rose Ferron prayed fervently for cures after becoming bedridden young and only accepted the idea that their unavoidable sufferings might be meaningfully offered for others when no healing was forthcoming. Just to keep matters from becoming too simple, I must also note that a few invalid reparatory sufferers seem to have been called to their odd vocation before becoming total invalids. Ironically, among these are some, like Marthe Robin, who seem the least likely masochists or neurotics.

To the legitimate reparatory sufferer let me apply another insight from Sanford's *Healing and Wholeness*. Again not writing specifically of saints, Sanford describes a permanent wound, often psychical—but sometimes physical, as with the apostle Paul who suffered "a thorn in the flesh"—that forces some individuals to develop spiritually or perish. Sanford warns against judging this "wound" as a sign of neurosis. Insisting, as I do, that each case is unique, he finds sometimes an illness or psychic disability arises from "a deep encounter" with the unconscious or God. Through such a wound, he says, pours a continual healing power as "a source of renewal and life."[14]

Sanford is speaking of "life and energy" flowing from this source for one's own psychospiritual development. As I see it, the rare genuine—and this is not a calling one verifies by oneself—reparatory sufferer has in this vocation a "wound" which is a source of life, not only for the individual, but for many others as well.

While some reparatory sufferers, like Brother Andre, are rarely bedridden, among inedics many are invalids. Unlike the neurotic invalid hiding from growth toward God and wholeness behind some disability, the holy inedic (invalid or walking) who is a reparatory sufferer is engaged in a much more cosmic drama than personal illness. She may have all sorts of symptoms today, none tomorrow, as she "takes on"—or is between—others' problems. Their lives perhaps so alike on the surface, the two types of invalids are as diametrically opposed as selfishness and selflessness.

Many inedics are also frequent ecstatic visionaries. Some are stigmatics. While all of this phenomena, especially in invalids, demand a scrupulously careful examination of both plain old virtue and, yes, mental stability, this group of people dismissed en masse many times as neurotics or "flakes" will get no such automatic treatment in these pages. Individuals ignored here are those like Julie Marie Jahenny, who in the nineteenth century sent word to various VIPs that she would perform a certain mystical phenomenon on a given day, then did so before the summoned onlookers. This eager self-exhibitionism has nothing in common with the inedic who set a bowl of stewed fruit on her bedside table, hoping to be declared a fraud so she could get on with her life of hidden service and prayer.[15]

Many inedics frequently—some even daily—experience visions while in ecstasy. As you may know, in mysticism ecstasy is the trance state in which an individual is totally caught up in enriching spiritual experience of the most compelling and immediate nature. In this state sensory life seems to freeze. A lighted match held to the skin causes no pain. A jab toward the eye elicits no blink. The entire physiology slows. Obviously, proneness to this sort of thing raises the question: could inedia be a way that the bodies of rare individuals react—as a more or less permanent modification—to frequent ecstasy? In favor of this hypothesis is the fact that inedics don't set out to learn to do without food like fakirs or other ascetics. Inedia in a number of ecstatic visionaries appears after their ecstasies were a well-established phenomenon, as though the functions needed for eating gradually became less and less able to rebound from their ecstatic freeze.

Unfortunately mysticism never seems to lend itself to the neat explanation. In this case one dangling end is the fact that some ecstatic visionary inedics cannot retain the unconsecrated Eucharistic wafer (see p. 183) but can receive and immediately evidence they are energized by a consecrated one *without anyone telling them which is which.* That speaks of a flatly supernatural situation.

Also the situation of the ecstatic does not resemble, as it

should if inedia comes from "vegetation," that of the fakir who must remain suspended in his self-induced trance in order to continue inedic and whose inedia will last not for years as with mystics but for about the same length of time as a hibernating bear's.

Ecstasies, instead, are generally quick, intense states lasting no more than a few minutes. Even in those rare inedics alleged to have had ten-hour ecstasies, the person will still, unlike the fakir, pass hours of her day not in ecstasy but relating to other people,† her body showing no signs of vegetative ecstatic residue. In fact, true ecstasy, as Evelyn Underhill notes, "is notoriously life-enhancing. In it a bracing contact with Reality seems to take place. . . . Often, says St. Teresa, even the sick come forth from ecstasy healthy and with new strength."[16]

Invalid inedics sometimes end an ecstasy cured. Other times, ecstasy seems to increase psychospiritual strength, either alleviating physical sufferings or giving new ability to bear them. Thus the lowered functions of ecstasy seem followed by a burst of new energy in one form or another.

Obviously the life-style of ecstatic inedic invalids is in many ways similar to the lives of non-ecstatic, non-holy invalid inedics, suggesting that not ecstasy but some rare physiological quirk of invalidism is the root of inedia. This would mean, while no slur on anyone's holiness, that the phenomenon of inedia is merely a footnote to the true physiology of sanctity. However, I note that some inedics who may take to their beds at the beginning or end of their careers may also pass years on their feet. All I can say is perhaps there are two types of inedia.

Lambertini implied that if inedia occurred where there was nothing like invalidism or ecstatic states to possibly suspend normal body functions, the phenomenon could be considered

---

† This will be true even of the invalid who, if she is holy, will manage to serve others somehow, like the bedridden inedic who sewed for the poor between her ecstasies.

supernatural. With today's slightly-greater understanding, three centuries after he wrote, of mind-body-spirit interaction, we can qualify this a bit. No one can explain inedia; but it is not unreasonable to suggest that in both the invalid and the active saint—or the invalid and active phases of the same individual's career—where holiness is real, a mix of physiological and psychospiritual factors could be involved, in addition to the directly supernatural ones cited by all inedics, from Giri Bala to Theresa Neumann.

The inedics themselves make it simple: Inedia is bestowed on them by God for His purposes. We recoil from such simplicity. Perhaps inedics make us uncomfortable because they assert so dramatically that none of us is really kept alive by food. We are all "living on God."

▲

And now that you know all about inedia, let us look again at Louise Lateau. If perhaps more than usually good and helpful to her parents on the family farm, she was still a normal child, apparently in no way given to ecstasies or strange phenomena.

Knocked down and trampled by a cow at the age of thirteen, she apparently suffered internal injuries. Painful abscesses resulted and the rest of her teens were blighted by ill health. At seventeen, in 1867, she lay dying, was given the last rites, and recovered after a novena‡ in a way others considered "miraculous."

Only three weeks later, more intense pain, more abscesses, more blood spitting, and other serious symptoms recurred. Again at the point of death early in 1868, the farm girl recovered a second time in a way that again seemed inexplicable. These brushes with death had served, it appears, to open the

‡ From the Latin for *nine,* a novena is a nine-day period of prayer focused on some special object, such as someone's healing (as in Louise's case) or preceeding some special occasion, such as the prayer for the coming of the Holy Spirit before Pentecost.

door for Louise into another sphere of reality. She went back to her chores. But she had begun to have visions.

About this time she began to experience the pains of unseen stigmata wounds. Gradually these became visible, beginning with bleeding from her side in April 1868. By July, every Friday Louise was having long ecstasies and bleeding from various wounds that replicated those of Christ.

Accompanying the visions and stigmata was a growing distaste for food. Always a small eater, the amount of nourishment the eighteen-year-old girl took dwindled continually although she still did hard manual labor every day except Friday.

On Fridays when her visions and bleeding incapacitated her, she never touched food at all. What she was taking at other times at this period amounted to no more than an ounce or two of bread, half an apple, or a spoonful of vegetables. After March 30, 1871, she could no longer eat even that: any solid food caused acute suffering. She did her best when her mother or confessor urged her to eat, but if she choked a bite down, her body threw it back. In no way had she decided like old St. Simeon to fast totally; she simply could no longer digest food. A physician reported that her gastric secretions were practically nonexistent. Milk, for instance, vomited back, showed no signs of curdling.

At the same time Louise became sensitized to the consecrated Eucharistic wafer. Although she could daily receive this—her only nourishment—without difficulty, she could not retain a nonconsecrated host even when it was presented to her under the guise of a consecrated one.

She is also among the inedics who do not drink. Even working on the farm in the heat of summer, she could not keep down—nor apparently did she need—even a spoonful of water. Somehow spared dehydration and nourished by no more than the Eucharistic wafer, Louise continued with her farm labors for five years until, at age twenty-six, in May 1876, she became bedridden. She died seven years later at thirty-three, having sworn to the end that she had neither eaten nor drunk anything for a dozen years.

The great expert on mystical phenomena, Thurston, who studied her case in more depth than I have been able to do, finds her truthfulness unquestionable.[17] As for the possibility that she thought she abstained from food, but—in a trance or sleepwalking—actually ate during the night, this he finds quite unlikely, as she would have had to do so for twelve years in the family's peasant cottage without ever being caught or food being missed. That her devout relatives might have abetted such a deception in the theologically stringent nineteenth century with its fear of hell and damnation, I must agree with Thurston, seems highly unlikely. Neither she nor they ever got anything—financial or otherwise—out of her condition. Thurston concludes the abstinence from food and water for a dozen years was real; but whether it was some rare, purely physiological phenomenon unrelated to mysticism, a rare bodily manifestation of holiness, a rare quirk of neurosis, or a wholly supernatural act of God, he can no more say with authority than anyone else.

Is this because the answer is so complex or too simple?

notes

1. Paramahansa Yogananda, *Autobiography of a Yogi,* pp. 531–40.

2. Deuteronomy 8:3. For the feeding by manna see Exodus.

3. Laleh Bakhtar, *Sufi,* p. 117.

4. Herbert J. Thurston and Donald Attwater, *Butler's Lives of the Saints,* Vol. 1, pp. 34–37. The three primary accounts of this ascetic include one by his disciple Antony.

5. Herbert Thurston, *The Physical Phenomena of Mysticism,* pp. 352–62 and 294–325.

6. Prospero Lambertini, *De servorum Dei beatificatione et beatorum canonizatione,* Book IV, Part I, ch. 27, quoted by Thurston, ibid., p. 362.

7. Clinical psychologist David Lukoff, in "The Diagnosis of Mystical Experiences with Psychotic Features," pp. 157–58, mentions many, including the ones I quoted: "positive disintegration" (Dabrowski, 1964), "creative illness" (Ellenberger, 1970), "problem-solving schizophrenia" (Boisen, 1962), and "spiritual emergencies" (Grof & Grof, 1985).

8. John A. Sanford, *Healing and Wholeness,* p. 71.

9. Michael Harner, *The Way of the Shaman,* p. 63.

10. John G. Neihardt, *Black Elk Speaks,* pp. 17–39.

11. Sanford, op. cit., pp. 67–70.

12. Evelyn Underhill, *Mysticism,* pp. 58–59 and 61–62.

13. Ibid., p. 59.

14. Our phone conversation and exchange of letters took place in late 1985 and in the first months of 1986. Rev. Ruffin has written of this subject in *Padre Pio*, p. 49.

15. Sanford, op. cit., pp. 34, 35–36.

16. This was Anne Catherine Emmerich, today dismissed by most Catholics but whose virtue has never been assailed.

17. Underhill, op. cit., p. 61.

18. See Thurston, *The Physical Phenomena of Mysticism*, pp. 348–51.

9 ▲

"living
on
god"?

In the mid-twentieth century, pictures of a Bavarian peasant woman appeared in America's *Life* magazine. They purported to show her bleeding from wounds like Christ's as, in ecstasy, she was caught up in visions of the events of Good Friday.* This writer, a little WASP child, recalls the bemusement and dismay with which she looked at the photographs. The strange lady seemed some kind of freak.

Theresa Neumann (1898–1962) caused similar reactions among many of her co-religionists. Catholic writers[1] joined Protestants and Materialists to propose in print that Neumann was a fraud or a hysteric. Others, including the Hindu saint Yogananda,[2] defended her as a genuine mystic. One item of

---

* One investigator names a Protestant, a Jewish, and a Catholic scholar who each found that in these ecstasies the uneducated woman "displayed unpremeditated presence of Aramaic words" she normally could not have known (Josef Teodorowicz, *Mystical Phenomena in the Life of Theresa Neumann*, p. 73).

controversy was the assertion that the stigmatic visionary lived, without water, solely on the Eucharist.

According to those on the spot, after mystical experiences at Christmas 1922, the twenty-four-year-old resident of Konnersreuth, Germany, could tolerate only liquids. On August 6, 1926,† she had a vision of Christ luminous, transfigured. Contemplating his glory, she later told her pastor, thirst and hunger for material food and drink left her forever. But to placate her mother, until that Christmas she continued to accept a few liquids—in total perhaps a cup a *week*—usually pouring them out when her parent wasn't looking because they made her vomit. From the opening of 1927, all that went down her throat was "a little spoon of water and about six or eight drops [more] after Communion to help her swallow" a tiny particle (less than a quarter of the whole) of a Eucharistic wafer.‡ After September 1927, even the spoon of water became unnecessary.[3]

Lack of food, mystics claim, is not lack of nourishment. Quoting Jesus' saying "My body is meat indeed," Theresa Neumann used to ask those puzzling, pondering, and probing her inedia, "Why can't that simply be the case if he wants it to be?" Joseph Teodorowicz, Archbishop of Lemberg, who made many investigative visits to Konnersreuth and produced a five-hundred-page study of the mystical phenomena in the Bavarian inedic's life, came to agree with the inedic's insistence that she lived on God.

In support of her claim he found many witnesses that Theresa was, in a completely mystical sense, not immune to hunger and thirst or the exhaustion that comes from privation.[4] The inedic said she was conscious of the nourishing presence of Jesus within her after receiving her once-daily Eucharist,

† In the Catholic liturgical year, this date is the Feast of the Transfiguration.
‡ Until June 1931, after which, her throat problem healed, she could swallow a whole Communion wafer.

usually until time to receive again. During reparatory sufferings she vomited at times and the tiny particle was recovered, intact, undigested, eight, ten, even eighteen hours after it was ingested.[5]

At times, however, seen as part of her reparatory sufferings for others, this nourishment disappeared before the next day's Communion. Father Hermann Joseph, a Capuchin Franciscan, pictures her in this situation:

> I was in Konnersreuth on the twenty-fourth of May, 1929 . . . in the sacristy about to vest for mass. Suddenly the door was opened and I beheld a countenance full of pain and interior sorrow such as I have never seen before, even in the dying. The eye reminded me of a person parched with thirst, using up his last bit of energy to reach the fountain of water before he sinks down powerless. It was Theresa Neumann coming [for the Eucharist].[6]

This was the inedic during one of her mystical states of vicarious (reparatory) suffering, at her "hungriest," so to speak. In such "a pitiful state of weakness," her "face pinched and sunken, . . . dark rings . . . under her eyes, . . . she could hardly sit on the chair" where she hid from sightseers behind the altar. But after receiving Communion, according to another observer, one Father Fahsel, "All these disappear," and "a distinct strengthening of the body is immediately noted." Fahsel said that on such occasions "one must agree with the pastor when he says: 'I do not know but Resl [Theresa's nickname] is always getting younger.' "[7]

Like all other inedics, Theresa Neumann also did without normal amounts of sleep. In a carefully controlled, non-Catholic psychiatrist-directed observation period, she slept ten hours in fourteen days, an average of an hour and twenty-five minutes a day. As the years passed, even this may have dwindled; Teodorowicz, writing at the end of the 1930s, estimated that

Theresa slept "only about two hours every week."[8] Another investigator put the figure at five hours a week. Either amount is not consistent with physical health or mental health, sleep deprivation being known experimentally to create psychic disturbance. Yet all who knew Theresa insisted on her down-to-earth normality.

Physiologically, her strange diet and sleep patterns did not make her resemble non-inedic mystics who fast and vigil rigorously (pp. 170–71). Let Teodorowicz recall his first view of Theresa nine years after she last ate:

> [I said to myself] hunger, sleeplessness and thirst must surely have left traces on her. . . . Perhaps she is emaciated to a skeleton and is more like a mummy than a living person. I open the door; I can hardly trust my eyes. Before me stands a person, thirty-three years old, strongly built, with freshness and will power in her attitude, . . . [whose] furrowless, even youthfully fresh countenance . . . [is more] full than lean.[9]

Indeed Theresa was the physical epitome of the strong, broad-backed peasant woman. She herself would tell how during World War I, with the able-bodied men at war, "the man's work devolved on me as the biggest and strongest" of a group of farm* employees: She "ploughed," "wheeled the manure on to the field," and "climbed up steps to the loft with sacks of grain weighing 170 lbs."[10]

Critics of mystical phenomena propose that "the mystical temperament"—dreamy, credulous, overimaginative, and inclined to psychic experiences—is behind much that is cited as "mystical." I find inedics' personalities, like their physiognomies, vary greatly. Some *do* have precocious experiences of a

---

* She worked from 1914 to 1918 for the same local man, her duties also including heavy work at the inn he ran.

psychic or spiritual nature. Theresa did not. Although she dreamed of being a nun, it was the exciting life in faraway lands of a missionary that interested her, not mystical pursuits.

Her pastor later recalled the eldest of the ten Neumann children was apt to look about in church and had to be disciplined for her talkativeness during services. If she was devout in an unexceptional way and unselfishly devoted to her strict parents, he found these qualities common in the village children.

At home she fought it out more than once with her siblings and seems to have been a typical oldest child—industrious but somewhat bossy and impatient.

As an adult, she remained more inclined to stubbornness than submissiveness, according to Teodorowicz. Overall, unlike some very feminine inedics, her temperament, like her strong body, had the brusque, unimaginative, sharply judging strength often associated with men. Typically her bishop observer notes, "She never took a liking for feminine handicraft. She feels herself [more] at home when oxen and horses are to be harnessed and driven."[11]

Ewald, a psychiatrist without belief in spiritual realities, characterized her as "no sneak, not shy, not particularly moderate; she did not readily give in and was not particularly good-natured, but she knew rather how to win out."[12]

A visionary, still she had no interest in fantasy of any kind. She never read a novel "because they aren't true." Asked to read a book of the earlier (now disfavored) inedic Anne Catherine Emmerich's visions, she replied to her pastor that she would if he insisted, but she didn't want to. He let her off and she never read it or anything else on mysticism. Her reading consisted of scripture and the Catholic catechism, a most unfanciful document in the first half of the twentieth century.

Anne Catherine had delighted in her beautiful visions, although she insisted she never took any theology from them. Passionately enamored of Jesus Christ, Theresa Neumann complained, "Why do I have to look at this?" of any vision, however beautiful, if Christ were not in it.[13]

She seems to have had no natural psychic ability, although after her visions began she gradually developed the precognition and other mental gifts associated with authentic mystics. She had no interest in her own feats however.

For a person this stolidly mundane how did the door open into the mystical dimension? As I see it, it started with battling a fire at her employer's. With the men away at war, as the strongest woman Theresa hauled thirty- to forty-pound water buckets, then took the most grueling position, standing on a chair for two hours lifting the heavy buckets above her head to her employer. Suddenly a bucket fell from her hands; she had seriously injured two vertebrae. Next she became a victim of her own feeling that she shouldn't sit around and be a drain on the farmer-inn keeper for whom she had worked since leaving school. Trying to hoist a bag of seed potatoes, her injured back went out, plunging her down the cellar stairs. Landing on the back of her skull, there was a fracture, hemorrhage, more spinal injury, and the start of vision problems that would end, after more knocks on the head, in blindness.[14]

Reams of material could be produced on the medical problems that began the day of the fire and reduced a strong woman to an invalid. But the bottom line, for our purposes, is that her illness is definitely a period of "creative disintegration" similar to the mysterious mind-body-spirit suffering of the African Dorcas before she accepted her call to become a shamaness.

Did anything neurotic mix into the organically caused illness of the twenty-year-old? Only the fifth doctor to treat her initially diagnosed hysteria to be involved. And he retracted this assessment as he studied her longer. However, medical men who never examined her and usually never met her have theorized atop those words for years, citing neurosis arising from causes such as her terror of fire (she denied any) to sexual libido (her sexuality was that of a woman whose plan is to become a nun as soon as her father returns from a war). Whether Theresa Neumann was fire-traumatized, sex-starved, or whatever, I find nothing alters one fact: In all the psychospiritual, bodily complexity of her human situation, blind and paralyzed, the young woman was goaded into contact with the same numinous realities that people of all spiritual traditions from the shamanistic to the Judeo-Christian have discovered in similar situations in the depths of one's own being or from an outer source.

Once this contact was flourishing, Theresa's varied disabilities were healed, one by one, in six ecstatic experiences from spring 1923 to fall 1925. If you don't believe the insistence of all the great mystics that ecstasy is healing, you may see this as proof the illnesses weren't real. I do not.

While her intake had dwindled to liquids during her invalid years, inedia occurred a year *after* she was fully recovered.

For the forty years or so after her inexplicable cures until her death at sixty-four of angina pectoris, Theresa Neumann remained a robust-looking, basically vigorous woman, although she was led by God, she believed, to take on the physical, mental, and spiritual sufferings of others at times. To heal others' illnesses and expiate their sins, as she saw it, the inedic often had symptoms of many varied illnesses, which disappeared when the period of reparatory suffering was over.

Celibate, she lived with her parents and was known as always busy, working about the house and garden, visiting the sick and dying of all the local hamlets, and enthusiastically carrying out her job of decorating the church as an expression of her love for God. Between ecstasies and the Friday sufferings that incapacitated her, she received family and friends, wrote letters, and led a life similar to that of millions of small-town folks.[15]

A Jewish businessman, Benno Karpeles, who met her noted the "fresh and healthy-looking peasant girl . . . certainly gave no signs of [living] . . . without taking any nourishment." He noted that during their two-hour conversation, Theresa dashed into the nearby church three times to supervise decorating for a big occasion. To Karpeles, Theresa was "a big overgrown child, with wonderful blue eyes, full of wit and sparkle."[16]

Perhaps a romanticized impression, but his description leaves no doubt that not only Catholics thought Neumann showed no signs of food or sleep deprivation. Could he and many others have been taken in for thirty-five years? That is, did Theresa Neumann look so well nourished because she was? Did she only pretend not to eat or drink?

To investigate this possibility, the local bishop† engaged a university lecturer in psychiatry, a non-Catholic named Ewald, to make a quiet examination. The Neumanns agreed reluctantly, Theresa pleading with her father to do whatever the bishop asked, Neumann *père* maintaining that the family weren't making any claims and wanted only to be left alone, so why should Theresa have to put up with all this?

For fifteen days in 1927 Dr. Ewald conducted his investigation for the bishop with the thoroughness for which German medical men are famed. Of his thirteen rules I give seven that pertain to inedia (the rest refer to general matters or the stigmata):

1. Four nurses would watch, in pairs, around the clock, each pair taking twelve hours and keeping meticulous records of everything pertinent.

2. Theresa would not be alone a single moment, day or night. The toilet was not to be used. Instead feces would be collected in a receptacle.

† Providing guidance to his flock on the legitimacy of alleged mystical occurrences within its ranks is part of a bishop's teaching responsibility. To help him, panels or individual experts on the subject in question are asked to investigate and report. As stigmatics were alleged "mental cases," Theresa's bishop chose a medical man who was also a psychiatrist to examine her.

3. The nurses would bathe Theresa with a damp washcloth only. No sponge could be used.

4. The water used for a mouthwash must be measured before use, then remeasured after she spit it out.

5. The few drops of water she was still using in 1927 to help get the Eucharist down her constricted throat must also be measured before she took them.

6. All excretions—urine, feces, vomit—must be kept, measured, or weighed and immediately sent to the physician for analysis.

7. There would be repeated weighing of the body and temperature and pulse measurements.

Blood and other tests, some of which Ewald did not tell her bishop or family about, were also made by the psychiatrist who in his own words felt "science recognizes no miracles, no interruption in the network of causality"‡ and was determined to prove it. What he proved instead was that Theresa Neumann's total intake for fifteen days was three Eucharistic hosts (each day she had a fragment equal to a fifth of one) and enough drops of water for swallowing them to total three spoonfuls. The human body being four-fifths water, on that intake her body, especially with blood loss, should have been a dried-up mummy. But there was no sign whatsoever of dehydration, her mouth, for instance, retaining normal moisture. Her weight went down after she bled on both Fridays from her stigmata but returned to normal the first week by Wednesday, the second week by Thursday.

Two days after the examination period Theresa conscientiously reported to Ewald "a slight bowel movement" of a type* catalogued in starvation physiology. (After 1930 bowel and bladder elimination, which had become more and more infrequent, apparently stopped entirely.)

‡ *Munich Medical Weekly* (No. 46, 1927)
* About a tablespoon, primarily mucus.

Ewald was less conscientious than Theresa. In a blatant breach of his agreement, he did not just hand his report quietly to the bishop but published it in a Munich medical publication.[17] Like most psychiatrists of the era, he was an atheist. Scrupulously honest in admitting Theresa inedic, he dealt with it in the only way possible for someone who recognized no mystical realities and whose ideas of mind-body interaction omitted spiritual influences: He said Theresa was a complex neurotic.

Over the next decade both critics and supporters clamored for bigger, better, longer, "more clinical" examinations. Theresa's response was always that she was willing to do anything her bishop asked. Refusing to forget how Ewald had betrayed his promise of confidentiality to make his eldest daughter a public spectacle, held up to the world as a nut, her father had other views. As head of the family he refused to sanction Theresa's going off to pass weeks or months under observation in some clinic to prove what he already knew and wasn't asking anyone else to believe. If she went anyway, he warned his door would be closed to her when she came back. Let others take that however they would and leave the Neumanns alone.

The obstinate old man had adherents who claimed no examination would ever satisfy those who found Theresa outside their belief system. If she were examined and anything supernatural cited, critics would cry "Catholic conspiracy" and "religious hoax." If she were examined by another atheist of non-Catholic background like Ewald, the examiner would have to take the tack that inedia proves "neurosis." These whispers in his ear solidified Neumann, especially when doctors warned him that experiments involving incisions into the stigmata or forced intravenous feeding might be part of a scientific inquiry. As the clamor continued, the Nazis came to power. National Socialism sneered at the weak Jewish God of Christianity. Now Theresa's father heard ominous rumors of getting the Konnersreuth stigmatic into a clinic and solving her riddle by means of injections. Lethal injections were a favorite Nazi murder method, and Neumann resolved more fiercely never to let his oldest child out of his hands.† Still pressured by his church and Theresa's detractors alike to give in, early in the Hitler era Ferdinand Neumann discovered that during the first investigation, supposedly safe because bishop-ordered, Ewald had made a number of unauthorized tests, including insisting on examining Theresa pelvically to determine her virginity. For the ultraconservative Bavarian peasant of his era, that was the final straw. I have seen a copy of his letter to the archbishop, which storms that his innocent daughter had been treated "the way they examine a harlot at the police station."[18] He closes with the declaration that since the Church's sponsorship of the first examination had proven no protection and his family's confidence had been so abused, he was resolved as head of the family to never permit another medical examination. And he never did, although Theresa remained willing.

Obviously Ferdinand Neumann's outrage can be interpreted as a clever ploy in a conspiracy, but if so what kind of conspiracy? The first examination had shown Theresa's inedia was not fraudulent. All who knew the Neumanns were adamant that if the inedic were guilty of fraud, her family would have been the first to accuse her. Significant also is that, as with Louise Lateau, these devout peasants strongly believed in damnation for those who maliciously use religion for nefarious purposes.

Teodorowicz once discussed the conspiracy charges with Theresa, who replied with some warmth, "Of what benefit would it be to my family to deceive the world and tell them I don't eat, if I do? Of what value would it be to us to plunge our souls into perdition through fraud and lies, through blasphe-

---

† She was in her late thirties, but as was not that unusual in father-daughter relationships of the era, Neumann claimed if she lived in his house, she had to follow his orders—or leave. He did permit, unofficially, a psychiatrist he knew and trusted named Witry to give her "a clinical exam" which was favorable to her [*Theresa Neumann,* Teodorowicz, p. 78]

mous confessions and communions?"[19] The bishop pondered and concluded only ambition and/or profit could be motives. As to profit, Ferdinand Neumann rejected out of hand a project to film Theresa's ecstasies which would have made him a wealthy man, while Theresa snapped, "I don't bleed for money."[20] As to ambition, the stigmata gave her enough fame for anyone without inedia, if fame was a goal. Actually, those who knew the Neumanns agreed that Theresa's notoriety was the family's "domestic tragedy."[21]

The Jewish businessman Benno Karpeles said, "In my whole life I have never seen a person who had absolute truth written on her face the way Theresa Neumann has."[22] Theresa herself said her parents were so strict on the point that she had never told a lie.

One of her critics, a Catholic priest, accepted these assessments. He charged Theresa, not with blatant fraud in claiming inedia but with a sort of unconscious deceit. Father Siwek proposed "Theresa does take natural nourishment but . . . for reasons of piety she can sincerely believe that there is no harm in affirming that she takes no food because she eats almost nothing."

Considering the seriousness of the questions put to her over and over on her total fast, this would demand a kind of moral imbecility on Theresa's part. While she was of only average intellectual ability, her moral intelligence was superb. And since her confessor and pastor Father Joseph Naber minutely examined her on this point, he, too, would have had to lack the ability to distinguish the half-truth from the whole in such a clearcut matter as whether one ate "a tiny bit" or "nothing." Simple parish priest Fr. Naber was, but not that simple.

A more intelligent charge than Father Siwek's was the assertion that Theresa was neurotic to the point of insanity in just this small area, so she could not distinguish the truth that she ate from belief that she didn't because of a morbid quest for "some kind of ascetic ideal in mortification by abstinence."

But this, too, would have demanded her family and pastor—and Ewald and his nurses—abet the conspiracy. And it asks for a temperament unlike the uncompulsive, unobsessive Theresa. Asked about her ascetic ideals, this down-to-earth woman replied:

> I don't consider the fasting anything in connection with the spiritual life. It is certainly good if somebody fasts, but it can also be good if someone does not fast. . . . I know that it is the great aim of men to come to the Savior, whether they eat or do not eat. In a certain respect, then, this great fasting is something indifferent as far as coming to the Savior is concerned, and in this light he who fasts does not merit any preferment over him who does not fast. If the question were for me to decide, I really do not know on what grounds I should decide in favor of the great fast for myself.[23]

And whenever she had guests, Theresa heartily urged them to have a meal.

1. Hilda Graef was a prominent critic.

2. He also visited her.

3. Josef Teodorowicz, *Mystical Phenomena in the Life of Therese Neumann,* pp. 325–26. See also Johannes Steiner's *Therese Neumann,* pp. 27–29.

4. Teodorowicz, op. cit., p. 326.

5. Steiner, op. cit., pp. 203–7, and Charles Mortimer Carty, "Who Is Teresa Neumann," p. 51.

6. Konnersreuth Yearbook, 1929, quoted by Carty, op. cit., pp. 47–48, and Teodorowicz, op. cit., p. 315.

7. Teodorowicz, op. cit., p. 327.

8. Ibid., p. 329.

9. Ibid., p. 54.

10. Carty, op. cit., p. 4, quoting Theresa's account to Father Leopold Witt, pastor of a parish close to Konnersreuth.

11. Teodorowicz, op. cit., p. 8.

12. Ibid.

13. Ibid., pp. 6–7.

14. See some medical details in Ibid., pp. 111–16, and Carty, op. cit., pp. 6–12.

15. Teodorowicz, op. cit., p. 258.

16. Steiner, op. cit., p. 87.

17. Dr. G. Ewald, "Die Stigmatisierte von Konnersreuth," supplement to *Munchner medizinische Wochenschrift* no. 46 (1927): See Teodorowicz, op. cit., pp. 329–32.

18. Dated Mar. 10, 1937. See Steiner, op. cit., pp. 79–80.

19. Teodorowicz, op. cit., p. 345.

20. Ibid., p. 347.

21. Ibid., p. 346. See also p. 20.

22. Steiner, op. cit., p. 87.

23. Teodorowicz, op. cit., p. 347.

▲ 10

two
more
inedics

▲ examined the case of Theresa Neumann at length because, not an invalid, she is the least easily dismissed twentieth-century inedic. This chapter takes a briefer look at two invalid inedics. In the process the reader will have an important chance to see inedia is not limited to Bavarians or people of Neumann's temperament.

▲

Born to peasants in the village of Balthasar among the piney hills off the Portugese coast, Alexandrina da Costa (1904–55), the younger of her family's two children, was a lively tomboy "full of wit and laughter." In church as a child she "furtively [tied] together the fringes of women's shawls as they listened attentively to the sermon." After mass she liked to rush out-side, hide herself behind a low wall and throw little stones at the emerging congregation.[1] And yet she was devout, too, seemingly born with a bent toward prayer.

After eighteen months' total schooling, when she was nine years old, her widowed, impoverished mother hired the strong, capable child out to a nearby farmer. When she was twelve, this employer tried to rape the pretty, vivacious girl. As spirited as she was strong, she managed to drive him off and ran home to her mother's.[2]

Her immune system perhaps weakened by trauma, that year she almost died of typhoid and had to be sent to a coastal sanatorium to recover. When she returned, no longer equal to farm work, she became a seamstress like her older sister.

From the time of the attempted rape, Alexandrina began attending daily mass. Always compassionate, two 1918 instances are known in which the fourteen-year-old stayed with old people who were dying and then prepared their bodies for burial in spite of a repugnance so great that she thought she would faint.[3]

There is nothing too unusual about any of this. Impoverished village girls grow up fast. But in March of that year her life changed forever. The would-be rapist had tried intermittently to get at her over the past two years. Now as she, her sister, and a friend sewed on the second floor of the da Costa home, he and two other men broke into the house. The girls barred the way with a heavy sewing machine, but the men broke through. Cornered, Alexandrina jumped out the window. Falling thirteen feet onto hard ground, in spite of intense pain in her spine she seized a piece of firewood and dragged herself up the stairs. Singlehandedly the slight teenager beat three adult men off the other girls. Only when they fled did she collapse. All were still virgins but for the heroine of the day the price was high. Over the next six years, in spite of the best treatment her mother's poverty permitted, including seeing a specialist, the injured spine deteriorated until by the age of twenty, vibrant Alexandrina's world had shrunk to a tiny upstairs bedroom.

Paralyzed, when doctors said there was nothing medicine could do, it was not her nature to give up. Bartering with God, she "promised to give away everything she had, to dress herself in mourning for the rest of her life, to cut off her [long, lovely] hair, if only she was cured."[4]

This poignant appeal for wholeness was answered by further deterioration. The last sacraments were given her several times in this period.

Alexandrina, from a mystical viewpoint, may be one of those rare souls for whom wholeness can only be found in utter brokenness. Those who knew her intimately were to see over the next years that she who had been a merry hoyden became, they believe, an enormous-hearted mystic precisely because she was forced to grapple with and heroically surmount dreadful physical, psychological, and spiritual suffering. Hope died hard in one so full of life. Only very gradually did Alexandrina accept the idea that what she did with her physical suffering might be her only means of making a creative response to life. Even in 1928 she told friends that if they heard singing in the streets, it would be her thanking God for her miracle cure.[5]

Perhaps a miracle of sorts did take place, because this healthy passion to be healed did not give way to bitterness or self-centeredness. The fire of her personality still blazed, but it became spiritualized. Her ardor for wholeness became the passion for that total wholeness found, mystics say, only in God. After seven years in bed, in 1931 she experienced an ecstasy. About 1933 visions of Christ began to call her to a special vocation of reparatory suffering to help others. By 1934 she writes in a letter that she can take only liquids "due to a swelling in my mouth." Even these often cause vomiting, she says, adding, as one would expect in that situation, that she suffers from not being able to eat and doesn't see how she can live much longer.[6]

In 1938 she began weekly relivings of Christ's Passion but never with visible stigmata. While it does not, to me, automatically discredit Alexandrina as a genuine mystic, one fact about these ecstasies indicates that her paralysis, in spite of what doctors say, *may* have had a nonorganic cause: During these weekly events the inedic was, just for their duration, able to move her paralyzed body. While I will not label this "neurotic," since it could be supernatural it shows that a psychosomatic element, i.e. mind (emotions and perhaps soul) acting on the body *may* have kept her paralyzed at other times.

After eighteen years of invalidism, on Good Friday 1942 the now thirty-eight-year-old ecstatic visionary believed Christ said to her: You will not take food again on earth. Your food will be my flesh; your blood will be my divine blood [the reference is to the Eucharist], your life will be my life. You receive it from me when I unite my heart to your heart. Do not fear.[7]

If Alexandrina's digestive functions had shut down for any nonmystical reason, either as a function of paralysis and body atrophy *or* from emotional factors, she *could*, of course, still have had such a vision. Its source, then, instead of the supernatural, would have been her own unconscious or "imagination." Because of this possibility, if the Catholic Church ever beatifies and/or canonizes Alexandrina as heroically virtuous, no decree will ever say that her visions or her inedia were supernatural. No decree will ever say they weren't. The Church's position will be that there is no way of sifting out the supernatural from the natural in areas such as visions* or inedia, even in the holy. They must be left to "human credence" —i.e. sort out the factors for yourself and call it as you see it.

However you call Alexandrina's vision, from that day for

---

* This stance is taken for the visions of all saints, not just inedics.

the thirteen years until her death, inedia was total except for the Eucharistic wafer. No water or other liquids were taken. "Why don't you eat?" investigating physicians asked. "I don't eat because I can't," she answered. "I feel full."[8] While some cried "Miracle," others accused the visionary, her mother and sister, and sometimes her spiritual director and/or the Catholic Church of "perpetrating a monstrous fraud." To answer the accusations, on June 10, 1942, when she had been inedic little more than a year, Alexandrina, at the request of the local bishop, entered the hospital of Foce del Duro in Oporto, Portugal. It was not Dr. Azevedo, her physician from 1941 until her death, who was to conduct the investigation. That was put in the hands of Dr. Enrico Gomes di Araujo. Araujo, a member of the Royal Academy of Medicine of Madrid and a specialist in "nervous diseases," had dealt with plenty of nuts. He planned to sort out all this "nonsense"[9] pronto.

Being moved caused Alexandrina terrible pain any time. When she arrived at the hospital after a trip over broken, rutted roads, she was in such bad shape for five days that Araujo expected her death. Understandably he wished to use intravenous feeding and medication but was reminded that Alexandrina was there only to establish the reality of her inedia and the normality of her mental faculties, nothing more. Without either of these helps, on the sixth day her pulse, color, and other vital signs returned to normal.

For one month she was never left alone. Dr. Araujo popped in often—especially at unlikely hours of the night. All the physicians and nurses began the study sure that if the so-called mystic were just kept isolated and under watch so she could not get food surreptitiously, dehydration and starvation would soon force her to ask for water and food. To their surprise this did not happen.

After thirty days, another physician, hearing of the test results, impugned Araujo's integrity, accusing him and the

203

nurses of colluding with the patient. Stung by this criticism after he had spent hours trying to convince Alexandrina that her belief Christ was sustaining her through the Eucharist was a delusion, Araujo insisted on meeting this physician's demand that a nurse of his choice (the man's own blood sister it turned out) be permitted another ten days' surveillance. This observer, too, found true inedia. Ironically, Araujo, who had wanted to show Alexandrina couldn't exist sans food, now had a colleague to back up his report that said, "It is absolutely certain that during forty days of being bedridden in hospital, the sick woman did not eat or drink."[10]

Araujo called it "scientifically inexplicable" but he would not state it proved, as Alexandrina believed, that complete nutrition and hydration came to her from the Eucharist she received daily. Dr. C. A. di Lima, professor of medicine at Oporto, also studied Alexandrina at this time. Doctor Lima issued a joint report, with her regular physician Azevedo, that the thirty-nine-year-old mystic's abstinence from "solids and liquids was absolute" from June 10 to July 20, 1943. They note:

> She retained her weight, and her temperature, breathing, blood pressure, pulse and blood were normal while her mental faculties were constant and lucid and she had not, during these forty days, any natural necessities.[11]

Studying the two reports, another doctor who was the president of the Society of Gastroenterology and Nutrition at Pernambuco and a professor of medicine at Recife and Pernambuco gave his medical judgment that the spinal cord disability, which he found the probable cause of the paralysis, did not cause the inedia. He also judged that the hospital investigation had ruled out fraud as a possibility while hysteria, he felt, did not fit the patient, especially since individuals competent to tell the hysteric from the true mystic put her in the latter class.[12] Alexandrina's Cause was opened in 1967.

▲

Invalid inedics tend to be dismissed as "weirdos" or "flakes." Marthe Robin (1902–81) is a definite exception. The late French Cardinal Danielou said the most outstanding person of his times was neither General de Gaulle nor John XXIII, "but Marthe Robin."[13] The Dutch-born writer of American best-sellers Henri J. M. Nouwen predicts Marthe's "life will make as much of an impact on the twentieth century as the life of St. Francis did on the thirteenth."[14] And a specialist in mystical theology calls her "another St. Catherine of Siena."[15]

Marthe was born March 13, 1902, the sixth and last child of small-acreage farmers in France's Drôme region. She would live her entire seventy-nine years in the house of her birth. On maps her village lies almost on a direct line from the seaport of Marseille to the industrial city of Lyon. Due to typhoid from a polluted well which killed a sibling, Marthe was a weak child who missed a lot of school and had little appetite. A friend remembers her at school throwing her unfinished hard-boiled egg into a field, asking the other "not to tell."[16]

She left school at fourteen, not unusual for a French farm girl. Of a happy disposition, she loved to bake, to exchange recipes with her friends, to embroider, to gather flowers for bouquets. Bringing the cows back at night, she was always fearful after some ne'er-do-wells once hid and scared her badly. In short she was a teen much like any other.[17]

Then, beginning in July 1918, the sixteen-year-old began having severe headaches and other symptoms. In the fall she collapsed. She was either in a coma or had some kind of "sleeping sickness" for many months. Her legs paralyzed, she was in great pain much of the time, crying out sometimes even when unconscious. At times she "came to" and was better. Doctors in July had thought of epilepsy. Now they spoke gravely of brain tumors. Over the years to come, meningitis, encephalitis, polio, and rheumatoid arthritis would also be considered possibilities.

Raymond Peyret, author of three books on his country-woman, theorizes "Jesus was using this illness to refashion Marthe and educate her at her depths."[18] Whether this is the case or not, on March 25, 1921, her sister Alice, who shared a bedroom with Marthe, was awakened by a loud noise to a beautiful bright light. Marthe agreed with her delight in the light but added joyously, "I also saw the Blessed Virgin."[19] The sick nineteen-year-old began to get better. She was able to be in a chair reading library books and doing embroidery to help pay for her medications.

Beginning to walk with a cane, she dreamed of becoming a Carmelite nun. Then there was another of those experiences which shape a life. Words in a book seared her soul: "You look for joy, peace, and sweetness; but it is suffering for which you must prepare." At the same time the now twenty-year-old heard the call "to give *all* to God."[20]

The rest of her life is the living out of that call and those prophetic words. But besides suffering, Marthe also found joy, peace, and sweetness—and communicated them, many say to an amazing degree, to others.

From November 1921, her health again declined. She was bedridden. Various treatments, including being "baked" at high temperatures for rheumatoid arthritis, brought no cure. By 1925 a sister witnesses "Marthe ate very little—she was content with a little fruit and a bit of liquid."[21] A year or so later, she was in a three-week coma the attending doctor predicted would end in death. During that "unconscious" period she later confided to her spiritual mentor that she had three visions of St. Therese of Lisieux. Therese told Marthe she would not die and her "mission would extend throughout the entire world."

Megalomania?

Marthe laughed about it rather than seeming to get puffed up. And the Foyers de Charity, which she founded, number by 1989 over sixty spread over five continents.

In 1927 it is said she was eating nothing "except a few tart candies brought by visitors."

Medical men from Lyons—Dr. Richard, a surgeon and clinical instructor; and Dr. Dechaume, director of the neuro-psychiatric clinic—studied Marthe at the request of the local bishop. Men of more integrity than Theresa Neumann's examiner, their twenty-five-page report went only to the bishop, with a copy to Rome. But since her death a portion of it has appeared in a book on the inedic by Jean Guitton, a member of the Academie Francaise who knew her personally. It is from this French-language source[22] I have taken all the medical details of her case, including the following sequence of events.†

After 1929, in addition to her paralyzed legs "contracted and twisted out of shape," she lost the use of her hands. In 1930 she became a stigmatic. From 1939, she went blind and even moving her head became almost impossible because it would fall to one shoulder and she couldn't raise it.

The portion of the report I saw states the doctors found no evidence of mental breakdowns triggering Marthe's physical disabilities. Nor is there mention of psychosis. They also rule out brain tumors or epilepsy. Encephalitis is deemed a possibility. Without going into more of the copious medical detail, the important point for our purpose is that the bishop, to whom the document was delivered, remained Marthe's great

---

† These details, especially dates, often differ from Peyret's first book, the only one translated to date. He probably had to work from hearsay, the report not being available at that time, immediately after her death.

supporter. This means fraud, too, was ruled out. Of course this is not to insist the inedia is supra natural.

According to this report, Marthe stopped eating in 1932 (Peyret and Guitton both say 1928 instead). Apparently because of her paralysis, she was unable to swallow. Even before that, the medical men note that she had great trouble with eating, vomiting most of what was taken. What the medical men say is backed up by those who cared for the totally paralyzed woman. First her parents. Then non-relatives after their deaths. All who were in contact with Marthe agree that for the forty-nine years from 1932 to her death in 1981, she drank nothing and ate nothing. The only thing that entered her body was the tiny Eucharistic wafer.

The Gallic mystic never made a big deal of inedia. Take Jean Guitton's conversation with her one morning. I translate his French:

GUITTON Well, Marthe, how're you doing this morning? You don't eat. You don't drink. You don't sleep. What a funny life!

MARTHE I'd love to be able to eat, to be able to drink a little. I compensate by imagining menus.

GUITTON We used to do that when we were prisoners [in World War II].

MARTHE Ah, do you know what I've been doing this week? I've prepared [directed, not physically put together] some packages‡ for prisoners—not prisoners of war but men on death row. I'm afraid one of them might already have been

‡ Called Marthe's baskets, these were made up of the gifts—fruit, rosaries, candy, etc. —given Marthe directly or collected at the end of Foyer retreats. It was her joy to send them to the poor and to missionaries, as well as to prisoners.

executed . . . Well, anyway the things I was putting in the packages of my prisoners I was imagining myself eating with them. But what did you eat yesterday evening, this morning? What did you have for lunch?

GUITTON I barely paid attention.

MARTHE You're wrong [to do that]. The odors . . . I remember . . . I always loved coffee. Hot chocolate I found flavorless.

GUITTON You know, Marthe, when I told one of my colleagues that you don't eat and that you don't drink, he told me that wasn't possible; he said certainly you slip out at night and rummage in your cupboard for a little cheese or drink a little water.

MARTHE Your friend's not wrong. I don't attach any importance to these fasts that Jesus submits me to. I'm on my farm in the house of my father with my cows. If I could drink the milk of my cows, I wouldn't deprive myself.[23]

I note one time she was roused, however, to remark, "I wish I could cry to those who ask me if I eat that I eat more than they do, because I am nourished by the Eucharist, the body and blood of Jesus. I'd like to tell them that it's they who block the effects in themselves of this nourishment."[24]

In addition to inedia, it is also maintained by those closest to her that Marthe Robin for a half century did not sleep. As I have said it seems to me almost impossible to prove someone never sleeps. Even her medical examiners write only, "Marthe says that since 1932 she has been unable to sleep." *If* this is true, I would consider it more certain evidence of mysticism than inedia. For while it is true that there are thousands of invalids and only a handful of inedics, still it is not impossible inedia comes from some complex bodily "shutdown" sans mystical factors. Sleep, on the other hand, is necessary for mental and physical health *except* where sleep's functions seem to be achieved through deep mystical states. If she never slept for almost fifty years, this would favor Marthe's being a great mystic whose inedia, too, may have been, at least primarily, mystical. But no one can make such a claim unless Marthe was observed round the clock for months on just this point. And I do not know whether such an investigation was ever made or not.

There are signs, however, which point to a high level of mysticism. These include Marthe's mental gifts of sanctity such as at times having knowledge of the future or the ability to read minds and hearts, bilocations, the fact that her frequent visions had profound mystical content, and that she could say of even very advanced mystical phenomena "Oh yes, I've experienced that. But it's superficial."[25] Above all is the fact that, with the utmost simplicity, humility, and laughter, Marthe Robin took the entire world to her heart.

A woman so paralyzed someone once told her she was "only a brain" ("and a heart, I hope," she corrected),[26] and who has all the sufferings of a stigmatic, could easily spill over with masochism or self-preoccupation. To read the lyrical joyswept prayers composed by this uneducated woman is to glimpse something of the bliss that bubbled out of the mystic's depths even as suffering, willingly undergone to benefit the human family, pressed her to the ground physically. Dozens of people of every background have left impressions of Marthe Robin because they found the crippled, blind woman unforgettable. I note how many mention "her youthful spirit and joy" and her sense of humor.

A physician and psychiatrist, Dr. Couchoud, who was considered a leading "anti-Christian thinker," was quoted in France's daily newspaper *Le Figaro*:

I have known . . . subjects with fragile blood vessels who, having meditated upon the Passion of Christ, display traces of blood on their bodies.* There are some of them in [mental] hospitals. But the case of Marthe is quite different; paralyzed, . . . her muscular system was completely atrophied, and she was unable to ingest anything. That, however, in my opinion is not the important thing. . . . The important thing is that she was a superior woman, that she had a kind of genius. I never conversed with her without taking away with me some kind of enlightenment that was nevertheless totally simple.[27]

A less famous person, Mrs. Helen Sorenson of Dijon, expresses thoughts that are typical:

In the month of August 1980, I had the great joy of meeting Marthe Robin in her dark little room; but what warmth, what enlightenment! I would have remained for hours, listening to her advice, her encouragement, her joyful hope. Her clear voice, which I would compare to a pure spring, was filled with gaiety and youth—a voice that proclaimed love and renewed one's strength to make progress in one's daily life.[28]

Mrs. Sorenson had lost faith in numinous realities twenty years earlier. Marthe gave it back to her.

In the context of such a life, Marthe Robin's inedia is extremely significant in one respect: whatever the causes of inedia in mystic invalids—physical, psychosomatic (spirit acting on body) or purely supra natural—I find it impossible to connect it in her regard to any neurosis, either simple or complex.

---

* His theory is useful with the mentally ill; it fails to help much with mystics like Padre Pio, whose deep wounds doctors could not heal although he healed normally otherwise and whose blood loss and diet make his life inexplicable.

notes

1. Francis Johnston, *Alexandrina,* p. 13. Johnston's English-language biography is based on the author's firsthand investigations in the inedic's home village and on the work of her spiritual director Fr. Umberto Pasquale, S.D.B., and contains some extracts from Alexandrina's autobiography.

2. Ibid., p. 14.

3. Ibid., p. 15. This contains an extract from the inedic's autobiography.

4. Ibid., p. 20.

5. Ibid., p. 21.

6. Ibid., p. 31.

7. Ibid., p. 70.

8. Ibid., p. 74.

9. Ibid., p. 78.

10. Ibid., p. 83.

11. Ibid., quoting the signed deposition of the two medical men.

12. Ibid., pp. 84–85, quoting portions of his report which appears to have been made at the request of her spiritual director.

13. Raymond Peyret, *Marthe Robin: The Cross and the Joy,* p. 130. This is the work given to English-speakers at the Foyers, which were founded by Marthe. The only thing available in English, it is not completely accurate in details of dates, medical data, etc., but it pictures her personality correctly.

14. In "The Passion of Marthe Robin," *Catholic Digest,* November 1987, pp. 30–39, condensed from a *New Oxford Review* article of May 1987.

15. Peyret, op. cit., pp. 77–78.

16. Ibid., p. 17.

17. Raymond Peyret, *Petite Vie de Marthe Robin,* pp. 29–30, and Jean Guitton, *Portrait de Marthe Robin,* p. 41.

18. Peyret, *Petite Vie,* p. 36.

19. Peyret, *Marthe Robin: The Cross and the Joy,* p. 27.

20. Ibid., p. 29.

21. Ibid., p. 36.

22. Guitton, op. cit., pp. 54–59.

23. Ibid., pp. 79–80.

24. Ibid., p. 164.

25. Ibid., p. 87.

26. Ibid., p. 65.

27. Peyret, *Marthe Robin: The Cross and the Joy,* p. 130. His comments were made to Jean Guitton, but I give the English-language source I have quoted.

28. Ibid., p. 125. I have excerpted a paragraph of Sorenson's much longer praise of Marthe.

II △

can blood smell like flowers?

Diseased by gangrene or other putrefying disease, human flesh stinks. According to observers of the sanctified body, flesh suffused with holiness sometimes smells too—of wonderful fragrances they term "the odor of sanctity." Here again is something that sounds bizarre. But think a moment. If under certain conditions the cells of the body can become cancerous* from such emotions as grief, anger, and despair, may they not become suffused with holiness too? Or to put it another way, if flesh can reek of the disease affecting a whole person—body, mind, and soul—then why may it not sometimes smell of a whole person's holiness as well?

I pose that question because I feel I have no choice. To

---

* See books like *Mind as Healer, Mind as Slayer* and *Love, Medicine, & Miracles*. No implication is meant that *all* cancer is emotionally caused. Most cases, doctors say, have roots in environmental pollution or such self-pollution as smoking or eating carcinogenic foods.

mention only Catholicism for a moment, in every century of the Catholic Church's existence, including this one, competent, skeptical observers of her saints testify that some—by no means all—sanctified individuals at times exude unearthly perfumes under circumstances ruling out fraud or delusion. In other cases, like the Shekinah Light that signals God's presence *with* a saint but does not emanate *from* the holy one's body, "heavenly" odors may accompany sanctity, it appears, without actually being emitted by the sanctified body. Usually seen as a sign from God of someone's holiness, it is said these fragrances may at times be a form of communication or signal a grace, such as healing, received from God through the saint's prayers.

This bizarre tradition of Catholicism, of which most Catholics remain themselves ignorant, fortunately for its credibility does not appear only among Catholics. In the Protestant branch of Christianity, for instance, delicious odors associated with the supernatural are not unknown. Episcopalian charismatic Agnes Sanford is among those who have had such an experience. In her autobiography, Agnes—whom some believe a saint herself—writes of the fragrance in connection with the School of Pastoral Care she and her husband, an Episcopal clergyman, ran for ministers of many denominations in order that "those who take part may have an *experience* of God." Some who attended, operating purely from a rational basis in their spiritual lives, found experiential (supra-rational) religion hardly their cup of tea. Agnes writes of one

> who came only out of desperation because his two little girls were born with cystic fibrosis and there seemed no way to heal them save by a miracle. Though he tried for their sakes, he simply could not accept any of our instructions, so foreign were they to the mechanistic and "rational" theology that he had been taught. . . . After our final meal, someone drew me excitedly into the chapel and

I went, wondering who had fallen apart now. There were fourteen ministers standing around in awe and amazement because the chapel was filled with the fragrance of a kind of heavenly incense, more sweet than any that man can make. No incense had ever been used in that chapel.

And this minister was on his knees in front of the altar, bathed in tears of joy. . . .

Since then I have often sensed the holy fragrance here and there in Lasell House, which . . . is filled with light and joy. When I mentioned this fragrance once to Tommy Tyson,† one of our leaders, he simply said, "Naturally. Don't you see the angels?" And when I mentioned it to one of the cooks, she said, "Of course. As soon as your school is over, all three of us go into the chapel and just sit there to soak it up."[1]

Non-Christian traditions report the same phenomenon. In Buddhist lore, for instance, is the tale of the great Japanese holy man Kobo Daishi. Long after his death, when the common people had turned this spiritual master, says authority Oliver Statler, "into a deity and savior," he appeared in a dream to a reigning emperor, requesting his corpse be clothed in new garments. In the course of this exhumation and reclothing, the high priest took his young acolyte's hand and "placed it upon the knee of the Daishi and ever after, this hand had a fragrant odor."‡[2]

Whether you believe this very old tale or not, would even what rationalists call "a pious legend" include reference to a supernatural odor if no one in Buddhism had ever experienced such a thing? I think not.

Besides being at times a sign of God's presence in special

---

† A well-known Methodist clergyman.

‡ The account is unclear as to whether the boy's hand touched a corpse or the knee of the dead holy man when he appeared in a vision to the high priest.

instances (like the one Agnes Sanford referred to) and at other times a physical by-product of sanctity, it is possible the ability to produce fragrances, like other arts of the fakir, may at times be learned. Indian holy man Paramahansa Yogananda wrote with a certain disdain of Gandha Baba, "the perfume saint," who could "give the natural perfume of any flower to a scentless one, . . . revive a wilted blossom, or make a person's skin exude delightful fragrances," an art, as Yogananda terms it, that the yogi mastered after twelve years' training with a Tibetan.* Yogananda did not claim what he called "an ostentatious display" was a fraud or illusion but objected to it in precisely the terms Buddha, Catholic sources, and others warn against such so-called "saints" who do spectacular things for display or show. Such "wonder workings," all their critics agree with Yogananda, are "spiritually useless" activities "having little purpose beyond entertainment, . . . [and] digressions from a serious search for God."[3]

They are also the exact opposite of the odors associated with the sanctified body. Any scent related to authentic holiness is always shrouded in silence on the part of the saint, unless it becomes so generally known that he cannot deny it without a lie. And even then there will be a real, not feigned, reluctance to talk about it.

If odoriferous parlor tricks have no place in this book, neither will many individuals who "died in the odor of sanctity." That phrase, seldom used today, is found frequently in older Catholic books. Just as we saw the halo in art used as a symbol, a sort of artistic shorthand, to indicate sanctity without any reference to luminosity, this phrase too was used, particularly in the nineteenth century, as a quick and easy way to suggest someone was a very good person, perhaps even—but by no means necessarily—a saint. And in its use no reference

---

* Others in India with this skill, which may be a magician's trick, of course, are mentioned by Paul Brunton in *A Search in Secret India.*

to odor was intended. When I wrote the still-living author of one such phrase, I received the answer, "Well, you know such things aren't meant literally."

One is glad then the phrase has been retired. For confusion arises from the fact that it can have an absolutely literal meaning. Indeed I am convinced that when first coined, the phrase was a literal description of instances when either during or just after death sanctified bodies gave off or were surrounded by what the writer William Thomas Walsh poetically terms "the good odor of Paradise." I believe this because not only do I find such testimonies regarding early Christian martyrs, grimy pole-sitters like St. Simeon Stylites, and great mystics like St. Teresa of Avila, but I find the same phenomenon has taken place at the deaths of some nineteenth- and twentieth-century saints.

▲

Grant me for a moment that fragrances do at times emanate from the sanctified body or signal God's presence, and the logical question follows: What do such odors smell like? Does God have a signature perfume?

No, Virginia, there is no eau de God. Witnesses' accounts show the odor varies, yet inevitably—with a few fascinating exceptions we will see more of later—the smells associated with sanctity invite words like "delightful," "delicious," or "heavenly." More precise descriptions have included the odors of roses, lilies, flowers of unknown varieties, sandalwood, incense, and even fine oriental tobacco.

Each individual, science tells us, has a unique scent that a sensitive nose, a dog's for instance, can identify. I know of no saint of whom it is said the odor of sanctity was always perceivable. But in certain saints, when the odor does appear, there seems to be an odor signature. St. Therese of Lisieux, for instance, is often associated with rose scents. In other cases the same saint will emit a dazzling variety of odors, it is testified—and even do so at times at the same moment, so that one individual smells one scent, another a second, and a third nothing at all. The odor of sanctity has been associated with

1. a live, visible, sanctified body.
2. the stigmata wound or blood of a saint.
3. apparent communication from a live saint who is not present (either by some form of projection or signaling an invisible bilocation, a topic treated later in this book).
4. an object or place strongly associated with a living saint who is not present, as if his or her odor lingers or penetrates deeply.
5. the deaths of some saints.
6. the corpses of some saints.
7. an object or place strongly associated with a dead saint, including the grave.
8. apparent communication by a dead saint or in regard to a dead saint without link to any material object or visible body.
9. visible after-death appearances by saints.

Obviously not all nine of these categories fall within the scope of this book. In this and the next chapter I will give examples of the odor of sanctity as it pertains to live saints, present or not. The phenomena relating to the holy corpse or after-death appearances I must treat in forthcoming books on those topics.

Because a saint emits the odor of sanctity in one of the nine instances does not mean unusual perfumes will be found in the others. And because fragrance is apparently emitted by a saint in one instance does not rule out the possibility that in another situation heavenly scents involving the same saint may not be emitted but have a purely numinous reference. As with the Shekinah Light versus luminosity from the sanctified body, distinctions between the two odors of sanctity will often be impossible. Which odors emanate from the saint, which bathe

the sanctified body from an exterior, numinous source, which are projected by the saint even at great distances, and which speak of the saint at great distances without coming from the sanctified body are matters you can puzzle over if you will. I ignore them, for the most part, because there is no way to unerringly make such distinctions.

For instance, take French Carmelite hero Père Jacques Bunel (1900–45), who went to a Nazi concentration camp for hiding Jewish children in the school he directed. Even before World War II showed the enormous sanctity of this man whose incredible combination of courage and charity cowed even the most bestial Nazis, Bunel's holiness is unmistakable. In 1926 this mystic was summoned by two of his blood brothers.

"Come at once. Mama's dying!"

"No, she won't die." The answer is calm. "I'll bring her Communion and God will heal her."

At the impoverished family home, both brothers watch Jacques, who is radiant, give their mother Communion, while the bedroom suddenly fills with an odor like roses. The dying woman falls peacefully asleep and recovers. When his brothers express their astonishment, Jacques tells them matter-of-factly, "God can do anything."[4]

Was the odor a numinous one, signaling God's healing presence and pleasure in Jacques' faith? Or did it emanate from the radiant and perhaps ecstatic priest? Take your pick.

As with luminosity, words are inadequate. Yet even if I could permeate this page, like one of those children's scratch-and-smell books, with the odor that sometimes emanates from the living Gino Burresi of San Vittorino, Italy, this would mean nothing unless you could visit the Tuscan priest yourself and rule out fraud or other explanations. I can offer no proof. I can only present the reports of eyewitnesses, people as skeptical, as discerning, and as intelligent as you and I. Whether what they smelled upset them or blessed them, they believe the phenomenon is real from personal experience. Make of it all what you will.

▲

One of the eyewitnesses who left an account of the Flemish Benedictine wonder worker known as Father Paul (Francis Luyckx) tells how she was kneeling in prayer in the Benedictine monastery chapel where Father Paul was present. They were alone in the church when, she says, "suddenly I perceived a perfume so delicious that I was quite distracted by it. I imagined that one of the lay brothers must have brought in a bouquet of flowers." Raising her eyes, she beheld instead of flowers Father Paul in ecstasy while "the atmosphere was scented with the most delicious perfume of roses and other flowers, such as I had never before experienced."[5]

Nineteenth-century sentimentality? Let's turn to Claretian priest Aloysius Ellacuria, who died at seventy-five on April 6, 1981, in a Los Angeles hospital. When he was in the hospital a few years earlier, the holy priest had had a vision of the Virgin Mary and was instantaneously cured of a brain tumor moments before surgery. That time the surgeon fell on his knees to ask the Basque-born priest's blessing.

Father Aloysius affected people like that. His holiness for years drew overflowing crowds to the Los Angeles Claretian chapel when he conducted services. The miracles of healing he worked and hints that he levitated and bilocated were also talked about during his pastorates in Phoenix, Arizona, and San Antonio, Texas. As one of his fellow Claretians remarked, "A man like Fr. Aloysius comes along once every two hundred years."

People have spoken of the odor of sanctity in Father Aloysius' regard. Here is one report by Francis Xavier Levy, a southern California engineer:

Almost always a distinct fragrant aroma surrounded Father. On one occasion I went into the chapel to pray and noticed that Father Aloysius was also kneeling in prayer. He concluded his prayers, and I was left alone in the chapel. In a few moments I was distracted by the characteristic aroma, which I immediately attributed to flowers apparently in the garden outside. By looking completely around the chapel, however, I learned that there were no windows open, and there were no flowers inside either. Why, then, the aroma? Soon, it dawned on me that even though Father had left, his aroma lingered for several minutes.[6]

Was Aloysius just a mighty user of aftershave? Francis Levy doesn't think so. When I interviewed him late in 1988, Mr. Levy pointed out to me that in 1961 when the above incident took place, there were far fewer aftershaves on the market, and their odors were fairly recognizable. Furthermore, he added, the odor he experienced on so many occasions when he was with his spiritual mentor came and went. Aftershave, the engineer pointed out, is there or it isn't; it doesn't flood the room, vanish, and flood the room again as the odor of sanctity can. Says Levy, "I would many times be in Father's presence and there would be no aroma. Then perhaps he'd give me his blessing and suddenly the aroma would wash over me. Then again if I expected it, nothing would happen. It always took me by surprise. And as unexpectedly as it came, it would also vanish."

I have spoken of how the odor of sanctity from the same saint may assume different scents for different individuals. At the same period that Francis Levy often smelled flowers around Father Aloysius, one of his children used to also speak of a wondrous odor associated with the saintly priest. Twelve years old, an age when one is always hungry, this child volunteered that Father Aloysius gave off "the wonderful smell you get when you walk into a bakery."

Finally, if it *was* aftershave, there is no explanation for two facts: a lot of people smelled the same wonderful aromas they associated with Father Aloysius, during his funeral and a friend, Mother Marguerite Carter, has experienced the same fragrance visiting his grave at the San Gabriel Mission.

▲

In the previous chapter I wrote of Alexandrina da Costa. Salesian priest Umberto Pasquale became a strong believer in Alexandrina's sanctity during her lifetime. Sometime after becoming the crippled woman's second spiritual director, he brought his sister to stay with the mystic for a few days. After witnessing Alexandrina in ecstasy, the visitor was unable to sleep.

> All through the night however, she was conscious of delicious waves of perfume coming from Alexandrina's room next door. The following morning she asked her brother for the name of the perfume used by the seer. Unable to tell her and because he had previously noticed it himself, he asked Deolinda [Alexandrina's sister]. She smiled and replied, "We don't use perfume. Do you think that this, the poorest house in the country, would be a house for perfume?"[7]

Writer Francis Johnston, who had a chance to speak personally with Father Pasquale and to use the priest's own writings on Alexandrina, reports that Pasquale eventually realized this fragrance, described as "like a breath of paradise," was a mystical phenomenon. It persisted for years, was noticed by hundreds of people, and followed Pasquale 150 kilometers away to his residence where it was noticed by others. A signed deposition from many who perceived it was eventually drawn up.[8]

If the Catholic Church eventually concludes its present investigation by beatifying Alexandrina da Costa, this will indicate conclusively the phenomenon survived a rigorous scrutiny to rule out fraud; however formal recognition of sanctity will rest, as always, on proof of heroic charity and other virtues—the odors surrounding the Portugese woman seen as no more than corroboratory evidence of her holiness.

▲

Born in an impoverished Arab village on the present-day road to Nazareth, the orphaned Christian Arab Mariam Baouardy (1846–78) fled the marriage arranged by her uncle. She had made up her mind to serve God alone. Eventually the runaway landed in Europe, where her "singularity" (read that "flakiness") got her dismissed from the first religious order to give her a trial. The Carmel at Pau, France, accepted her. A contemplative order, Carmelites are professionals in the mystical life, not easily taken in by the inauthentic. They came to believe "la petite [the little one]," as Sister Marie of Jesus Crucified was affectionately called for her simplicity, was a being totally centered in God so that her levitations, stigmata, visions, and other phenomena could be seen simply as bodily manifestations of her sanctity. The Carmelites observe that at times "delicious perfume" or "sweet fragrances" apparently emanated from the stocky little Arab,[9] who has recently become one of the few stigmatics to ever be beatified.†

Padre Pio is among the most-studied stigmatics of all time. From the United States, Pascal Parente,‡ a professor of mystical theology at Catholic University, spent time in San Giovanni observing him, as did Charles Carty, a priest-journalist

---

† Lutheran minister C. Bernard Ruffin, who has studied this phenomenon, says of several hundred stigmatics observed since the late Middle Ages, only sixty-one had been beatified or canonized by the 1980s.

‡ He wrote *A City on the Hill,* since replaced by more thorough biographies such as Ruffin's.

who specialized in separating inauthentic from genuine mystical phenomena. The many other experts who made on-the-spot studies of the phenomena surrounding the mystic included medical men of expert credentials. All agree that Padre Pio emitted perfume. From all accounts, the fragrance varied greatly. Common were odors of violets, lilies, roses, or even fresh tobacco. But there were also such bitter odors as iodine or even carbolic acid.[10]

An early investigator notes,

> Caustic substances destroy odors; therefore if . . . out of humility or obedience, in order to hide his own perfume, [Padre Pio] were to use any of these . . . , they would destroy all the other smells, whereas actually [at a given moment] some recognize the perfume of roses, some of lilies or violets, and still others can smell only carbolic acid.[11]

And most important—because it eliminates the possibility of fraud—others at the same time smelled nothing.

The opinion of some friars who lived with Padre Pio is that when perfume was noticed, it was often a sign that God had bestowed some grace through the intercession of Padre Pio. Padre Alessio speaks also of these fragrances acting as little nudges, as to remind people, for instance, to pray.[12] I recall the testimony of Emmanuele Brunatto who had led a totally debauched life until, living in "a putrid Naples alley" with "the lowest kind of prostitutes," he became obsessed with the idea of visiting Padre Pio. Brunatto's pilgrimage to San Giovanni is one of those great conversion stories* in which a whole life takes a sudden U-turn from self-destruction toward sanctity. Suffice to say here, when he made his sordid confession to Padre Pio—who with the gift of reading hearts already knew it

* The best English account is in Ruffin's *Padre Pio: The True Story.*

all better than he did—Brunatto noticed that with the words of Christ's forgiveness "from Padre Pio's mouth there came an intense perfume of roses and violets, which bathed my face."[13]

Back in 1918 when Padre Pio first evidenced the visible stigmata, his Capuchin superiors ordered an investigation by various physicians charged to heal the wounds and determine whether they were self-inflicted, that is, fraudulent, or connected to psychological imbalance. Dr. Luigi Romanelli, chief physician of City Hospital in Barletta, Italy, was one of the first to examine the wounds. When he first met Padre Pio in 1919, Romanelli remarked to another friar, "I think it very unsuitable for a friar to use perfume." Pio, of course, did not use cologne. He did not use scented soap either. For the next two days Romanelli smelled nothing. Before he left the friary, however, he got a final whiff as he went up a stair of the same odor. Eventually, to Romanelli's chagrin, he discovered that Pio's blood could smell of flowers. He is said to have exclaimed, "But this is incredible. I hardly believe it!"

"I hardly believe it myself," poor Pio is said to have responded wearily.

Romanelli consulted with several scientists who assured him blood cannot have a sweet odor. Undoubtedly none had ever read—who has?—*The Life of St. Veronica Giuliani,* a stigmatic nun of whom it was reported when her "wounds were open they emitted so delicious a fragrance throughout the whole convent that this alone was sufficient to inform the nuns whenever the stigmata had been renewed."†

Gamely, Romanelli recorded the facts as he found them: Not only did the stigmata smell sweet but "when the blood is coagulated or dried on some garment that Padre Pio has worn, it still retains its perfume."[14]

† St. Veronica was the type of stigmatic whose wounds are not "permanent." Such stigmata may only appear or may only open and bleed, as with Theresa Neumann or Louise Lateau, on Fridays or seasonally as in Lent.

When Pio's wounds were bandaged for eight days under observation so the wounds could heal—they did not—the world of science began to understand that these stigmata could not be explained by fraud. As medical men saw firsthand Pio's stability, sense of humor, and chagrin rather than pleasure over the "fame" the wounds brought, psychological instability had to be ruled out. But there was always the distinct possibility that, as with inedics, the stigmata were psychosomatic, not in a derogatory sense but meaning they were a phenomenon arising out of the whole person's sensitive physiology, profound spirituality, and mental absorption on the Passion of Christ. Accepting this "explanation," which leaves out any supernatural imposition of the wounds or "mystical grace," was unfortunately made a little harder because of the persistent perfumes that hinted at less explicable mysteries.

Dr. Giorgio Festa, another physician, came down from Rome to study Padre Pio. Festa had no sense of smell. But he found out about the sweet smell of Pio's blood anyway from a little cloth stained with Pio's blood. He says:

> I brought [it] back with me to Rome for a microscopic examination. I personally, being entirely deprived of the sense of smell, did not notice any special emanation. But . . . persons with me in the automobile on our return to Rome from San Giovanni, not knowing that I brought with me that piece of cloth enclosed in a case, despite the strong ventilation owing to the speed of the automobile, smelled the fragrance very distinctly and assured me that it precisely corresponded to the perfume that emanates from the person of Padre Pio.[15]

Even odder, for a long time afterward the doctor received inquiries from patients who came to his office about the perfume filling the room. The scent was traced to the little cloth stained with old blood, which Dr. Festa kept in one of the office cabinets. As many of us know, the natural smell of human blood is not particularly pleasant, while the smell of old blood, which breaks down rapidly, is downright putrid.

In the following chapter on odors of sanctity as a means of communication, I give other instances where people far away from Padre Pio experienced perfumes they associated with him, but without any object being involved.

Not all stigmatics evidence the odor of sanctity. Theresa Neumann, for instance, did not. Still Pio is not the only stigmatic of recent times whose wounds gave off an inexplicable perfume. There are two twentieth-century laywomen I have testimonies on whose cases I omit only because one's Cause is not yet open and the other's is stalled due to such phenomena in her life as inedia. Happily I can point to Blessed Sister Marie of Jesus Crucified (Mariam Baouardy), the phenomena of whose life have been well scrutinized. Blessed Marie, whom I mentioned as emitting the odor of sanctity, also at times had open stigmata wounds. Among the records kept by her Carmelite observers at Pau is a note dated February 27, 1868, which mentions that they had carried her to the infirmary because she was suffering intensely from wounds in her hands and feet. All evening those near her took in a strong, sweet odor for which there was no discernible cause. The implication of the report, which is in French,‡ is that this fragrance was from the nun's stigmata.[16]

Finally, there are the odors from the stigmata of Gino Burresi. We will look at the case of this living Italian stigmatic (1932–) in the next chapter.

‡ Now translated into English, *Mariam: The Little Arab: Sister Marie of Jesus Crucified* by Amédée Brunot is available from Carmel, 87609 Greenhill Rd., Eugene, Oreg., 97402.

notes

1. Agnes Sanford, *Sealed Orders,* pp. 251–52.

2. Oliver Statler, *Japanese Pilgrimage,* p. 159.

3. Paramahansa Yogananda, *Autobiography of a Yogi,* pp. 54–59.

4. Michel Carrouges, *Père Jacques,* p. 77.

5. Edward van Speybrouck, *Father Paul of Moll,* p. 154.

6. Francis X. Levy, *Our Guide,* p. 13.

7. Francis Johnston, *Alexandrina,* pp. 98–99.

8. Ibid., p. 99.

9. Amédée Brunot, *Mariam: La petite Arabe: Soeur Marie de Jésus Crucifié,* pp. 44–45, 157.

10. See Charles Mortimer Carty's chapter "His Perfume Odor" in *Padre Pio: The Stigmatist.*

11. Ibid., p. 36, quoting Alberto Del Fante.

12. John A. Schug, O.F.M. Cap., *A Padre Pio Profile,* p. 59.

13. C. Bernard Ruffin, *Padre Pio, The True Story,* pp. 159–61.

14. Quoted by Carty, loc. cit.

15. Ibid., pp. 30–31, quoting Festa, author of *Misteri di Scienza e Luci di Fede.*

16. Brunot, op. cit., p. 45.

12 ▲

a
means of
communication

Paul Chacon, a Los Angeles banker, recalls:

> In 1970 Father Thomas Matin, my spiritual mentor,
> and I were in Europe on a pilgrimage. Father Thomas was
> a holy priest*—the sort who is up at two or three in the
> morning giving the homeless money for something to eat
> and a place to stay. He was very interested in stigmatics
> like Theresa Neumann† and Padre Pio who had died just
> two years earlier. But Father Thomas knew that I had
> always poohpoohed the whole thing, saying stigmatics'
> wounds could be faked or psychologically induced.

---

* A friend of Fr. Aloysius Ellacuria's, Matin is buried near him at Los Angeles's San
Gabriel Mission. Both graves receive many visitors, who sometimes credit one or the
other of the Claretian priests' prayers with great favors.
† Matin wrote *The Mystery of Konnersreuth* about her.

In Italy, without specifying what he had in mind, Fr. Thomas took me to a place called San Vittorino. He said he wanted me to meet someone who lived there.

When we arrived Brother Gino wasn't home. Fr. Thomas got talking with another priest who was Brother Gino's spiritual director and he showed us to Brother Gino's room. The first thing I noticed was that the room was filled with some wonderful scent.

"Boy, this guy uses really good cologne," I said to myself, thinking the less of him for it. Eventually we were sent to a place where Brother Gino was giving a talk to some nuns. But when we got there he had already left.

We returned to our hotel where Father Thomas showed me a glove with blood on it which had been worn by Brother Gino. This, too, was heavy with perfume. By now I had caught on to the trick Father Thomas was playing on me, that this Brother Gino was a stigmatic. I exclaimed that this religious—who is supposed to be following a vow of poverty—certainly didn't deny himself the best fragrance. I kept making critical remarks like this, but Father Thomas said nothing. The following day we went again to San Vittorino but missed Brother Gino again.

I said to Father Thomas, "Come on. Let's get out of here and go see something worthwhile." [Matin in reply just suggested to Chacon he go pray in the church.]

I did. And when I finished my prayer and came out, there was Brother Gino surrounded by people who were all trying to kiss his hand. He gave me a very long, penetrating glance that made me wonder what this funny look meant. At the same time, I smelled, even as far from him as I was, this wonderful perfume.

I went over to the group and, doing as the locals did, I too tried to kiss his hand, but he refused to let me. However we were invited in with all the others and Brother Gino talked at length. I recall that he made some predictions which have come true about the Italian political situation. He also mentioned that a pope would have an attempt made on his life while he was out of Italy on a trip, a prediction which also came true when Pope Paul VI went to the Philippines. During this talk, Brother Gino continued to stare at me.

After a time he said that if anyone wanted him to bless articles such as rosaries and religious medals, he would be glad to do so. He did this for everyone, but again, when I followed Father Thomas up, he singled me out for refusal.

Shortly afterward he went into another room and Father Thomas followed him. Later they called me in. They removed Brother Gino's bandages and I saw his stigmata. I was so moved I began to cry.

Brother Gino's response was to hug me.‡

After Brother Gino hugged me, the perfume stayed with me for four days.

As we left, he said he would be praying for me.

Two or three months later, I was at home in Los Angeles watching television with my mother. I had no thought whatsoever of Brother Gino but suddenly I experienced his characteristic odor. It lasted no more than three minutes at the most. I asked my mom if she smelled anything.

"Nothing," she said.

A week or two later I dreamed of Brother Gino one night. I awoke from this dream and the room was filled with the same aroma, not exactly roses, not exactly lilies, but a fragrance that is unusual and distinct. Again it lasted no more than two or three minutes.

I believe God graced me on those occasions, possibly through Brother Gino's prayers for me.[1]

‡ In a personal interchange, Chacon was also told something regarding his future which seems to be coming true.

Who is this Brother Gino who could move a thirty-five-year-old American banker to tears? A clever manipulator of men with self-induced wounds he uses to play on people's spiritual instincts? Or a genuine mystic?

Gino Burresi (1932–) was for years a lay brother and is now an ordained Catholic priest in the religious order known as the Oblates of the Blessed Virgin Mary. Oldest of the six children of Tuscan tenant-farmers, from his earliest years he pestered his parents to let him enter a religious order. By fourteen he was being given a trial run by the Oblates.

He never went home.

Ten years later the twenty-four-year-old mystic received invisible stigmata, a phenomenon that, as in the case of Padre Pio, foreshadowed later visible wounds.

Padre Pio's wounds became suddenly visible in 1918. Starting in 1968, the year of Padre Pio's death, Father Gino's have gradually become fully visible. For instance, a seminarian who helped change the bandages over the lance stigma about ten years ago said at that time that the wound was so deep he saw right down into Gino's heart.

Father Robert Fox, an American Catholic priest and writer from South Dakota who knows the stigmatic personally, told me the stigmata not only emit perfumes but—bizarre as this sounds—the scents change with the liturgical seasons.[2] Bitter in Lent, they become sweet during such periods as Advent and Christmas.

Father Gino himself says he smells nothing; but the perfume of his blood is so strong, according to Father Fox and others, that the stigmatic's presence can at times be detected by scent before he enters a room. Father Fox also spoke of riding with Gino in a closed car: The scent became so strong the American priest had to open a window.

The odor is not just from the stigmata. Physician Alfonso

Bernardo, Burresi's doctor, says at times the perfume comes from Brother Gino's "entire body."[3] Someone close to Burresi recalls that the mystic was one day bathed in sweat during an ecstasy. His friend witnessed that, changing Burresi's wet undershirt, "It did not have the odor of sweat at all. It was just perfume."[4]

▲

Far from a somber and medieval figure, Father Gino is described as a very contemporary man. Well over six feet tall and robust, his personality is good-humored and playful and he is particularly fond of young people. It's a habit of his to bestow humorous nicknames on those he gets to know. While collecting material on the stigmatic for a book, Father Fox got one of those nicknames: Gino laughingly called him "the fox who discovers everything." Yet while the mystic seemed to find the project personally distasteful, Gino cooperated with the American author because his superiors had asked him to.

When they met for the first time, Father Fox took Gino's hand to kiss it in a European gesture of religious respect. Says Fox, "I experienced the sweetest perfume, quite indescribable, a perfume that seems to penetrate the lungs and refresh the soul." Later he quizzed Gino about the perfume, asking to what he attributed it.

Brother Gino answered, "I think that when a soul lives with Christ, Christ lives in him and in some way will manifest himself. In some he will manifest himself by a perfume, in others in another way, . . . It is [always] Christ who manifests himself."[5]

Apparently at times the perfume is an embarrassment to Gino. He told Father Fox about the time he washed the mittens he wears to cover the hand wounds in disinfectant in order that the strong smell would cover any odor of perfume that day. To his chagrin the first person he met commented at once, "Oh what strong perfume!"[6]

If Gino is a fraud, this story obviously is untrue. If he is genuine, this is evidence that the phenomenon has nothing in common with the "perfume saint" scorned by Yogananda.

Dr. Bernardo, who said sometimes the odor is not from the stigmata but from Brother Gino's entire body, issued a statement with his wife, Dr. Maria Mato, also a physician. After noting "there is no natural explanation for the perfume," the doctors note a number of oddities:

- The perfume remains a long while on his handkerchief, even though there is no blood on the handkerchief.
- The perfume is not smelled by all simultaneously.
- A body can't produce the perfume.
- The aroma can't be analyzed.*
- It is not a chemical reaction.
- Blood does not give a perfume.

Yet the two doctors find that Brother Gino's blood *does* give off a wonderful fragrance and that the odors associated with him are most frequently linked to his wounds and his blood, as far as they can tell.[7]

But not always. From American banker Paul Chacon's account, although Chacon himself carefully makes no claims, some people would conclude that Brother Gino's perfume crossed the Atlantic Ocean and the American continent twice to reach Chacon in California after Brother Gino assured him on their parting, "I'll be praying for you."

Father Fox knows of similar incidents. Anxious to do nothing to sensationalize the living stigmatist, Father Fox for the most part omits details of this phenomenon from his book on Burresi. He does cite by name one individual, however, who

---

* It would emit no perfume when being analyzed, Dr. Mato says.

has smelled Brother Gino's fragrance across thousands of miles: Joseph Breault, a fellow Catholic priest who is French Canadian by birth and American by citizenship. Fox writes in what I can be certain is meant as an understatement that at such times Breault feels "as if Brother Gino must be thinking of him."[8]

Father Fox feels less compunction about sharing his own experience. I have told how on his first meeting with the stigmatic, the South Dakota priest smelled a perfume that seemed to originate in the stigmata wound of Burresi's hand. That same day Father Fox returned from San Vittorino to Rome. There the same perfume from time to time inundated him. Without any prompting, others in his party of Americans mentioned the same experience. Father Fox also discovered that unscented cards with printed prayers which the stigmatic had given him to distribute periodically gave off the same perfume.[9]

Physician Alfonso Bernardo recalls this experience from his student days:

> On October 5, 1972, I was studying medicine in Bologna and I happened that day to be in Rome, 20 kilometers away from San Vittorino, after having met Brother Gino. I was visiting my aunt, telling myself that roses don't bloom in October; yet I could experience that same perfume for two consecutive hours . . . [which I had experienced earlier the same day] 20 kilometers away.
>
> My aunt, who did not know Brother Gino, came to perceive the same perfume. We went into the garden, still smelling the same perfume. My aunt, who knew Padre Pio, and had smelled [Pio's] . . . perfume, although I had never mentioned Brother Gino to her, said "This is the perfume of sanctity."

After making clear that there were no flowers in the garden and explaining that he remained silent about the event because it was so important to him spiritually, Bernardo continues:

> Two months later, around Christmas, I went to thank Brother Gino, because my exams had gone well. My aunt came with me to meet Brother Gino and then recognized the same perfume we had experienced two months previously.[10]

Dr. Bernardo also told Father Fox (from whose book *The Call of Heaven* I have quoted the doctor's various statements) a brief anecdote that points to Gino's playfulness and love of teasing. A Catholic priest who had met Gino said to others, not to the stigmatist, that he did not believe in "this odor business." Traveling shortly afterwards, he was enveloped by strange perfume. Apparently the medium contained a definite message because he took the trouble to return to San Vittorino and chide Gino, "Really, you shouldn't have played this joke on me."

Brother Gino only responded wryly, "Well, you didn't believe."

All anecdotes regarding Burresi are, of course, tentative in the sense that he is alive and not yet given the yea or nay of his church's official after-death investigation. That investigation is well under way on Padre Pio and there are many witnesses who insist they experienced Padre Pio's fragrances during his lifetime while he was far from them. While some took this as invisible bilocation (see ch. 17) others claimed Pio could project perfumes at will as a means of communication.

A man who spoke of this from personal experience as well as thorough research regarding others' experiences was Alberto Del Fante, who had been trained as a lawyer before becoming a journalist. Active in anti-Catholic organizations in 1930, Del Fante authored several articles debunking Padre

Pio, this "cunning priest who knew how to deceive." Then, in Del Fante's own words, "There occurred the *unexpected, unmistakable, and indisputable* healing of my nephew."† Perplexed, the journalist, who was an atheist, traveled to the remote monastery in backward southern Italy to see this fellow for himself.

By 1950 he had made thirty such trips and written two books on Padre Pio. In one of those turnarounds so common in those who met the Franciscan, he now regarded "the cunning deceiver" as his spiritual mentor. Del Fante believed that "each particular case" where someone far from Pio smelled one of the priest's characteristic fragrances

> reveals the manner in which Padre Pio follows souls, and how he guides, counsels, and comforts, using this divine gift. Many of these souls are suffering . . . [many are] begging for his powerful intercession with God. There are mothers with sick children, fathers asking help in financial difficulties. . . . He makes them aware of his perfume to warn them not to be afraid, but to hope, to pray . . . [and] to steer always toward the right goal. Their spirits become serene and their hearts are filled with hope because they no longer are alone, but feel they are sustained by a supernatural strength.[11]

Del Fante's rather exalted tone may sound overzealous but remember, he writes as a convert to Pio's cause. That Pio effected changes in people through the odd medium of odor was something Del Fante had personally experienced. On that first visit in 1930, when he arrived a man who believed in only the material and left one who saw a whole new universe full of immaterial realities as well, he was followed about San Gio-

---

† The boy had an abscessed kidney. Padre Pio told the child's father it would be cured a certain day. It was.

vanni by a smell "like some very fine Oriental tobacco." Oddly enough this particular odor was often reported by Pio's converts.

A year later Del Fante reports a different odor. He had been visiting his parents with his wife and children, returned home and went to the typewriter. He now had a new habit—a moment of prayer before beginning work. This time he forgot. He writes:

> I was suddenly aware of a delicate scent, which I did not at first recognize. Padre Pio's odors do not have the quality of commercial perfume; they resemble each other but are not the same. This was the smell of incense.[12]

Aware that he might be imagining something, Del Fante called the family and their maid.

"Do you smell anything?" he asked.

All but one immediately replied, "Yes, incense." The littlest child smelled something but could not identify the scent. Del Fante's interpretation: Padre Pio was reminding him of his forgotten prayer.

All such reports are subjective, of course. Even if Del Fante showed there was no incense on the premises, even if Padre Pio confirmed his interpretation, some will believe, many will not.

Another testimony, again confirmed as to the presence of an odor by witnesses, comes from an Italian schoolteacher. A widow, Annita Righini of Leguigno di Casina wrote her six-page testimony on October 25, 1948. Because of its length, I summarize her report.

During her summer vacation, the schoolteacher organized a trip for herself and two friends to see Padre Pio. Although the threesome stayed near the monastery five days, getting up at 2 A.M. each morning, Righini never made it into Padre Pio's confessional. In that period just after World War II, the lines were that long. Anxious about her daughter's health, the best she could manage was the superstitious-appearing act of giving the child's photo and some articles of her clothing to another friar who had Padre Pio bless them. As they were returned to her, the friar commented that Padre Pio expressed great hope for the child's recovery.

During her stay Padre Pio had given her a long, knowing look. She had the distinct feeling that he knew her and had been expecting her, an intuition her companions seconded. She had also received Communion several times from his hands; yet Righini began her homeward trip in a snit. In the train compartment were five other pilgrims, all speaking excitedly of the ways in which their various contacts with Padre Pio had blessed them. Only she had been unable to talk personally with the stigmatic. Petulantly, the widow began to complain aloud. Hadn't *she* initiated the trip? It was unfair her companions had succeeded where she had not.

Responded one pilgrim, "Ah, Signora, don't complain; you'll see that you will receive greater blessings than we!" At that moment the complainer was enveloped by a wave of the perfume associated with Padre Pio. After a time the others smelled it too, but only for a moment, while Righini continued to bask in the fragrance for a long while. The others cheered, "You see, Padre Pio wouldn't let you down!"[13]

The reader will find dozens of such testimonies in the many biographies of Padre Pio. Impressive as they are, their weakness is that the average witness is anxious to verify the reality of the odor; he or she is much less anxious to share the interior spiritual experience the odor spurred or signaled. A testimony like the one above, for example, gives no hint of the psycho-spiritual effects of the incident; yet obviously more occurred than just perfume on a train. Fortunately the next testimony focuses on these interior effects, which are the heart of the phenomenon of the odor of sanctity as a means of communication. Mother Caterina Cuzzaniti, superior of the College of Santa Maria di Bagheria at Palermo, Italy, writes:

On the evening of the 18th of November, 1948, shortly before retiring we had been talking, as often happens nowadays, about the conversions brought about by the very rev. Padre Pio. With rather a feeling of disappointment I was saying that I had not had any answer to a letter that I had sent to him. I had sent a second one by hand through someone who was going to San Giovanni Rotondo [the friary where he lived], and who had placed it directly in the Father's hands. Although I had not received any answer to this one either, I was sure that my prayers had been answered, and I had obtained what I had asked for. . . .

Having retired, I awoke at about 4:30 (I consulted my watch). I put out the light, but no sooner had I placed my head on the pillow, than I was struck by a sweet and most unusual perfume, which at first I could not define, but which became stronger and stronger. It was a delicate and most aromatic kind of incense, but there was something different about it, something beautiful, that cannot be described in words. I remained with my head glued to the pillow, breathing this most delicious scent and aware of being surrounded by some element of the supernatural.

. . . My brain was actually intoxicated by the persistent perfume.

. . . I came to the conclusion that through this perfume the good Father had given me the proof that he had granted my request as expressed in the letter I had sent him. . . .

At this thought my emotion was increased to the point of tears. I could do nothing but pray and give thanks. I felt myself in the presence of God, as though in a church. I also felt that the Father was in the room, and in those precious moments I recommended to him all the intentions that were nearest to my heart: my own poor soul, and several people who were suffering. . . .

When at last the perfume began to fade away, I still retained in my nostrils that indescribable scent. I heard the parish clock strike; it was 5:45. One hour and a half had passed. I could not close an eye, and only at dawn did I get some sleep.

[Since] . . . a great peace and tranquility have remained within me, and I feel like a child in its mother's arms. I am also aware of a sweet odor of incense which speaks to me of God, of goodness and mercy, and lifts up my soul to Heaven in an unceasing hymn of thanksgiving to my Creator.[14]

Of course all this could be delusion. But both psychologists and spiritual directors say the aftereffects, or "fruits," of self-induced experiences are usually hyperarousal, not the "great peace and tranquility" which, at the time of Mother Caterina's testimony, had endured six months from the night she believes Padre Pio paid her an aromatic visit.

▲

In the previous chapter I limited reports to instances of saints' bodies and/or stigmata emitting wonderful odors. In this chapter, to these were added the phenomenon of "projected" or bilocatory perfumes. A fourth instance of odors related to the sanctified body concerns perfumes so strong and so persistent that they linger around a place or cling to an object after the saint's contact ceases. Engineer Francis Levy, in the previous chapter, mentioned how the floral odor of Claretian priest Aloysius Ellacuria lingered in a chapel the holy Basque had vacated. Dr. Bernardo mentioned the puzzling way a handkerchief of Gino Burresi's holds the perfume associated with him.

I know of no instance where the scent is permanent in regard to any place or object: The odor of sanctity, like a breeze, always comes and goes. But it can certainly come and go for a long time. Odors associated with St. Teresa of Avila,‡ a sixteenth-century mystic, still turn up in her Carmelite convent in Spain I am assured by those who live there.[15]

Turning back to the nineteenth and twentieth centuries, objects belonging to Padre Pio at times gave off his odor. A Capuchin father from Sicily had a bit of linen that had touched the lance stigmata in Padre Pio's side. As he showed the fragment to a woman, she suddenly cried out over the "wonderful perfume" that "refreshes my whole body!"[16]

Her fellow Carmelites mention that the coat and even a veil belonging to Bl. Marie of Jesus Crucified had a lovely odor after she had taken them off.[17]

Paul Chacon, whose saintly spiritual director took him to meet Father Gino Burresi when the Italian was still a lay brother, told me:

> When I was at San Vittorino, where Father Gino lives, they gave me a little clot of his blood which had the same characteristic aroma. When I got home I used to take it out occasionally and the scent always remained. This continued even after seven or eight years had passed. Others smelled it too.

Eventually Paul put the fragrant clot into his safety deposit box for safekeeping, so he no longer experiences the odor. But as he says, the clot should have ceased to smell of Gino's fragrance long before he locked it away.[18] Besides which, I add, the odor of old blood is hardly fragrant. Paul Chacon,

‡ Other holy people of whom this phenomenon has been reported include twentieth-century individuals, among them a Buddhist, but after-death phenomena are outside the scope of this book.

who once sneered at Burresi for using expensive cologne, assured me today of his conviction that Father Gino uses no perfume at all and that the wonderful odor that has clung inexplicably to a clot of his blood is the odor of sanctity.

Odd as it sounds, his twentieth-century physicians Maria Mata and Alfonso Bernardo have said that a representation of Christ in Gino Burresi's room also sometimes emits the odor associated with the Tuscan priest.[19]

An even odder tale can be told of the controversial stigmatic Rose Ferron (1902–36). I have several thousand pages of well-documented testimonies regarding the holiness of this French-Canadian who lived and died in Woonsocket, Rhode Island; I have omitted Rose from this book in spite of this wealth of material because her Cause has never been opened due to others who insist she was a fraud. But I permit myself one anecdote, an unpublished testimony given January 17, 1960, by Anatole Lemire of Woonsocket, one of Rose's numerous brothers-in-law.

Lemire was there one night when Rose was vomiting. According to his taped testimony, he had seen her bring up this type of green matter with blood in it before and the ejected matter always stank, as would be expected. This night, he tried to pass the mystic a larger pan while she leaned toward it. Unfortunately, she missed and vomited all over his shirt. To his shock, says Lemire, "The only thing I could smell [from the garment] was a sweet odor." He ends his account by stating that, odd as it may sound, from that day on the shirt always had the same sweet smell.[20]

I can't leave the odor of sanctity without reiterating that the phrase "died in the odor of sanctity" is rooted in literal description. Without getting into fragrant corpses, bones, graves, or other after-death phenomena, an area so big I am tackling it in a separate book, I want to sketch one death and its immediate aftereffects so you won't have to take my word for that.

Sister Maria Assunta Pallotta (1878–1905) of the Franciscan

Missionaries of Mary was nobody special. An Italian peasant girl, she left her rather bewildered family—not overly religious, none of them could fathom someone wanting to join a religious order—to become the kind of a missionary who mends the socks and cooks the meals while "more gifted" sisters are out in a strange land teaching, doctoring, tackling social injustice, and otherwise trying to make the God of love they believe in visible. It is said, however, that that God is less interested in the importance of accomplishments than in how and why they are done. Sister Assunta's great desire, her special vow, was to do everything, however banal, for the love of God. Some would insist the socks she mended and the meals, however humble, she cooked in Italian and Chinese convents were of greater service to the world than most contributions found in history books. Why? Because, in their view, by her purity of intention and the love in her heart, she was helping bring about the great metamorphosis that all faiths yearn toward, whether they call it "the classless society," "nirvana," or "the kingdom of God."

Whatever you make of all that, the fact is that at only twenty-seven years old, nursing other nuns and Chinese orphans, Assunta caught typhus. It was a light case but the simple young nun said flatly she was going to die. The disease took an unexpected turn. And Assunta was on her deathbed. As is customary, the other nuns and a priest, along with some Chinese women who worked with the sisters, all gathered around the dying sister's bed. From an account furnished by her order, I translate from Italian what happened next:

> Twenty minutes before the passing of Sister Assunta. . . . the room was inundated with an inexplicably delicious perfume. The Superior did not suspect anything out of the ordinary. The priest present, she believed, must have opened a bottle of scent and shaken it around to dispel the bad odor. The priest also smelling the perfume

had the same thought, that Mother Sinfonia [the Superior] must have sprinkled perfume. Then someone asked someone else if they smelled the perfume and this led to asking who was responsible. Everybody smelled it. No one had used it. Suddenly there was an intuition that something prodigious was taking place. A realization came that this perfume was supernatural, a testimony to the holiness of the young woman in agony before them.

Following Sister Assunta's death, the odor stopped. The next day, however, it reappeared and diffused itself more largely. Traversing the courtyard of the convent, one received strong whiffs of the perfume, as if a bird was swooping to and fro, leaving an odor signature of his passage.

During her illness Sister Assunta had been cared for in three different rooms. These three for three days were drenched in this odor. . . . The scent also followed the coffin along the funeral route. When the sisters and their co-workers returned to the house from the cemetery, the entire house was impregnated with this sweet perfume which lasted until the next day. For three days everyone participated in the joy that the smell left in one's soul.

The long, detailed report mentions other particulars. For instance the last linens used by the dead woman were washed by a Sister Evasio who testified that they gave off the same fragrance.

What was the fragrance? Some said they thought it was a roselike scent, others said violets, some thought it a mixture of lilies and roses.

Talked about excitedly, the phenomenon started a pilgrimage to the town of Tong-eul-keu where Sister Assunta died, so that, according to the report, "Chinese of all ages, conditions and beliefs" smelled the fragrance. It is also significant—to rule out a hidden machine pumping out fragrance—that some who came smelled nothing. With a touching simplicity in both the reporter and some of the people, it is said, "a few Chinese who came and smelled nothing concluded this was a result of their sins. They rushed off to confession, then returned and this time, they, too, smelled this mysterious odor of paradise."

Could it have been some seasonal blossom carried into the dying woman's room and elsewhere by the wind? The investigation answered:

> The first part of April was not spring in this part of China. There were no blooming flowers in the fields; everything was dry because of the frost; nor were there any trees blooming.

Reasonably the phenomenon's exponents ask:

> If the wind had been carrying the perfume, one would have to explain why it brought it to, and only to, the spots intimately associated with Sister Assunta. Why never in other houses. . . .

And finally in their coup de grace they offer the testimony that the Chinese locals found this *a new and singular fragrance outside their experience.* "For them," says the report, "it was clearly a supernatural event."[21]

No one had ever given Assunta Pallotta any thought. Her own fellow nuns had smiled at or in some cases—all nuns certainly not being saints—even ridiculed her simplicity. But now when miracles of healing, that is instantaneous, permanent cures of serious, organic illness, took place in various parts of the world after individuals asked the dead nun's prayers, the penetrating scrutiny of Catholicism's Congregation for the Causes of Saints was turned on the young peasant. Another impressive phenomenon when the body was moved was its extraordinary preservation. All culminated in 1954 with the beatification of Assunta Pallotta, formal recognition not of odors or incorruptibility but of the more important fact that the simple Italian had indeed done all for the love of God —and done it with heroic wholeheartedness.

All of this for a nun who would have been barely remembered in her own order if it hadn't been for a sudden gust of perfume.

Which leaves the interesting question, if you are a curmudgeon who insists there has to be a machine blowing perfume in there somewhere, how did the perpetrators manage instantaneous cures—none of them local—which a commission of medical men called "humanly inexplicable"?

After Assunta, Gino, Padre Pio, Father Aloysius, and the others, perhaps you feel you have a handle on the odor of sanctity. For me, questions linger. Is the odor, as I suggested in the previous chapter's opening, in some cases manufactured in the body, holiness spilling over, from time to time, in olfactory form? Or is the scent, when it occurs, only apparently emitted by the body and actually always deposited around and through it? Does its presence ever have an existence apart from signaling graces poured out on and/or through the saint?

I can offer no certain replies.

Why the sanctified body at times apparently exudes a sweet smell instead of the more fetid odors of ordinary flesh and by what mechanism God or saints waft odors through thin air or encapsulate them momentarily in objects like handkerchiefs, nun's veils, and old blood remain matters beyond this puny brain. But if this does happen—and the sheer bulk of testimony is certainly compelling—then this I do know: Blessed literally are those who smell them.

notes

1. Interviews July and Nov. 1988.

2. Interviews in 1980 and 1981. Wherever Fr. Fox told me things which later appeared in his book, I cite the book as a source that can be checked by readers.

3. Quoted in appendix to Robert J. Fox's *The Call of Heaven: Br. Gino, Stigmatist,* p. 180.

4. Ibid., p. 111.

5. Ibid., pp. 150–51.

6. Ibid., p. 185.

7. Ibid., p. 180.

8. Ibid., pp. 97–98.

9. Ibid., p. 15.

10. Ibid., p. 179.

11. Carty, op. cit., pp. 33–34.

12. Ibid., p. 33.

13. Ibid., pp. 41–46. Addressed to Alberto Del Fante, her report is dated Oct. 25, 1948.

14. Ibid., pp. 46–50.

15. Letter to me, dated June 29, 1983.

16. Letter from a Capuchin to Del Fante, cited by Carty, op. cit., p. 37.

17. Amédée Brunot, *Mariam: La petite Arabe: Soeur Marie de Jésus Crucifié,* pp. 45–46.

18. See note number 1.

19. Fox, op. cit., p. 180.

20. Transcript of interview taped by John Baptist Palm, S.J., to whom I am indebted for its use.

21. Carlo Salotti, *Suor Maria Assunta Pallotta,* pp. 273–78. Based on the Process testimonies and other official documentation, this 1929 Italian-language biography, published by the saint's order, was furnished me from their archives.

▲13

levitating
in
los angeles?

Southern California in the early nineteen fifties.

Father Aloysius Ellacuria, a Claretian priest in his mid-forties, gives conferences or says mass from time to time for various groups of cloistered nuns. They notice that sometimes their visitor is subject to raptures during the most prayerful points of his mass. Once at a Carmelite convent, three extern* sisters, along with a laywoman who is present for the mass, note that during one of these ecstatic states of consciousness, Father Aloysius' body rises several inches above the floor.[1] A nun in a second Carmelite convent in the area will later recall

---

* In a cloistered community one or more sisters will be designated "extern," meaning an individual who goes out of the cloister, on the community's behalf, to run errands, shop, etc. These women, alone among the Carmelites, were physically in a position to see Father Aloysius' feet. Their cloistered companions, in that pre-Vatican II era, could only tell Father Aloysius was in an ecstasy by the fact that the Mass they were hearing through a screen stopped until he suddenly heard a doorbell and came to.

to this writer one of Father Aloysius' fellow Claretians† telling her he had seen the Basque-born mystic levitate.[2] Respecting the mystic's privacy, the sisters whisper among themselves about the levitations but they do not speak of them to the priest or to outsiders. But a fifth Carmelite sister who lives in the Carmel of another Western state will mention Father Aloysius when the subject of levitation comes up between us one day about three years after his death at age seventy-five in 1981. My friend Sister Veronica recalls particularly talk that the Claretian novices Father Aloysius was in charge of in that era had seen their mentor risen from the floor.

What makes Sister Veronica visibly light up, as she recalls her contacts with Father Aloysius through conferences when she was a novice, is *not* ecstasy or levitation. It is his wonderful sense of humor, the simplicity that made him so easy to be around, and the extraordinary spiritual intensity with which he said Mass.

Spain, 1968.

Astute businesswoman, wife of a successful dentist, and mother of three daughters, Katherine Morrow has joined a number of other Americans on a pilgrimage with Father Aloysius to his native country. This day Katherine excitedly tells her friend Mary Levy that, saying mass, Father Aloysius kept holding on to the wine-filled chalice he was elevating for adoration as if it were rising and he being irresistibly pulled with it. While he struggled to pull the chalice down, Katherine says to Mary, it seemed to her and other observers that Fr. Aloysius rose off the floor. Although the altar obscured his feet, the short, stocky Basque's head was so high above the altar that

---

† There has been no confirmation of this from his Claretian Congregation, which nevertheless affirms that Father was "a very holy priest."

his feet could not have continued to touch the floor. Mary Levy believes her friend because Katherine is noted as a person of great acumen, devout but not credulous. In 1988 Katherine is ill and in her eighties, but she has not forgotten that she twice saw Father Aloysius struggle against his rising body in Spain and later witnessed the same phenomenon as he said mass in the basement of his Claretian order's establishment in Los Angeles. Remembering Fr. Aloysius as the family's old friend who sometimes spent the night at the Morrow home and loved something good to eat, she would rather tell her interviewer, "How much I loved him! Fr. Aloysius was so kind to everyone. Nothing was too much for him to do for someone!"[2]

Paris, 1975.

Mother Marguerite (Carter), a Massachusetts native who has spent a lifetime working in education, health, and care for the impoverished in Oklahoma and Southern California, is on another pilgrimage of Americans led by the holy Claretian. She says:

> We were in the Rue de Bac chapel belonging to the Sisters of Charity of St. Vincent de Paul.‡ We were excited that Father Aloysius was saying mass for us there.
>
> I recall we were unable to use the main chapel and were up on a balcony off to one side. We were kneeling on the floor because there were no benches when suddenly at the offertory Fr. Aloysius cried out, "My God . . ."
>
> Naturally everyone looks up and there is Father Aloy-

‡ Famous among Catholics as the place where in 1830 a young French nun named Catherine Laboure (1806–76) had several momentous visions of the Bl. Virgin Mary.

sius lost in ecstasy and a good four inches off the floor. You could see the space under his shoes.

Mother Marguerite is happy to tell me about Father's levitations, bilocations, and other mystical phenomena; but she becomes most animated when she talks about the healing power that flowed out of his great love affair with God. The lively eighty-two-year-old, who knew him for forty years, bubbles over with humorous anecdotes about Father Aloysius' healings: an American hippie's crippled dog down in Mexico, a dying Mexican carried into the church using a bedsheet for a stretcher in Phoenix, the mother of a movie star in Beverly Hills. "Oh my and *how* he had the gift of healing!" she chortles. "He cured every sister I ever took out there from Oklahoma whether she had arthritis so bad she couldn't move or cancer."[3]

Healing, yes, but levitating? Could someone have really levitated in Los Angeles, the American city of flakes and fantasy? Could a human being *anywhere* actually defy gravity to rise, unsupported, from a few inches to much higher? Even at the outer limits of physiology, can this be considered within human potential?

To answer that, let me say for starters there are a goodly number of other nineteenth- or twentieth-century testimonies by witnesses as normal as those I just quoted on Father Aloysius.

A phenomenon that has been with us down the centuries, entire groups, at times, have left depositions that someone levitated. For instance:

> On one occasion at Santa Fiora in the house of the Duchess Sforza, when she was present with a crowd of other people, Passitea [Crogi, who died in 1615] was surprised by a rapture, under the influence of which she remained raised from the ground at the height of a man. The

Duchess, who was a witness of the occurrence, caused an attestation of the fact to be drawn up, which was signed by all present.

Such accounts sometimes include meaningful measurements of both height attained (a few inches appears most common) and how long the levitation lasted. For instance, of the same mystic it was testified:

> According to the violence of the ecstasy she was lifted [at various times] more or less from the ground. Sister Felice deposed that she had seen her raised three arm's lengths and at the same time that she was completely surrounded with an immense effulgence of light. This lasted for two or three hours.[4]

On rare occasions individuals have even touched or stood under levitating bodies in full daylight, which goes far to rule out any apparatus that conceivably could be hidden if a levitator were observed from enough distance or seen in murky light. For instance, Anne of the Incarnation, a companion of the great Teresa of Avila, testified under oath after the saint's death:

> Between one and two o'clock in the daytime I was in choir waiting for the bell to ring when our holy Mother [Teresa] entered and knelt down for perhaps the half of a quarter of an hour. As I was looking on, she was raised about half a yard from the ground without her feet touching it. At this I was terrified and she, for her part, was trembling all over. So I moved to where she was and I put my hands under her feet, over which I remained weeping for something like half an hour while the ecstasy lasted. Then suddenly she sank down and rested on her feet and turning her head round to me she asked me who I was and

> whether I had been there all the while. I said yes, and then
> she ordered me under obedience to say nothing of what I
> had seen, and I have in fact said nothing until the present
> moment.[5]

If one isn't there to see it oneself, skepticism is not only unavoidable in the face of levitation anecdotes, it's essential so one isn't gulled. And one can gull oneself. Researchers find the brain's limbic area can generate feelings of floating or flying. This rules out of serious discussion anyone whose claim to levitation is unwitnessed. Authority on mysticism Evelyn Underhill, in fact, dismissed all levitation this way. In her landmark *Mysticism,* referring to a mystic who, as she carefully phrases it, "felt as if he were lifted from the ground," she immediately adds "the sense of levitation" is "a frequent physical accompaniment" of "shiftings of the level of consciousness." And when she must refer to St. Teresa of Avila's autobiographical writing on the subject, Underhill says, "This carrying-away sensation may even assume the concrete form which is known as levitation: when the upward and outward sensations so dominate the conscious field that the subject is convinced that she is raised bodily from the ground."[6] One cannot blame her for ignoring the testimonies of those who *saw* Teresa and other mystics raised. Even a scholar may be quickly labeled a nut.

Science has no help to offer as to how the phenomenon works. Insisting that gravity is not breachable, scientists have never taken levitation seriously enough to even postulate how it might work. Alone Thelma Moss, when she was a medical psychologist at UCLA's Neuropsychiatric Institute doing research in parapsychology some years back, is said to have shown that four people working with body and vocal rhythm, can create a kind of levitation in a fifth passive individual.[7] By trying to reproduce levitation, even in the form of a parlor trick, Dr. Moss stands alone in the West as having at least postulated the phenomenon had discernible causes.

Yet Tibetans, Hindus, Moslems, Spiritualists, and Transcendental Meditators join Orthodox and Catholic Christians in claiming levitators. A universal myth? I prefer to take this universality as suggesting this mystical phenomenon is *not* a myth but exists at the outer limits of human psychophysical potential.

Asking levitation be taken seriously is not made easier by the fact that the levitator most often cited in the last century is a person surrounded by an aura, not of holiness but of unanswered questions. Scotch-born, American-raised Daniel Dunglas Home (1833–86) reportedly floated out one window and in another seventy feet off the ground in a dimly lit room (his critics stress the poor lighting) in the presence of three well-known Englishmen, including two peers of the realm. A fourth investigator, scientist Sir William Crookes, not present on that occasion, said he also witnessed levitations by Home.

His extraordinary psychic (others charged magician's) gifts Home attributed, without making anything religious of it, to the assistance of "discarnate spirits"* who, he said, used him as a medium. Born a Scotch Protestant, Home entered the Catholic Church on the ground that "with so many spirit-manifestations in the lives of the saints," Catholicism "provided an atmosphere in which he would be more at home." He was not formally a Catholic long however. The opportunistic levitator was booted out, in the late nineteenth-century furor between Christianity and Spiritualism, with the comment over his shoulder that if he *was* messing about with spirits, as he claimed, they must be dark ones and furthermore any phenomena in his life bore only the most superficial resemblance

---

* According to Michael Harner, shamans, too, rely on spirit help. Whether the "spirits" are objectively real or projected parts of the shaman's personality is a matter of debate.

to anything holy. Even if one thinks the Catholic Church hard on Home, the latter remark was correct. Known for feats, not holiness, he exhibited himself willingly and, while maintaining his amateur status by not accepting fees, was amenable to expensive presents from admirers.[8] Authentic saints, of course, flee all that with horror. Over the years many efforts to expose Home as a fraud came to naught. Yet today many still suspect his levitations and other phenomena were superb illusion similar to the fakir who climbs an unattached rope until he vanishes, a feat of magicianship par excellence.

If he was using magic to pad natural psychic gifts, Home had lots of company. Ex-Spiritualist minister-medium M. Lamar Keene details in *The Psychic Mafia* how fraudulent levitations of people or such items as voice trumpets are manuevered during seances to gull the unwary.[9] Christian Fundamentalists tend to feel about all mystical phenomena "if it ain't Christian, it ain't—or if it is, it's of the Devil." Keene's eye-opening book offers sometimes hilarious and often melancholy proof that levitation—and all phenomena for hire or show—is less apt to be directly Satanic than to remind us that "a sucker is born every minute."

Turning to levitators from the world's great faiths, some Islamic sources mention al-Hallaj (858–922). This Sufi was condemned to a horrible death by those within his tradition who considered him a heretic. Later generations in Islam esteem the mystic as a great saint, much as Joan of Arc was burned at the stake by fellow Catholics, then canonized.

In *Autobiography of a Yogi,* Paramahansa Yogananda devotes a chapter to fellow Hindu, Bhaduri Mahasaya,† "the levitating saint."[10] Yogananda also heard of a levitation from the widow of deceased Hindu holy man Lahiri Mahasaya (no

---

† Yogananda notes Bhaduri was considered odd among Hindus because for twenty years he never left the house where he levitated before groups of visitors. If he practiced magicianship, this would be pertinent, but Yogananda judged he was authentically holy.

relation to Bhaduri). Mahasaya's widow, Srimati Kashi Moni, told Yogananda:

> It was years before I came to realize the divine stature of my husband . . . One night . . . I had a vivid dream. Glorious angels floated in unimaginable grace above me. So realistic was the sight that I awoke at once; strangely the room was enveloped in dazzling light.
>
> My husband, in lotus posture, was levitated in the center of the room, surrounded by angels. In supplicating dignity they were worshipping him‡ with palm-folded hands. Astonished beyond measure, I was convinced that I was still dreaming.
>
> "Woman," Lahiri Mahasaya said, "you are not dreaming. Forsake your sleep forever and forever." As he slowly descended to the floor, I prostrated myself at his feet.
>
> "Master," I cried.[11]

My guess is that many a husband has enjoyed something similar in fantasy but few in reality end as Mahasaya did with a wife who was her husband's fervent disciple.

▲

‡ For those husbands rushing out to get *Autobiography of a Yogi,* I note this peculiarity, which some will find comical, others irritating, and all confusing. The author recasts Western theology to fit Hinduism and uses Judeo-Christian terms loosely. Here, for instance, angels worship a man, which in Western theology would be ridiculous; motioning toward the "angels," the husband tells his wife to bow to each of these "saints." In Western spirituality, an angel can never become a human being (nor would want to), nor does a saint, even after death, become an angel. The Western reader cannot tell whether Yogananda paints an after-death appearance by Hindu saints or a visit by celestial spirits. When Yogananda wrote, in the 1940s, Christianity and Hinduism weren't even on speaking terms, so his was a step in the right direction. And it is only natural he would privately interpret another tradition in the light of his own. Today, with much more ecumenical contact, members of the great world faiths emphasize using one another's vocabulary more accurately.

A few words from Catholic theologians on the phenomenon. Where fraud is ruled out, three possible explanations are postulated for levitation:

1. It may be strictly a neutral phenomenon tapping an as yet unknown force of nature or rare psychic ability.
2. It may be of God as He acts in the sanctified body directly or by His angels.
3. It may be Satanic,* counterfeiting mystical phenomena to confuse those seeking the truth or physically attacking the holy.†

In theory, then, I could propose St. Teresa of Avila levitated because her body was acted on by God, Daniel Home levitated because he had rare psychic gifts, and Mahasaya levitated, aided by the devil, to torment his poor wife! I am kidding, of course. Distinctions are not so easy. In actual fact, because it is so difficult to distinguish the purely supernatural from the psychophysical even in saints, levitation is never acccepted as "miraculous proof" of sanctity in Catholic investigations. Assuming the presence of the crucial virtues of heroic charity, heroic humility, heroic trust in God, etc., well-verified levitation can be accepted as "corroborative evidence" of sanctity however. This is important for us because it means testimonies of levitation are not just ignored but looked at carefully to rule out fraud, delusion, and hearsay.

If holiness in Catholicism does not always include levitation —and certainly like all traditions Catholicism has more nonlevitating saints than levitating ones—genuine levitation among Catholics is regularly associated with holiness. Testimonies from Beatification Processes and other trustworthy

* Many Catholic writers prefer to see all demons as internal, Jung's "shadow side" of the personality, but this is literally meant.
† Some twentieth-century saints claim such attacks, including Fr. Aloysius Ellacuria and Marthe Robin. For an unverified example, see the autobiography of Catholic lay evangelist J. Roy Legere, *Be My Son* (Ave Maria Press), p. 133.

sources simply contain too many eyewitness, broad-daylight accounts for the relationship to be coincidental. German investigator Joseph von Gorres (1776–1848) concluded, as far back as the first half of the nineteenth century, that at least seventy-two Catholic saints were levitators. Herbert Thurston in his twentieth-century study *The Physical Phenomena of Mysticism* claims he could easily name sixty levitators and lists twenty‡ from just one 218-year period, 1531–1791, while in his twentieth-century revision of *Butler's Lives of the Saints** the Jesuit investigator finds over two hundred saints showed some form of the phenomenon.†

Christians debate whether Jesus levitated. Some cite his being carried by Satan to the temple pinnacle and to a mountaintop (Matthew 4:5 and 8), while one writer insists Christian levitation begins with Christ's Ascension.[12]

Down the centuries accounts of Catholic levitators keep popping up. This is not to say there aren't some shadowy figures along the way, like the hermit St. Mary of Egypt (c. 500). Mary can be dismissed because there is no proof she even existed, let alone levitated. But some of the accounts that sound the most preposterous prove to be absolutely authenticated. For instance, the highest levitations ever attributed to a Catholic saint are as well attested as accounts can get. St. Joseph of Cupertino (1603–63) was seen "over their heads" by a Spanish ambassador and his wife. In one friary where he lived seventeen years, over seventy occasions of levitation were recorded. Removed from his own Franciscan order and sent to a competing group that would be happy to prove him a fraud, Joseph gained their testimonies as well that he often flew seven or eight feet up to kiss the statue of Jesus and that he flew carrying heavy things in his arms—including at least once an-

---

‡ Only seven were canonized, so levitation does not make anyone a shoo-in for official sainthood.

* Done with Donald Attwater.

† See chapter 15 for a second type that *may* have psychophysical roots.

other friar. Even Pope Urban VIII saw him levitate. And the great Lambertini (p. 41) personally acted as devil's advocate during his Cause and after the most penetrating inquiry declared that "eyewitnesses of the most searching integrity" proved "the famous upliftings from the ground and prolonged flights of the aforesaid servant of God when rapt in ecstasy." Apparently Joseph levitated so much because this was his particular bodily reponse to rapture. And all accounts agree that just a thought of God or even the sight of anything vaguely religious enraptured the man.[13]

▲

In previous chapters I did my best to favor luminosity testimonies where the sanctified body emitted light rather than was bathed in the Shekinah Light, to favor perfume testimonies where the body emitted scent rather than was surrounded by odors of an apparently external, supernatural nature. Similarly, in the next chapter my focus is not the levitation, which falls under the theological classifications (p. 263) of an outer (angelic, Satanic, or divine) mover. I will not be reporting on the saints who say the devil threw them out of bed, for instance. Where I can tell the difference, occasionally tricky, I want to focus on the enraptured levitation that may come from within the person or, as the theologians put it, "taps an as yet unknown" psychospiritual-physical agent. If—as perplexing as the thought may be—it appears that human beings do levitate, and that overwhelmingly those who do so are holy, the obvious question is, can we finger the psychospiritual-physical connection between sanctity and levitation?

To a degree I think we can. Speaking in nontheological terms, levitation of the primary type appears an extreme manifestation of the "walking on air" sensation of blissful love. "I have always walked down this street before / but the pavement always stayed beneath my feet before"[14] goes the love song.

Saints in rapture—and sanctified levitators of the first type always appear enraptured—are bursting with a love that towers over springtime romance the way an elephant looms over an ant. If your first love made you feel you were walking on air, isn't it possible the sanctified body, ravished by the love of God, at times breaks through gravity and actually rises in bliss?

In support of this possibility, I produce the celebrated Doctor of the Church—and levitator—St. Teresa of Avila. Asked by her spiritual directors to write about her mystical experiences in order to help others, this commonsense woman humbly described levitations that various onlookers witnessed (see one observer's account, p. 258). St. Teresa says, in an account I abbreviate greatly to stress the connection she makes between rapture and levitation:

> [Rapture] comes, in general, as a shock, quick and sharp, before you can collect your thoughts, or help yourself in any way, and you see and feel it as a cloud, or a strong eagle rising upwards and carrying you away on its wings. . . . I repeat it; you feel yourself carried away you know not whither. . . . (You) feel how delicious it is. . . . (At) times it was impossible to resist at all; my soul was carried away . . . and now and then the whole body as well, so that it was lifted up from the ground.[15]

Mystical theologican John G. Arintero (1860–1928), whose own Cause is under way, also ties levitation to rapture and describes rapture in a way modest St. Teresa simply passes over. This Spanish Dominican writes:

> When the prayer of union begins and all the faculties are bound in such a way that they no longer disturb the quietude of the will, this sleep is gradually changed into swoons of love, spiritual transports, and ecstatic faintings

> and raptures. In these states the soul, lost in the ocean of divine goodness, is . . . taken out of itself, . . . dissolved and absorbed in the love of the supreme Good. . . . Rapture elevates one, transfigures, and tends to lift him into the air.[16]

If this is all correct and rapturous love between God and a person cause levitation, the real wonder may be that so many mystics are earthbound. Why don't they all levitate like St. Joseph of Cupertino and St. Teresa?

I believe the most likely answer to this is that physiognomies vary tremendously in their sensitivity to emotional states. In this view some enraptured mystics, much more resistant than others, will remain gravity-bound, while more sensitive organisms will tend to rise—and a rare few actually do so—just as in water some bodies sink like a stone, others tend to float, and a few are unusually buoyant.

To support my statement that some "tend" to rise, which you may note I took directly from Arintero, let me give Paul Chacon's statement to me regarding Fr. Aloysius Ellacuria when I asked the Los Angeles banker if he had ever seen Fr. levitate:

> One day Fr. Aloysius was giving us a day of recollection. As he was talking about the Lord, I noticed he was standing on the tips of his toes. He maintained this odd position for perhaps five minutes, and during this time he was extending his arms and talking without any of the trembling in the body or legs that would seem normal in that circumstance.
>
> I said to myself, "This guy's going to take off." I really thought he might rise off the ground. But he didn't. I mentioned what I had seen to my friend Bill Landa, who said he noticed only how caught up in talking about God Fr. Aloysius was.[17]

The incident took place in the 1960s and there are testimonies from the 1950s that Fr. Aloysius was already a levitator. I agree with Paul that here is a mystic teetering on the edge of a rapture and, not just coincidentally, also teetering on the edge of levitation. As further evidence I point to an incident when Theresa Neumann was in ecstasy. Seeing Mary led into heaven in her vision, Theresa "cried, 'Take me along!' and raised her hand. Observers said she was "standing on the very tips of her toes so that you had to look to see whether she was still on the floor or not."[18]

There are of course many people, among them plenty of her coreligionists, who do not believe even a St. Teresa of Avila levitated. They do not suspect deliberate fraud but some kind of limited or, on rarer occasions, mass hallucination. To better understand such criticism and to at least pose some of the questions it raises, here is a typical nineteenth-century testimony, sincere and under oath, of one Father Gardette, a chaplain to the Chalon-sur-Saône Carmelites, on St. Jean Marie Vianney, the Curé d'Ars:

> One day my brother, who is Curé [parish priest] of Saint Vincent at Chalon-sur-Saône, came with me to Ars. In the evening, whilst the Servant of God [Vianney] recited night prayers, we took up a position facing the pulpit. About the middle of the exercise, when M. Vianney was saying the Act of Charity, my brother, whose eyesight is excellent, saw him rise into the air, little by little, until his feet were above the ledge of the pulpit. His countenance was transfigured and encircled by an aureola. My brother looked round, but witnessed no commotion among those present. So he kept quiet, but as soon as we came out of the church he could no longer refrain from speaking of the prodigy he had beheld with his own eyes; he spoke of it to all who wished to hear, and with much eagerness.[19]

The reader will see at once that sincere testimony by an educated man about a great saint may still leave many questions. Even the careful measurement is not much help, except to those familiar with the pulpit. Was the ledge at the top or bottom? I *assume* it was near the bottom since the levitation could have only been a few inches as there was "no commotion." The witness spoke of it to others but no mention is made as to whether anyone else volunteered they noticed the Curé's feet had temporarily parted company with the floor. Maybe others had but Gardette, speaking years later for his dead brother, forgot? Or maybe only this one individual noticed the levitation.

That seems possible. Few people check to see if their spiritual leader's feet remain on the floor during religious services. And if the levitation were less than half a foot in dim nighttime light (the Curé died in 1859, before electric lighting) and his feet very likely visible only to a few spectators in the church anyway, the observer may simply be the only one who noticed.

But what about the halo and transfigured face? With these factors, shouldn't someone else have noticed? Must we now conclude the viewer suffered an attack of overactive imagination? Some will say yes. Others may believe the observer had a vision, that is, saw something real but not material, a personal numinous grace if you will. And some will insist he was just the only observant spectator present.

I can only end these speculations by reiterating three things. First, we are dealing in accounts of any mystical phenomenon with all the imprecision and capacity for error and self-delusion of human beings. Second, we are dealing as well with the unfathomable mysteries of numinous reality, that is so simple a child can understand it and so ineffable the mightiest brain can not unravel its secrets. Finally, I remind the reader that the most extraordinary event may be reported in grossly inadequate fashion; the most question-proof report may be pure fabrication; and the truth or falsity of one levitation report has no automatic bearing on the next. If you've got all that firmly in mind, you're ready for the next chapter, which looks at some levitators of the nineteenth and twentieth centuries.

notes

1. Mother Marguerite Carter verified the extern sisters' report (they are all now deceased) for me during her fall 1988 visit to the Carmel in question. I spoke to Sister Lucy late in 1988. My interviews with Sister Veronica regarding Fr. Aloysius date from 1984–89. I do not name any of the Carmels in order to protect the privacy these nuns need for their work of contemplation.

2. Interviews by phone with Mary Levy and Katherine Morrow in Nov. 1988.

3. Series of interviews with Mother Marguerite in Oct. and Nov. 1988.

4. Herbert Thurston, *The Physical Phenomena of Mysticism,* p. 29.

5. Her deposition was taken at Segovia in 1595 or 1596.

6. Evelyn Underhill, *Mysticism,* pp. 186, 376.

7. Thelma Moss, *The Probability of the Impossible,* pp. 133–35.

8. Ibid., pp. 117, 131. Also Dr. L. Rumble, "Spiritualism and Psychical Research," pp. 8, 27.

9. M. Lamar Keene, *The Psychic Mafia,* pp. 100–3.

10. Paramahansa Yogananda, *Autobiography of a Yogi,* pp. 70–76.

11. Ibid., pp. 323–24.

12. Robert D. Smith, *Comparative Miracles,* p. 37.

13. *Bibliotheca Sanctorum,* Rome, 1965, Vol. 6, pp. 1300–3. Reference furnished by the archivist for the Congregation for the

Causes of Saints, Oct. 17, 1985. See also the entry under the saint's name in the revised *Butler's Lives of the Saints.*

14. Alan Jay Lerner, "On the Street Where You Live," from *My Fair Lady.*

15. *The Autobiography of St. Teresa of Avila,* E. Allison Peers' translation, p. 190.

16. John G. Arintero, *The Mystical Evolution in the Development and Vitality of the Church,* pp. 264–65.

17. Interview with the author in July 1988.

18. Johannes Steiner, *Therese Neumann,* p. 177.

19. Francis Trochu, op. cit., pp. 542–43, from Process testimonies.

14 ▲

two
centuries
of levitators

Perhaps because the phenomenon is so "unnatural," levitators may easily be reduced in our minds to cardboard figures. This makes nothing more important than to keep firmly in mind, as we gaze at levitators of the past two centuries, that these are real people who often began life spiritually pretty much like the rest of us. Take our earliest verified nineteenth-century example,* Andre Herbert Fournet, for instance.

As a child in a devout family, he found religion boring and wrote in his book "This belongs to Andre Fournet, a good boy, although he is *not* going to be a priest or monk!"[1] Always in mischief at school, he once ran away, only to be returned and

---

* St. Julie Billiart (d. 1816) is also said to have levitated in ecstasy before the young religious community of which she was co-foundress. But in tracing the English accounts back to the French-language memoirs of her co-foundress who was present, I find the account of this occurrence does not mention it included levitation.

soundly thrashed. As a young man, he went to Poitiers ostensibly to study law and philosophy, actually to whoop it up away from his pious mother. He seems not to have hit the books at all—at least the next detail is of his enlisting and his horrified family buying his way out of the army. Then the bewildered mother tried to settle him as a clerk but his abominable handwriting made him unemployable. As a last resort the family shipped the ne'er-do-well to his uncle, who was parish priest in some poor backwater.

What a nagging mother failed at, the holy uncle accomplished. Andre settled down so thoroughly that he studied theology, was ordained a priest, and became his uncle's assistant. After the older man's death, he went home where "his liberality to the poor and his winning personality soon endeared him to the whole parish." For a while he kept up entertaining friends in a manner befitting his class of origin "but the casual criticism of a beggar led him to give away all his silver and every article of furniture that was not absolutely necessary."[2] That new simplicity next spilled over into his sermons.

"Your Reverence used to preach so finely that no one understood you," the sacristan remarked one day. "Nowadays we can all follow every word you say."[3]

In 1789 the French Revolution broke out, a revolt by the rising, middle classes against abuses of power and a no longer workable system in which those who governed as King, ministers, and Church leaders all usually came from the same aristocratic families. While the rural areas tended to look more kindly on their clergy, in the industrializing cities the Church was attacked as the accomplice of an oppressive regime. Many priests and nuns would die during the next years. Fournet's bishop ordered him to flee to Spain.

Five years later, ignoring the threat of death if discovered, he felt he must return. Incognito, he celebrated masses in barns and escaped capture at times by a hairsbreadth. In an era of violence and hatred, "an all-embracing charity and straightforwardness" had joined simplicity as "the keynotes of Fournet's character." Returning good for evil, the once truant schoolboy—by the same simple, agonizing process described in chapter one—had become a Christlike figure. The divine love first glimpsed in his holy uncle in Fournet's maturity spilled out of him so lavishly that testimonies recount physical healings and even multiplications of food for those in need. The saint survived the Revolution terror. Living to eighty-two, he even founded a new order of nuns in the land where religious congregations had been outlawed. Witnesses for the Process deposed that in front of entire congregations the man's ardor, as he said mass or preached, sometimes literally carried him off the floor.

I translate the following incident from the Process testimony of a nun:

> In the year 1819 or 1820 the Servant of God passed three months at Issy, near Paris, in our congregation's recently founded house there. While the Servant of God [Fournet] celebrated the mass, Sister Marie Alexandrina saw him elevated off the floor, remaining immobile in this position during the period of the elevation [one of the most solemn points of the service].
>
> Fearing to be mistaken, she alerted the [other] nuns and begged them to observe whether she truly was seeing the Servant of God levitated above the ground. These circumstances continued for the space of eight days in conjunction with the masses said by the Servant of God.

The same Process witness also tells how two nuns, Sister St. Martin and Sister St. Francis of Paola, saw Fournet another time levitated as he prayed before a cross on a day when the parishioners of La Puye were having a procession to the site, situated near the nuns' garden.

In what is apparently a separate incident (the Italian of the

Process is unclear), the witness next mentions a boarding school girl of La Puye who pointed out to her teacher, Sister St. Vincent de Paul, that the priest was elevated above the floor. The teacher informed Sister St. Martin, and "all of them," says the Process witness, saw the incident. Whether that means the threesome or includes others, I cannot say. The incident, however, was well known and often related among the community of sisters where it occurred, a group that saw Fournet not only as their founder but as a reliable guide to the heights of Christian spirituality.

Still another incident involves a member of the nuns named Sister Monica. This sister, the Beatification Process witness who was her friend relates, found herself in the church at La Puye near three or four other nuns while the saint was kneeling with his arms extended like a cross as he prayed under the church bells. The other nuns were whispering among themselves, "Look at the priest! Look at the priest!" Monica paid no attention but went on with her own prayers. However, she was scarcely out the church door when the others were excitedly telling her they had seen Father Fournet elevated above the church floor, no part of his body in contact with any means of support.[4]

One must be suspicious of any second- and third-hand testimony but where there are first-hand accounts accompanying it and we are dealing with witnesses of solid reputation, I think levitation is almost an exception. From personal experience, I find reasonable that neither Sister Monica nor her friend would forget such a startling event: I never met Father Aloysius Ellacuria but I will never forget being told by my friend, Sister Veronica, that certain individuals had seen him levitate. The vital thing of course is that the original witnesses can be trusted as to both integrity and freedom from delusions! In the case of the man today known as St. Andre Fournet, the fact that each case involved more than one witness is a plus. Finally the best corroboration that he may have been a levitating saint seems to me his life blazing with ardent love.

▲

You may recall St. Gaspar del Bufalo, the saint with the (in English) funny name whose specialty was converting bandits and the hit men who tried time and again to assassinate him (p. 149). A native of Rome who died there in 1837, Gaspar left behind a number of witnesses who swear that his frequent ecstasies at times resulted in levitation. For instance at Campoli Appennino in 1824, Gaspar was saying mass in a little country church with another priest, Domenico Silvestri (who later joined the order the saint founded), acting as altar boy. This other priest testified:

> [Later] my aunt assured me that she had seen Father Gaspar risen above the altar steps about four or five inches (half a hand's span) after the Consecration.

Three years later:

> at Pereto, where he gave a mission in 1827, he was waiting in the small Church of the Savior for some priests to whom he was to give a lecture.
> Praying before the tabernacle, he was suddenly observed to start as if an electric shock had transfixed his body. Immediately he rose almost a hand's span [nine inches] above the ground. Neither knees, hands, nor any other part of his body was in contact with any surface.

Materials supplied by Gaspar's religious congregation indicate there were other occasions including one when:

> During the mass at the time of the elevation of the host, he was observed floating in the air above the altar at Pievetorina in St. Augustine's Church.[5]

Because the Italian gives no measurements for the last incident, it is not possible to tell whether Gaspar's feet were observed to be higher than the altar or his head so much higher than normal that his feet had to be off the ground, or whether he was in one of those mystical flights like those of St. Joseph of Cupertino that are the rarest form of this phenomenon.

▲

St. Gaspar's contemporary St. Maddalena di Conossa (1774–1835) was the daughter of a nobleman. As a young woman Maddalena renounced her family's wealth and went to live with society's poorest in Verona. There she worked in a hospital, aided children who were imprisoned or abandoned, and began teaching religion in local churches. In 1803 she founded a school for the poorest children of the city (Napoleon himself gave her an abandoned convent). By 1808 she had created a new woman's order in service of the poor, today called in her honor the Daughters of Charity of Canossa. The rest of her life Maddalena was busy opening more schools, colleges, and retreat centers, all for poor youths of both sexes. To assist her nuns she also founded an order of men. "Love for the poor devoured her like a fever," remarked John Paul II as he officially canonized her October 2, 1988. That love, the Process testimonies affirm, also at times flowed over into ecstasies, visions, and rapturous levitation.

For instance, one time the saint visited some priests in Venice to help them set up a charitable institute. Her hosts told her traveling companion Sister Anna Rizzi that some of their number saw the ecstatic aristocrat raised from the ground to the level of a crucifix under which she had been praying. As their "thank you" for her help, the men gave Maddalena that crucifix when she left.[6]

▲

Three Process witnesses reported levitations by St. Joseph Benedict Cottolengo (1786–1842), a man whose charitable enterprises still thrive in Turin, Italy, today. But none of the three had personally seen Cottolengo levitate, so without impugning them, I pass over these accounts.[7] Another individual I only mention in passing is French mystic and foundress Mother Marie of Jesus (Madame Josephine du Bourg) who died in 1862. Herbert Thurston says many nuns were eyewitnesses to levitations by Mother Marie, another foundress. While I have verified with the Congregation for the Causes of Saints that she is a candidate for beatification, I have been unable to obtain the testimonies Thurston refers to.[8]

▲

The Spanish noblewoman Joquina de Mas y de Vedruna is still another of those giants of practical charities Western spiritualities produce in such abundance. The young (she was thirty-three when her husband died) widow of a Barcelona attorney and mother of eight founded the Carmelites of Charity, one of the nineteenth-century's many new congregations dedicated to nursing and teaching. It was hardly the thing expected of a woman of her class.

"How could you be so stupid as to involve yourself in an undertaking this absurd?" the aristocratic widow was scolded by a marchioness, while kinder critics pitied "the poor thing driven crazy by her husband's death."[9]

Seventeen years a wife, at forty-two a foundress, she died at seventy-one having borne paralysis for several years with great fortitude. The testimonies gathered before she was officially canonized in 1959 under Pope John XXIII report that "several times when at prayer" she was seen, her head haloed with light, "lifted from the floor in ecstasy."

The first time this occurred the witness was one of her children. Later, various nuns of her order caught her elevated. One witness for the Process recalled two dead nuns' experiences. I quote the witness:

> One time Sister Apollonia Camps, now dead, with whom I lived, told me that she saw the Servant of God [Joquina] who was reciting some prayers to the Holy Trinity in ecstasy, all resplendent [with light] and at the same time raised from the earth. Also, in another instance, Sister Teresa Casany, now dead, with whom I lived, told me that one night, she observed a great splendor in the cell of the Servant of God. Recalling that the Sisters' rule called for little light to be used in the cells, she raised the curtain of Mother Joquina's cell and, with wonder, observed the Servant of God luminous and raised in the air higher than the bed on which she slept.[10]

▲

In my book on physical healings that have occurred through the prayer of saints, *Nothing Short of a Miracle,* I devoted two chapters to the healings of Bavarian-born Father Francis Xavier Seelos, who came to the United States as a missionary in 1843. Seelos was a lively fellow, quick to laugh and open in heart and hand to anyone in need. Members of the Redemptorist order he joined considered young Seelos a saint even when he was a novice, an opinion shared by Americans in all the cities and small towns from Wisconsin eastward where he was stationed or stayed briefly on the preaching tours which are a Redemptorist specialty.

At Cumberland, Maryland, he was pastor of the Catholic church, as well as teacher and prefect of Redemptorist seminarians from May 1857 to 1862. During this time a young fellow from Prussia by the name of Andreas Franz was a candidate to become a Redemptorist brother. Eventually Franz decided religious vows weren't his calling and went to Baltimore, where he married and became a tailor. He never forgot Father Seelos however. After the saint's death, when testionies to his virtues were being collected, Franz came forward. Among the things he wanted to share about the much-loved Seelos was this:

> On one occasion I went into the chapel at Cumberland, and there I saw the Servant of God [praying] on his knees with his arms extended, and, as it seemed to me, elevated from the ground about a foot. It was during the day about two o'clock in the afternoon, during the period of time the Servant of God gave to his devotions.[11]

While some might find the Prussian tailor's cautious "it seemed to me" indicative of lack of certainty, I find it reassuring. While he has seen something so striking it remains in his mind for over forty years—he testified before the Baltimore tribunal November 27, 1901—under oath, as a rational man talking of something as "wild" as levitation, he can only say, "This is how it seemed to me." With any single witness, hallucination is *always* a possibility. One thing, however, is clear. Buried in New Orleans's landmark St. Mary's Assumption Church, whether he levitated in Maryland or not, Seelos's virtues are such he seems certain to one day join the canonized saints.

▲

Mariam Baouardy (Sister Marie of Jesus Crucified), the Christian Arab from Galilee who died in 1878 in Bethlehem, definitely levitated, according to detailed eyewitness accounts by groups of witnesses. It's the way she did it that perplexes me, gliding up the outer edges of trees or hopping like a bird from branch to branch, then teetering ecstatically into the breeze on the twig-like branches of the uppermost heights. I felt Daniel Dunglas Home a magician because he didn't go straightforwardly up but out one dimly lit window and in another, both at the same height.

In Sister Marie's case, I wondered if she was a natural gymnast. In a sense this is silly of me: She was a housemaid before becoming a nun, not a circus performer while the onlookers to her levitations, wily nuns adept at spotting phonies, had no such qualms. They testify, as do lay people who lived with her before she entered the Carmelites, that Mariam was as honest as the day is long. The Carmelites judged her a saint, an opinion corroborated by her official beatification. Still, Mariam's is definitely one of those cases where one sees the genius of her church's refusing to cry "Miracle" when someone levitates or to claim to sort out the innate psychical gifts, if any, of a given saint from the mystical ones.

Hindu holy man Paramahansa Yogananda ascribed the levitation of a fellow Hindu to mastery of *pranayama,* the controlling of life force through the breath. Through such learned techniques, Yogananda claimed, the body "loses its grossness" so that it rises "or hops about like a leaping frog." It seems clear that Mariam had no mastery of *pranayama* but instead was mastered by her rapturous love for Jesus—but she certainly hopped about like a leaping frog. This parallel with something Hinduism finds learnable may point to a physiological basis for Mariam's bodily activity during certain early states of rapture in her life.

Like a frog, yes. However the nun who liked to call herself *"le petit rien"* [the little nothing] and whom the other Carmelites called simply *"la petite"* [the little one] *most* reminds me in her levitations of a deliriously happy child skipping for joy. See what you think:

The phenomenon was noticed the first time June 22, 1873, in the garden of the Carmel at Pau. Noticing her absence at supper, the mistress of novices searched for her in vain in the cloister and the orchard until one of the sisters heard someone chanting "Love! Love!" Looking up, she saw the little one balancing without any support at the absolute summit of an enormous lime tree [this would be about fifteen meters or roughly forty-five feet from the ground].

Informed, the prioress arrived. Faced with this phenomenon, the prioress didn't know what to do. After praying [about it], she addressed the little one, "My sister, Marie of Jesus Crucified, if Jesus wishes, come down by obedience without falling and without hurting yourself." At the moment she heard the word "obedience,"† the ecstatic came down "with a radiant face" and perfect modesty, stopping at several branches to chant "Love!"

"Barely was she on the ground," notes one witness, "than as if to compensate our [reverend] mother and our sisters for the anguish we had in searching for her and then seeing her perched so high, she embraced us with a sort of drunkenness and affection impossible to express."

This particular phenomenon took place only in this one brief period of Mariam's life. Perhaps while raptures at first overpowered her, in time she learned to handle ecstatic states without those visible manifestations mystics find so embarrassing. From the two-hundred-page book, the authentic compilation of everything pertaining to Mariam, that the Bethlehem Carmel sent me, I find she was observed in "ecstatic ascen-

---

† Like many orders, Carmelites vow poverty, chastity, and obedience. The last is regarded as the hardest and a touchstone of genuine sanctity, since it involves the ego death or humility to abandon one's own will. It would never include accepting orders against morality or human dignity.

sions" eight times, seven from June through August 1873 and a final one a year later, July 5, 1874.

"Why do you rise like this?" the Mother Superior interrogated her.

"The Lamb carries me in His hands," Mariam answered, speaking of Jesus with typical unselfconsciousness. Another day she explained that "if I obey quickly, the tree becomes like this," and she put her hand close to the ground.

Because of its exceptional nature I am going to quote more details on Mariam's case (I translate from the French material which has since become available in English):

> Certain Carmelites wanted to get to the bottom of this thing, so they spied on the little one. One day, one of the lay sisters who was working in the garden witnessed one of the ascensions: "She [Mariam] had seized the extremity of a branch so little that a bird would have bent it, and from there, in an instant, she had been raised on high." On the fifth of July, perched on the lime tree, she said to the prioress: "I was on that [branch] over there and I came here. See, my sandals are left there." [In a letter to this author, the nuns explain that these sandals were merely rope soles held on the feet by cords that were easily caught as the levitator "flew" up into the tree.]
>
> On July 19, 1873, she had a moment of hesitation when ordered to descend. She begged to be given longer with "the Lamb." "No," insisted the prioress "by obedience, descend." She obeyed, but the moment of hesitation had been fatal: The vision had disappeared. "The Lamb is gone," she sighed; "He left me alone to descend." And in effect it was with effort this time that she returned to earth, and she paid by four sorrowful days‡ for the unhappy moment. The July 25 levitation lasted from four to

‡ Probably by losing the experiential sense of God's presence.

seven in the evening; the one of July 31 from recreation which followed the evening meal until nine o'clock.

It speaks against any hidden wires that she did not always ascend the same tree. A priest who studied her case wrote:

> Sister Marie rose to the summit of trees by the extremities of the branches: she put her scapular* within her hand, seized with the other hand the extremity of a little branch on the side of the leaves and in the wink of an eye glided by the exterior of the tree to its summit. Once risen, she held herself on branches too feeble to sustain, normally, a person of her weight.

Apparently she could at least sense a rapture coming on at times and make an effort, however futile, to hide. A nun who was with her in the garden one day reported Sister Marie said to her, "Turn around." She did, then looked quickly back and saw Sister Marie already at the heights of a lime tree, balancing on a little branch like a bird and singing ecstatically of divine love.

Another witness tells of seeing Marie "with resplendent face" sitting at the top of a tree on a branch that should not have sustained her. She came down "like a bird from branch to branch with great lightness and modesty."

With reluctance I admit that the information supplied by the Bethlehem Carmel also contains one account of a earlier levitation which is even odder than flitting about in trees.

In 1868 Mariam passed forty days and nights in a strange state that she and the other Carmelites believed to be reparatory suffering. It is said it was a state of torment and attempted degradation by Satanic forces who tried to shake her commitment to God by every kind of temptation. Be that

---

* A loose part of religious clothing liable to snag somewhere.

as it may, at the end of the fortieth day, as Mariam had fore-told, all this ceased:

> The moment the hour of midnight came, the observers saw a complete change. After the temptations, the humili-ations and disfigurements of the little one, owing to her struggles against evil, now there was a true transfigura-tion.
>
> The novice [Marie] rose several hand spans above the bed while her visage became luminous, her eyes shone like two dark diamonds and a marvelous smile blossomed on her lips.

The nuns present fell on their knees. They reported it seemed Mariam at that moment was so united with God that the onlooker who saw her saw Him.[12]

▲

One morning in December 1878, eighteen-year-old Evasio Garrone and a companion named Franchini acted as altar boys during the mass of St. John Bosco. At the moment of the elevation they saw the visionary and great man of action slowly rise above the floor until they could not reach his cha-suble.† Bewildered, Garrone, who had been a store clerk until that August when Bosco took him in so he could get an educa-tion, rushed out to call another priest, Father Berto. Unable to find him, he returned in time to see the enraptured, luminous priest‡ slowly descend until his feet once more touched the floor. The levitation had lasted for about ten minutes, accord-ing to the written report of Garrone, who became a priest himself.

After mass and Bosco's long prayer period immediately fol-

---

† The uppermost garment worn by priests only when celebrating mass.
‡ See p. 78.

lowing, the youth brought the saint coffee and asked, "Don Bosco, what happened to you this morning . . . ? How did you rise so very high?"

Don Bosco gave him a meditative look. Then he asked, "Why don't you have a little coffee with me?"

Garrone got the hint and dropped the subject. Two other times he saw the same phenomenon.[13]

While Bosco never spoke a word about his own levitations, this father to several thousand disadvantaged youths did occasionally acknowledge the phenomenon in their ranks, which include several canonized or beatified individuals.* Father Giovanni Battista Lemoyne, a spiritual son of the saint who met him in 1864 and spent his life collecting testimonies to the saint for the monumental twenty-volume *Memorie Biografiche* and other books on the saint, has left this witness:

> One day Don Bosco accompanied a priest to see the altar of Mary Help of Christians [the church Bosco had built in the midst of one of Turin's worst slums]. Behind the altar of the sanctuary, he found a lad elevated in the air, ravished in adoration. At the approach of Don Bosco and the other priest, the ecstatic youth came down like a feather carried away by the wind. Don Bosco sent him away as if nothing unusual had happened. Then turning to the priest, he said, "These things seem to be of the Middle Ages, yet they happen even now."
>
> Once again, upon entering the . . . [sanctuary] at an hour when the church was deserted, he saw a pupil . . . raised in the air before the large picture above the main altar. . . . Don Bosco would tell some of these things, saying humbly "Don Bosco is a poor priest but he has

---

* Among them are teenager St. Dominic Savio, Bl. Michael Rua, Bl. Don Orione, Bl. Luigi Guanella, and Ven. Philip Rinaldi, among others, as well as unofficial saints such as Francis Besucco, whose biography Bosco wrote.

many saintly boys who draw many blessings [on him] from God."[14]

The Flemish Benedictine wonder worker Abbot Paul (Francis Luyckx) preached, taught, and breathed one topic: the love of God. Even his personal letters open and close with such phrases as "O love! O infinite love of Jesus! O excess of love!" With levitation linked to rapturous love, it seems fitting there are those who assert Father Paul was also a levitator.

One woman, kneeling alone in the church where Father Paul was preparing to give her Communion, later testified:

> I raised my eyes and to my great astonishment, I saw Father Paul standing before me in ecstasy, raised a considerable distance above the ground, and holding the sacred host. I cannot tell how long he continued in this attitude, but I think it was at least five minutes. It would be impossible for me to describe how attractive . . . the Rev. Father appeared.[15]

Another woman reported she "sometimes saw Father Paul raised above the ground." Apparently at such moments he felt himself being swept away by rapture, because this witness notes that he would first try to distract her by some comment like "Just look at those beautiful pigeons in the garden." She would look at the pigeons and turn around to find the Benedictine lost in some ecstatic vision of his own. She says at those times he would levitate to a height of a few feet for about ten minutes.[16]

A third witness tells of an 1889 visit to Fr. Paul:

> In the course of the conversation he suddenly stopped and exclaimed, "For the love of Jesus!" and as if wrapt in ecstasy he was raised about three feet above his chair and

remained thus eight or ten minutes; then he slowly descended upon his chair and resumed the conversation.[17]

▲

With St. Gemma Galgani (1878–1903), we not only breach the twentieth century, we get inside the rapturous vision, for once, to see what a saint saw† as she was overwhelmed by love and lifted from the earth. As far as we know, Gemma's "numerous levitations" all took place in relation to a large representation of Christ crucified, which hung on the wall of the dining room of the Giannini family of Lucca, Italy. The beautiful, young, orphaned daughter of a pharmacist lived with the Gianninis.

To Padre Germano, her spiritual director, Gemma confided that one day as she was preparing the table for dinner, she was carrying on an interior dialogue with her beloved Jesus. Looking up at the very expressive and almost lifesize crucifix high on the wall (in photos sent to this writer, its top is just below the ceiling, and the knee of Christ's figure is almost at the top of the room's door), she was overwhelmed by love. Like someone looking at a photograph who impetuously kisses it, Gemma was overcome with the desire to kiss the lance wound in the crucifix's side. She expressed this desire to Jesus. The next thing she knew, she rose and—in rapturous tears—was able to carry out her desire.

Padre Germano adds that in September 1901, while busy again with some housework, Gemma had a longer and more profound ecstasy or rapture.

"Jesus, let me come to you. I'm dying of love," she cried. In what was obviously a vision, as she described it to Father Germano, the crucifix seemed to come alive and stretch an arm to

---

† English schoolteacher Teresa Higginson (1844–1905) left three letters to her spiritual director with such details and was observed levitating by Canon Musseley, a priest in Manchester, England in October 1891 or 1892. I omit Teresa because of as yet unresolved questions which have stalled her Cause.

her while she rose to embrace Him. That time she levitated as high as the heart wound.

To commemorate "the number of times" this sort of thing happened in the dining room, a lamp is kept perpetually burning under this crucifix today at No. 31 Via S. Gemma.

Father Germano never personally saw Gemma levitate. He took her word, not just because he *had* experienced so much of the other phenomena of the stigmatic visionary's life personally but because he knew "her two major characteristics were extreme humility and simplicity." Simple and spontaneous as a child, he swore Gemma would neither have shammed mystical experiences, nor was she egotistical enough for delusions.

For those not about to take any flaky stigmatic's word that she levitated, fortunately there was a witness among the dozen or so members of the Giannini family. The child Elena Giannini once ran to her Aunt Cecilia, shouting, "Aunty, come see Gemma. She's flying!" Only because Elena too died young is her firsthand testimony not found in the Process before Gemma's 1933 beatification.[18]

Like many stigmatic visionaries, St. Gemma has been dismissed by most modern Catholic writers as some kind of nut. Let me add then that because there was so much unusual phenomena in Gemma's life, great care was taken in the investigation to make certain of both her mental stability and all absence of fraud. The investigation was resolved in favor of Gemma's phenomena being side effects of sanctity in large part because of the Giannini family and Father Germano. Each had carefully verified so much pertaining to the young mystic because of their own initial doubts. And each came to believe implicitly in Gemma's holiness only after, at times, painful incidents. Tests they set to "trap her" only revealed the heroism of her virtues. Another major factor in the rapid (1940) canonization was the extravagant outpouring of inexplicable healings for those who asked the dead mystic's prayers.

Around 1945 Charles Poirier, Catholic priest at a spot called Longueuil in French-speaking Canada, spent several weeks making frequent visits to an elderly man‡ to prepare him for death. Poirier says:

> This old man attested with the utmost seriousness and in full recognition that he was about to appear before God, that he used to go see Brother Andre [Bessette at the Montreal shrine where the healer lived and worked], and spend the night sharing the [saint's] tiny room above the chapel. [On those occasions] two times he saw Brother Andre raised above his bed.[19]

This is the only witness, so again we must consider the possibility of delusion.

Theresa Neumann, the Bavarian stigmatic who died in 1962, is attested by priests, an abbess, and other lay onlookers to have levitated, according to investigator Johannes Steiner. One such occasion was in the monastery church of St. Walburn in Eichstätt:

> The Abbess, Maria Benedicta von Spiegel, suddenly noticed that, at consecration time, Resl [Theresa's nickname] had fallen into a state of vision; she had been sitting lower than the Abbess at the beginning of her vision state but now she was about the same height. Later examinations proved that she had been levitated about one step from the floor.

Another incident Steiner uncovered was at the Steyler monastery in Tirsehenreuth on the Feast of the Assumption, August 15, 1938. A group of lay people and priests all saw Theresa "actually raised a little bit from the floor and hover-

‡ By the name of Moise Poirier—he was not related to Fr. Charles.

ing in the air for a while."[20] Steiner spoke personally to a Mr. Dost from Hildesheimer, one of those witnesses, on September 24, 1950. Although I have written to Konnersreuth where Theresa lived, I cannot verify, or add to, Steiner's work. Fr. Anton Vogl, who is in charge of answering letters like mine, writes me that those who can testify "that Theresa Neumann at times levitated are no longer alive."[21] If they left testimonies, as I suspect some did, these are not yet available to researchers.

I mentioned (see note p. 264) that few levitators have been beatified or canonized. Sister Marie of Jesus (Mariam Baouardy) made it to beatification recently in spite of phenomena as "suspicious" as levitations in her life, because she had her fellow Carmelites to vouch for her genuine holiness. The young canonized laywoman Gemma Galgani had connections to the Passionist order, which took up her Cause. As another laywoman stigmatic visionary with no connection to any religious order (her spiritual director-confessor, for instance, was a parish priest rather than a member of some group like the Passionists or Franciscans), Theresa Neumann may one day end up only a footnote in books on mystical phenomena. That, of course, will not invalidate, nor would a successful Cause prove, that she really levitated.

notes

1. Herbert J. Thurston, S.J., and Donald Attwater, *Butler's Lives of the Saints*, Vol. 2, p. 304. The article on Fournet is based on the biographical summary of the bull of canonization, found in the *Acta Apostolicae Sedis*, vol. XXV (1933), pp. 417–28 and other sources.

2. Ibid.

3. Ibid.

4. *Posito super virtutibus*, Rome, 1900, Summarium, n. XV, pp. 544–45.

5. Amilcare Rey, *Gaspare del Bufalo*, Vol. 2, pp. 490–91, quoting various firsthand witnesses. Rey says the saint was also seen levitated while preaching (p. 276). Furnished by the saint's order, these incidents were translated from the Italian by Herbert de Souza, S.J.

6. *Posito super virtutibus*, Rome, 1905, Summarium, n. XVIII, p. 288.

7. *Posito super virtutibus*, Rome, 1896, Summarium, n. XIX, pp. 729, 738–39, 753.

8. Herbert J. Thurston, *The Physical Phenomena of Mysticism*, p. 155, quoting G. Du Bourg, *Une Fondatrice au XIXième siecle* (Paris, 1914), pp. 241, 256. "The Congregation for the Causes of the Saints," letter to me dated Dec. 28, 1988.

9. Thurston and Attwater, op. cit., vol. 2., p. 373.

10. *Posito super virtutibus*, Rome, 1931, Summarium, n. XIX, p. 452.

11. *Copia Publica Transumpti Processus Ordinaria Auctoritate Constructi in Curia Ecclesiastica Baltimorensei*, folio 167r.

12. Amédée Brunot, *Mariam: La petite Arabe: Soeur Marie de Jésus Crucifié*, pp. 42–44, 65, 86.

13. Eugenio Ceria, *Memorie Biografiche di San Giovanni Bosco*, Vol. 13, pp. 701–2.

14. John Baptist Lemoyne, *The Venerable Don Bosco: A Character Sketch*, p. 107.

15. Edward van Speybrouck, *Father Paul of Moll*, p. 154.

16. Ibid., p. 156.

17. Ibid., pp. 156–7.

18. Germano di S. Stanislao, *S. Gemma Galgani*, pp. 263–65. Other material, including the anecdote regarding Elena Giannini, is from "Santa Gemma e Il Croccifisso Di Casa Giannini," prepared for me from the primary sources in their archives by the Passionist nuns at St. Gemma's shrine, Lucca, Italy, through the kindness of Lucia Sbragia of San Francisco, a native of Lucca.

19. Étienne Catta, *Le Frère André (1845–1937) et l'Oratorie Saint-Joseph du Mont-Royal*, p. 847, quoting Poirier's report to Aimé Trottier of the Montreal shrine.

20. Steiner, *Therese Neumann*, pp. 59, 177. Done in the late 1930s when Theresa still had almost a quarter century to live, Josef Teodorowicz's fine work on the mystical phenomena of her life does not mention levitation, indicating it was a phenomenon of her maturity.

21. His letter is dated October 9, 1985.

15 ▲

fast
travelers
indeed

Sister Dolores Cazares, a dynamic American nun who works in youth ministry, and some relatives were vacationing for a few days in France in 1975 before attending the first international Catholic charismatic conference in Rome. Walking along a street in Nice, the energetic Dolores had left her mother and cousin some paces behind as she stepped out to cross a boulevard.

She was in the middle of the street when suddenly, turning out of the crossroad, a motorcyclist roared into the intersection. Traveling extremely fast, he had to lean heavily into his turn. This meant he had no chance to maneuver, and he was headed straight for Sister Dolores.

"I'm dead," was all she could think. Mid-stride at that moment, her foot came down not in a tangle of motorcycle and bodies—but on the opposite curb several steps away.

Shocked, the young nun could only conclude, "the Lord still has some work for me to do."

Two male pedestrians who saw the impossible were shocked too. They kept turning around to stare at her for the next several blocks.[1]

▲

If you are a skeptical person, as I *hope* you are, your reaction to Sister Dolores' story, her awed observers notwithstanding, is probably something like "Oh, she just had an enormous burst of adrenalin from fear and jumped several feet." That would have been my reaction at one time, even though it meant a woman had to move faster than a speeding motorcycle. Today I say to you, read this chapter, then take another look at this incident: You may still say "Adrenalin"—or you *may* see other possibilities.

In the last two chapters I put before you the idea that under the influence of rapture, human feet may at times lose contact with the floor. This chapter will look at two other types of levitation or closely related phenomena in which (1) the sanctified body moves—sometimes miles—from point to point in moments *or* (2) its feet apparently glide over rather than touch the ground, propelled in a manner and/or at speeds beyond known capabilities.

With a moment's reflection you will understand why this chapter must be short: Few bodies glide over or just above the ground. However, those rare occasions *can* be observed. When a body moves from point to point in an inexplicable way, as Sister Dolores did, this can only be observed if the distance is a very short one. Since the phenomenon usually involves longer distances, even miles, or situations where the saint is alone, there are almost never witnesses. Instead we usually have only the word of the saint who experienced this strange phenomenon. What permits us to believe "transportation," as some have called it, really occurs is that on the rarest occasions of all there *are* witnesses of sorts.

And, as with levitation, we find the same or similar phenomena in other traditions. Religious historian Mircea Eliade finds traditions of "traveling immense instances in a flash" in both Buddhist and Hindu lore. He mentions that among the Buddhist arhats, one finds even a specialized verb *rahatve* (in Singhalese), meaning "to disappear" and "to pass instantaneously from one place to another." Such experiences, says Eliade, are found also throughout shamanism and archaic spiritualities. Eliade mentions such phenomena as being (1) mystical, interiorized, nonconcrete (i.e., psychological) experiences or (2) illusions, and also seems to refer to (3) concrete experiences expressed in the Hindu saying "with such a body, the yogin goes where he will."[2]

Michael Harner, the New York professor of anthropology who is a practicing shaman, details one phenomenon that may be pertinent. Harner speaks of emergency situations in which an Australian aborigine shaman or a Tibetan lama may "engage in *fast traveling*—a trance or Shamanic state of Consciousness technique for running long distances at a rapid rate."[3]

Dr. Harner is talking of a learned ability utilizing mind-body oneness to a very high degree through an act of the will. Obviously that is no description of Sister Dolores' experience. And because of these volitional, learned aspects, *fast traveling* is certainly not the same phenomenon as this second type of levitation as it appears in holy people; however, it is close enough that, if you can accept *fast traveling* as a physical reality for a shaman in an altered state of consciousness, the second type of levitation seems physiologically reasonable for saints, who are often (see pp. 15–16) in an altered consciousness even when they engage in mundane activities.

Jews can point to scriptural figures like Elijah (I Kings 18:46 and II Kings 2:11) or possibly Enoch (Genesis 5:24) who have moved in rare ways or been carried off by God, as well as to modern mystics like Rabbi Israel Spira (see p. 304). There is also the great eighteenth-century mystic the Baal Shem Tov, who I am told evidenced this phenomenon many times. Interestingly, his Hasidic tradition does not conceptualize the phenomenon as someone being transported but as the geography to be traversed shrinking momentarily. Thus the Baal Shem Tov is said to have strode across a great abyss between mountains as if it were only a crack—because for a moment it was. What I find intriguing about this way of looking at the phenomenon (which is as reasonable as the idea of being carried by an angel or lifted, speaking figuratively, by the hand of God) is that in the altered consciousness of mysticism, where hours often shrink to moments, this could so easily be a mystic's perception of what had occurred—which is not to cast my vote to box God in to either concept.

All denominations of Christians share the tradition of Christ's disciple Philip. After baptizing an important Ethiopian, Philip disappeared, "the spirit of the Lord" having instantly transported him from the site of the town of Axotus (Acts 8:39–40).

Christ himself may have evidenced the gliding just above the surface phenomenon when he "walked" on water (Matthew 14 or Mark 6). As a child I puzzled how Jesus "passed through the midst of them" (Luke 4:30) when an angry mob was dragging him up a hill to throw him over a cliff. Today I think this may be an example of the transportation phenomenon.

Throughout this book, as you know, I have tried to focus on bodily phenomena we can legitimately theorize as rooted within the physical potential of the psychospiritually whole— i.e. holy person. The gliding phenomenon falls into this category. Transportation is something else. I cannot speak for Eastern spiritualities or shamanism. But *all* Jewish or Christian sources speak of something happening *to*, not *in*, the sanctified body. Transportation is typically credited by Jews to the direct action of God, by Christians to God in the person of the Holy Spirit or through angels. The only variation on this theme consists of instances when both Jews and Christians feel God acted in response to the intercessory prayers and/or merits of dead relatives or saints.

Now it is true that a Jewish or Christian saint who experiences something does not thereby become infallible in explaining the phenomenon. And this is even more true regarding something like transportation, a phenomenon invariably accompanied by total lack of recall. This amnesia I first thought could be shock following an energy explosion in the psychophysical self which rockets the individual to a desired destination as a total survival response to emergency. Unfortunately for my effort to situate the phenomenon *within* the saint, transportation does not always take place in emergencies. In all honesty then, I must say that with this phenomenon of the sanctified body, we *may* have reached the end of psychospiritual bodily potential and entered the realm of the flatly supernatural event.

▲

In the first chapter on the classical type of levitation, I mentioned the seventeenth-century Sienese Capuchin nun Passitea Crogi, as a well-verified indication that levitation is neither just a biblical nor a modern phenomenon among Catholics. Passitea can fulfill the same function for this chapter, for "she was often transported from place to place without moving her feet and without touching the ground," says Herbert Thurston, quoting her biographer, "a learned professor of Arabic" with "a quite unusual sense of the value of evidence." As some of that evidence the story is told of Passitea's expedition with another nun, Sister Diodata, on a muddy day. At journey's end Sister Diodata "was covered with mire," while Passitea's feet had somehow covered the same terrain without getting "even a speck" of mud on her.[4]

Now to some nineteenth- and twentieth-century examples. You recall the Benedictine abbot Father Paul, who at times levitated upward in rapture. This saintly abbot also exhibited the second type of levitation, according to a community of nuns he used to visit at Bruges. These sisters said "they noticed that the Rev. Father while passing from one room to another, hardly moved his feet but seemed to glide over the floor rather than step upon it."[5]

Twentieth-century French parish priest Jean Edouard Lamy seems to have experienced both gliding and transportation. He confided:

> I have been . . . brought from one place to another without knowing anything about it. I used to say "My God, how tired I am." I was in my parish [in the town of La Courneuve near Paris] far away, often at night, and I found myself carried to the Place St. Lucian all at once.

One hopes the saint needed to go to the Place St. Lucian! "How it happened I don't know," he insisted, yet on the other he openly credited "the holy angels" with upholding him in his weariness.

In fact to give you the whole scoop, Lamy didn't just credit invisible angels. One of those saints who apparently have expanded sensory abilities (a topic so huge I reserve it for another book), the holy priest openly claimed to intimates to *see* angels. For instance, he said they were there during World War I when he ministered, alone, to whole trainloads of wounded and dying soldiers. And he spoke of something like the phenomenon we are discussing:

> I climbed the whole length of the [train] carriages hand over hand. When I had to go up sixty or eighty times and

> much more . . . the holy angels used to help me. *You do
> not feel heavy to yourself when they are there.*

Claiming to see angels, was this "priest of the ragpickers,"
as Père Lamy was often called for his charity to the poorest of
the poor, perhaps just a dotty old man?

Two bicyclists who ran into him in 1924 on the road from
Rivières-le-Bois to Le Pailly didn't think so. Comte Paul
Biver, Lamy's friend and biographer, heard from villagers of
the tale these two were telling in the local cafés and saloons,
for which they were called liars, even drunkards. Biver got the
saint's side from Père Lamy, who explained that one evening
just before sunset, when the low sun makes it harder to see, he
was walking back to town from the shrine of Our Lady of the
Woodlands:

> I bent my head, leaning forward so as not to have the
> sun rays in my eyes. I therefore saw nothing, half blind as
> I am [Sight in his right eye was lost in his soldiering days,
> and his left eye seriously weakened by poison gases when
> he ministered to almost a thousand wounded during a
> 1918 disaster]. . . . of what was . . . in my path. Sud-
> denly there rose against me . . . a cyclist. I should have
> been knocked down in one turn of the wheel, but lo, the
> holy archangel Gabriel seized the bicycle by the two
> wheels and put it neatly on one side. He lifted the bicycle
> and the rider, and put them both down on the grass that
> fringes the road. Weight is nothing to an archangel. They
> find everything so easy! I saw the cyclist standing open-
> mouthed, looking at the angel and at me. I had a mad
> impulse to laugh, seeing the face of the poor boy.

Hurriedly the old priest went on his way as the bicyclist
kept shouting "like a madman" to a companion cyclist who

was coming up fast, "There are two of them! There are two of them!"

Lamy told Biver that, yes, he had been asked questions about the incident but he "pretended not to understand."

I dare no comments.

At certain times, perhaps when he was in mild states of ecstasy (from one description of "the air of happiness on his face"), onlookers witnessed the seventy-year-old Lamy walking at a speed of about eight miles per hour despite the fact that he suffered from heart disease so severe he could normally only shuffle along with a cane. The aged priest "who dragged his feet so painfully . . . and seemed out of breath after the least walk" also raced up a muddy, slippery hill that others were afraid to tackle, prayed at the top, then sped down as fast as he went up. Interrogated by his companions as to how he had done this, he credited it to the intercession of a saint, adding, "It is a mark of mercy from this holy priest [St. Peter Fourier] to an old scallywag, who isn't worth the trouble."[6]

Thurston tells of a Sister Marie della Passione (d. 1912) who moved in a similar fashion, according to a letter dated June 3, 1913, by a nun of her community. Sister Maria Prassedes writes:

> I was still a novice and on those last occasions when Suor Maria della Passione was able to come down to the choir to receive Holy Communion, the Rev. Mother Superior bade me take her back to her cell, because, as she was so ill, she had to return to bed almost immediately after Communion was given her. Well, no sooner had we left the choir together than I noticed that the servant of God, though she was in a most suffering state, mounted the stairs in an instant, as if she flew on wings, while I, though I was in perfect health, could not keep pace with her; so much so that it seemed to me that she never touched the

> ground but that she really flew up the flight of stairs
> which led to her cell.[7]

In over a decade of inquiries I have been unable to run down
this Sister Marie, so I can offer only Father Thurston's reputation as verification that she and the witness's letter are genuine.

Because of the nature of this phenomenon, some incidents
are not only unwitnessed but so equivocal that the temptation
is to drop them, in spite of the fact that they may, of course, be
genuine. Let me give two examples so you can see for yourself
how impossible it is to separate the ordinary, adrenalin-
sparked escape from transportation:

While still a laywoman, Margaret Hallahan, who later
founded an English congregation of Dominican nuns, used to
go about England's factory towns at night visiting the workers,
the sick, and the poverty-stricken.

> One snowy night [in 1842 or 1843] she was coming
> home alone. The road was unfrequented and indescribably
> dirty, while at one side lay a large, unfenced pond. Marga-
> ret made a false step in the dark and found herself strug-
> gling in the mud and ice of the pond; she had absolutely
> lost all sense of direction and in the darkness ahead lay
> death. She had recourse to prayer. Then somehow, she did
> not know how, she found herself again on the footpath.
> She came home drenched with water up to the waist and
> could never say how she had passed this dangerous spot,
> though she always retained the impression that she had
> been supernaturally carried through it.[8]

I wrote the English Dominicans founded by Mother Margaret. They do not think there is anything to fuss about in her
experience. In other words, they vote for adrenalin. Yet
Mother Margaret thought there was something more and

Margaret was a tough, slum-bred cookie, not some pious soul prone to overly fertile imaginings. In the end, I can neither say this is transportation—nor can I swear it isn't.

The second example, even more equivocal, concerns a saint in whom the highest mystical phenomena mingled with the most down-to-earth practical abilities. Italian-born Frances Cabrini (1850–1917) was a penniless woman who built hospitals, schools, and orphanages in strange countries as if it were all just another day's work. Yet this modern business genius could also, like some medieval saint, make the sign of the cross over a burning orphanage and put out the fire. Or buy property for a song because every modern means of finding water had failed, point "There" after prayer and uncover an abundant supply.

As a child, this woman who would become America's first citizen saint was playing alone on the banks of the Venera River. Into a tiny boat she deposited violets, pretending they were missionaries on their way to China, something she hoped to be herself in a few years. Wading out too far to shove her boats into the swift-moving current, the little girl lost her balance. She could not swim and there was no one around. As the water spun her away, she suddenly felt unseen arms lift her and set her gently on the ground a few feet away from the riverbank. Cabrini apparently believed this was a supernatural experience, and biographers have made much of it. Her spiritual daughters, as unpretentious as the saint herself, make no claims: They simply state the saint was never able to recall how she got from the swift waters to the bank.[9] Since mental blankness seems to invariably accompany transportation and can also be part of shock, this detail again neither proves nor disproves Cabrini's feeling that she had not saved herself.

Hopefully these two incidents clarify why neither we—nor sometimes the saints themselves—can be sure who was transported and who was not.

One saint who actually left us his own account of such an

unwitnessed experience is St. Anthony Claret (1807–70), an energetic and eminently practical, successful young Spanish businessman who set financial success aside to become a priest and eventually a leading figure in the spiritual revival in nineteenth-century Spain. In a chapter of his autobiography with the very modern title "Why I Gave Up Manufacturing," the saint writes:

> Because I had been working so hard, I didn't feel very well during the summer. I began to lose all appetite, and the only relief I could find was to go down to the sea, wade in it, and drink a few drops of the salt water. One day as I was walking along the beach on my way to the "old sea" on the other side of La Barceloneta, a huge wave suddenly engulfed me and carried me out to sea. I saw in a moment that I was far from shore, and I was amazed to see that I was floating on the surface, although I didn't know how to swim. I called out to the Blessed Virgin and found myself on shore without having swallowed even a drop of water. While I was in the water, I had felt exceedingly calm, but afterwards, on shore, I was horrified at the thought of the danger I had escaped through the help of the Blessed Virgin.[10]

South African-born Pentecostal minister David du Plessis (1905–87) was a pivotal figure in twentieth-century ecumenism whom *Time* once characterized as "one of the most prominent Christian leaders in the world." In his autobiography he tells of experiencing transportation. Du Plessis relates that he was once reconciling two estranged members of a Pentecostal congregation when:

> I heard the Lord speaking clearly to me, "You are wanted at that house, at once."
> "I can't be there at once," I said in my mind. . . . I

turned to the two men. "Brethren, I've just heard from the Lord, I believe, and he says I am needed at that house. Now that you two are reconciled, I'll go on and you can come more leisurely. I'll run as fast as I can."

And I walked quickly away. From the side of the house I went to the front and made a right turn toward the gate. It was in a hedge of trees. As I moved quickly toward it, I thought to myself, "It's about a mile. If I go to the right, it's in the middle of the block, then uphill and around some other houses. If I go to the left, it's more level and I can run faster."

This all happened in two or three seconds. I went through the gate, and heard it click behind me. I turned left, the level way. And that's all I can remember. When I lifted my foot to run, I put it down at the front door of the man's house.

I stood still for a moment. "How did I get here? Where did I come from? I can't remember anything. Did I go to sleep?"

Entering the house, du Plessis discovered he had indeed been needed—and needed at once. No sooner was his work there accomplished then

one of the men [present] heard a knock and went to open the door. In a few moments I heard voices, loud and agitated. I went to the door and there were my two friends. "This brother says you've been here twenty minutes," one exclaimed, turning toward me. "We've just now arrived. You left us twenty minutes ago. How could you be here twenty minutes?"

"Well," I said, "I've been here some time. I wouldn't know the exact time."

. . . [Someone] interrupted. "When David walked into the room with the Bible in his hand, I looked at my watch.

And when you folks came, I looked again. Twenty minutes had passed."

"But how can that be?" they almost yelled.

"Well, I don't know," I said. "I ran."

"Which way did you run. We saw you go. You told us you were going to run, and we heard the gate click. And when we got to the gate, we looked to the right and there was no David. We looked to the left. No David. We thought you had gone into the house, so we opened the door and shouted. But they said they hadn't seen you."

I shrugged my shoulders. They charged on. "We decided we'd walk on, and when we come we find you're already here—and have been here twenty minutes! Impossible!"

It was then that I realized I must have been transported by the Holy Spirit.

David ends his detailed account by recalling another Protestant leader he knew who was transported and whose followers were so impressed that, in a manner of speaking, "they began to worship the man." It ruined him, du Plessis added soberly.[11]

St. Anthony Claret called on the Mother of Christ to intercede with God when he was swept out to sea. When he was in need, twentieth-century Hasidic Rabbi Israel Spira* also sought intercessors. Spira was an unwilling participant in one of those devilish games played in Nazi concentration camps by SS men and collaborators. In the middle of the night prisoners were suddenly rousted from their vermin-infested barracks. Exhausted by slave labor, disease, and malnutrition, they were ordered to jump across an enormous pit. Those who landed in the crater would be machine-gunned. Among the prisoners, the rabbi waited his turn with a friend, a nonbeliever who said, according to the account in *Hasidic Tales of the Holocaust:*

* Ninety-seven years old in 1989, this Hasidic master resides in Brooklyn, New York.

"Spira, all of our efforts to jump over the pits are in vain. We only entertain the Germans and their collaborators . . . Let's sit down in the pits and wait for the bullets to end our wretched existence." . . .

"My friend," said the rabbi, . . . "man must obey the will of God. If it was decreed from heaven that pits be dug and we be commanded to jump, pits will be dug and jump we must. And if, God forbid, we fail . . . we will reach the World of Truth a second later, after our attempt. So, my friend, we must jump."

The rabbi and his friend were nearing the edge of the pits . . . [which] were rapidly filling up with bodies.

The rabbi glanced down at his feet, the swollen feet of a fifty-three-year-old Jew ridden with starvation and disease. He looked at his young friend, a skeleton with burning eyes.

As they reached the pit, the rabbi closed his eyes and commanded in a powerful whisper, "We are jumping!" When they opened their eyes, they found themselves standing on the other side of the pit.

"Spira, we are here, we are here, we are alive!" the friend repeated over and over again, while warm tears streamed from his eyes. "Spira, for your sake, I am alive; indeed, there must be a God in heaven. Tell me, Rebbe, how did you do it?"

"I was holding on to my ancestral merit. I was holding on to the coattails of my father, and my grandfather and my great-grandfather, of blessed memory," said the rabbi and his eyes searched the black skies above. "Tell me, my friend, how did you reach the other side of the pit?"

"I was holding on to you . . ."[12]

notes

1. From a talk given at the Southern California Renewal Communities conference, Sept. 1988, Anaheim, Calif. Details verified by phone Nov. 1988.

2. Mircea Eliade, *Shamanism: Archaic Techniques of Ecstasy,* pp. 408–11.

3. Michael Harner, *The Way of the Shaman,* p. xviii.

4. Herbert Thurston, *The Physical Phenomena of Mysticism,* p. 29, citing L. Marracci, *Vita della V. M. Passitea Crogi Senese* (Venice, 1682), p. 148.

5. Edward van Speybrouck, *Father Paul of Moll,* p. 156.

6. Paul Biver, *Père Lamy,* pp. 101–3, 172–75.

7. Thurston, op. cit., p. 30, quoting L. M. Fontana, *Vita de la Serva di Dio, Suor Maria della Passione,* 2nd ed. (Sconsaro, 1917), p. 294.

8. S.M.C., *Steward of Souls,* p. 50.

9. Compare, for instance, the biography *Mother Cabrini,* by a Daughter of St. Paul, pp. 20–21, with *Mother Frances Xavier Cabrini,* by one of her spiritual daughters, Mother Savrio de Maria, pp. 28–29.

10. *Autobiography of St. Anthony Mary Claret,* ed. Jose Maria Vinas, p. 21.

11. David du Plessis, *A Man Called Mr. Pentecost,* pp. 84–87.

12. Yaffa Eliach, *Hasidic Tales of the Holocaust,* p. 4.

▲16

bilocation:
what is
it?

Try this riddle: how are saints at times like subatomic particles?

The answer I take from *The Dancing Wu Li Masters,* an
overview of the new physics. A particle, we learn, used to be
thought of as "confined to a region in space." Either here or
there, it certainly could not be in two places simultaneously.
Then came "the astounding discovery" that subatomic particles constantly appear to be making decisions in reaction to
decisions other particles are making as far away as another
galaxy, without even a millisecond intervening.

And that, to answer my riddle, is how some saints *at times*
are like subatomic particles: Both can be found experimentally
to be *here* and in some inexplicable way *simultaneously there*
as well.

The author of *The Dancing Wu Li Masters* postulates "the

philosophical implication of quantum mechanics is that all of the things in our universe (including us) that appear to exist independently are actually parts of one all-encompassing organic pattern. . . . No parts of that pattern are ever really separate," he says.[1]

Mysticism would put it that all that is is so caught up in and sustained by God that space and time (arguably only intellectual constructs after all) in God are not the barriers we imagine.

▲

All that said, we still don't know much about the phenomenon known as bilocation or how it works. The most negative view is that bilocators are psychotics who infect others with their delusions in a kind of group psychosis. To see how this view arises—and it is not related to any particular tradition—let's look at a man whom many of his countrymen in India dismiss as a mental case and con artist, while his supporters swear he is holy, and offer testimonies that he bilocates.

In 1940, when he was fourteen, Sai Baba (born Satyanarayana Raju in 1926), according to the authorized biography put out by his followers,

> gave a shriek and leaped up grasping his right toe as if he had been bitten. Although no scorpion or snake was discovered, he fell as though unconscious and became stiff. He did not speak and his breathing became faint. When such an occurrence happens to Sai Baba now (thirty years later), devotees do not feel shocked, for they are accustomed to his leaving his gross body and going out in the "subtle" body to other places.

"Unconscious" throughout that first night, his spiritual children believe the young boy "was actually supraconscious." As evidence they cite an incident of clairvoyance or bilocation: At the same moment that friends were in a temple that night, offering sacrifice on his behalf, Baba said, "The coconut has broken into three pieces." Shortly the friends returned with three, instead of the usual two, pieces.

> Sathya revived in a day or two, . . . [but there was] a complete transformation of the personality. . . . He sang, spoke, and behaved in a strange manner. Also his body would become stiff intermittently,* and he appeared to leave the body and go elsewhere.
>   . . . The District Medical Officer from Anantapur . . . judged that the illness was allied to fits, that it was a type of hysteria unconnected with the alleged scorpion sting . . . and administered a course of medication. This was strictly adhered to for three days, but the symptoms of laughing and weeping, eloquence and silence continued as before. Sathya sang and spoke about God; he described places of pilgrimage to which no one had gone before; he declared that life was all a drama. Astrologers said it was a ghost that possessed the boy. . . . Magicians ascribed the condition to a sudden fright which must have set Sathya's nerves awry. The priest advised . . . a consecration rite in the temple.[2]

This is only a portion of the long account by those for whom Sai Baba is spiritual mentor of the theories and treatments bruited about before some people concluded the teenager was a remanifestation of a dead holy man who must be revered, not medicated. In spite of the brevity of my extract from the English-language biography published by his followers, in which

---

* This catatonic state can be a symptom of severe mental illness *or* of spiritual experience. As Evelyn Underhill points out in *Mysticism,* [p. 360] the ecstatic body state by itself tells us nothing: All depends on *content.*

they so lucidly picture what can be equally interpreted as a "breakthrough illness" or a psychotic breakdown, you can see why Baba—like some Catholic inedic bilocators† in the West —is controversial in India. Holy or a nut (one longs for one of those inquiries that are the specialty of the Western mind), Sai Baba is hardly your typical Hindu saint. More important, you can now see how, even in the face of well-attested bilocation accounts by supporters, some people dismiss the phenomenon as group delusion or group psychosis.

Clinging to the fact that at least a goodly number of bilocators have undergone a relentless scrutiny of their mental health, let us turn to other possibilities.

Bilocator Padre Pio explained the phenomenon to someone by saying he was sometimes in two places at the same time by "a prolongation of personality." Bilocation is called by others "visionary participation," which indicates their view that the bilocator sees rather than goes. That makes bilocation a synonym for clairvoyance, the ability to see actions or objects which are physically far removed in space or time. Taking an opposite view, some authorities say bilocation is the ability to induce a vision in a targeted recipient. Now not only does the bilocator not go but the "seeing" is attributed to someone else. In this theory the varied types of bilocation are then categorized under the three classic types of visions: physical, imaginative, and purely intellectual.‡ Of course, how a saint "induces a vision" remains as fuzzy as how one "prolongs personality." Also unclear is how one knows, if one only induces a vision, that it succeeds.

† I think particularly of American Rose Ferron, whose supporters have amassed at least 2,000 pages of testimonies, including well-attested reports of bilocations and healings but whose bishop refuses all discussion of her case, implying either that he dismisses inedic, stigmatic visionaries in general or that he has evidence she was a fraud or a nut. In England, Teresa Higginson's bilocations are also attested by some, scoffed at by others.

‡ For explanations of these, see any standard work on mysticism, such as Anglican Evelyn Underhill's *Mysticism.*

A once-esteemed, now frowned-on early nineteenth-century Catholic visionary from Westphalia took another tack. Anne Catherine Emmerich (1774–1824), who allegedly bilocated frequently, said "the [guardian] angel calls me and I follow him. . . . He takes me among persons whom I know either well or slightly, and again among others who are entire strangers. We cross the sea as quickly as thought travels."[3]

But how did she follow? Is the sea crossed "as quickly as thought" because this is all in the head? Shamans often speak, in terms similar to Anne Catherine's, of journeys with spirit guides. Sometimes shamanistic "trips" are drug-induced (which I realize doesn't automatically prove they aren't real bilocations). And researchers now know the brain can send us on trips too. Besides flying-type sensations (see f.n., p. 16), stimulating the proper area of the brain can give individuals *sensations* of "divided consciousness." These may be the "witnessing oneself" experienced in the out-of-body experience. Or the sensation may be that of being in two places at once.

To know the brain can do this helps distinguish the false bilocation from the true. But it doesn't explain true mystical bilocation in which a second party, who is in good mental health, identifies the presence of a saint in a second place while someone (besides the bilocator) confirms the saint has not left a primary location. Nor does it shed light on events such as inexplicable healings that may "confirm" the visit.

In understanding bilocation I personally get farthest when I start from the way love intuitively recognizes no barrier of time and space, permitting us to somehow *be with* those we love wherever they are. From this stance I find the phenomenon simpler to grasp—and comforting in its implications. Just as luminosity can be seen as a sanctified degree of the bride's joyful radiance and levitation as a holy extension of the natural jump for joy, bilocation in this view appears to be the ultimate in a human ability that expresses itself at lower levels in extrasensory perception (ESP).

With ESP members of our human family project feelings of need or concern to somehow touch those not present. A typical example: One is depressed, and a much-loved cousin not heard from in months phones saying, "I woke up feeling I'd better call you." Infrequently ESP can even include the form of psychic projection known as the out-of-body experience (OOBE). My friend Marlene O'Neil recalls a time when she had just put her feet up for a few moments rest in a Minnesota employees' lounge where two other people were chatting. Fully conscious of their conversation—although she appeared to be dozing to observers—Marlene felt herself rise in a white mist out of her body and look down on the scene from above. The next instant she was looking down on her mother's home in California and her mother was crying. Moments later, back in her body and "awake," she placed a long-distance call. Her mother picked up the phone—crying.

Because of such episodes, nonsaints may be called bilocators too—with two important qualifying remarks. First, it appears nonsaints bilocate only in the lower, that is, psychic, or nonphysical modes. Second, their bilocations are strictly within the confines of normal ESP attachments: mother and child, spouses, or other intimates. Only very infrequently, if ever, will an OOB type ESP like Marlene O'Neil's occur with someone known only slightly or with someone tied to one by birth or marriage but not particularly liked. And I have never heard of such things occurring with someone not known at all or for whom one had strong negative feelings and no special ties.

The bilocations of the holy show saints tap into a rarer and more latent human ability than ordinary ESP. Always at the call of God, the saint projects more of herself, as we will see; most important, she projects more broadly in love and service to even those personally unknown but loved in God.

If we are talking of a human ability—even one so rare it occurs in its full-blown form only in the saints—the *concept* of bilocation should be found in various traditions. And it is.

I have mentioned the spirit-guided journeys of shamanistic spiritualities. In shamanistic traditions there are also journeys of one's own spirit without guides. In 1889 Oglala Sioux mystic Black Elk (b. 1863) experienced what he would later call a spirit journey. In Paris as part of a Wild West show and pining for home, one day as he sat at a table in some French friends' home, he suddenly felt the house and all in it, including himself, caught up. Transferred to a cloud, he was carried, he says, over lands and the ocean until eventually

> I was right over Pine Ridge [South Dakota], and the cloud stopped. I looked down and could not understand what I saw, because it seemed that nearly all of my people of the different bands were gathered. . . . I saw my father's and mother's tepee. They were outside, and she was cooking. I wanted to jump off the cloud . . . but I was afraid it would kill me. While I was looking down, my mother looked up, and I felt sure she saw me. But just then the cloud started back, going very fast. I was very sad but I could not get off.

After a return over land and the ocean, Black Elk was transferred once again from the cloud to the house, which settled again on the earth. The moment it touched ground, he came to normal consciousness in a sickbed. He was told that, sitting at breakfast, he had looked up and smiled, then fallen like one dead from his chair. For three days* his friends had only occasionally been able to find any breath or heartbeat. He told these non-Indians nothing because he felt they would not understand. Because of his "illness" he was given a ticket home. After a long journey by ship and train, he hitched a ride in a

---

* Time in mystical experiences is often experienced as being much briefer than its duration in nonmystical reality.

mule-drawn wagon and so returned to the reservation. He reports:

> When I got to Pine Ridge, everything was just as I had seen it from the cloud. All the Lakotas were there, as I had seen them, because that was the year of the treaty (1889). . . . I had been away nearly three years and knew nothing about this foolish thing until then.
>
> My mother's tepee was right where I had seen it when I looked down from the cloud, and other people were camped exactly where I saw them.
>
> My parents were in great joy to see me and my mother cried because she was so happy. I cried too. . . . My mother told me she had dreamed one night . . . that I had come back on a cloud, but could not stay. So I told her about my vision.[4]

Besides recognition by shamanistic peoples, the idea of somehow being in two locations predates Christianity as one of the recognized yogic powers mentioned in the Yoga Sutra of Patanjali in the second century before Christ. Paramahansa Yogananda's autobiography, for instance, devotes several pages to the bilocation of another Hindu, Swami Pranabananda. Yogananda says he was visiting Pranabananda when the latter, in meditation before his eyes, apparently personally delivered a message at that moment to someone else. On another occasion Yogananda tells how his personal mentor, holy man Sri Yukteswar, appeared to him in Serampore while Yukteswar was either en route there by train or still in Calcutta. Stunned by the sudden appearance of his guru in a room with an iron-barred window and a closed door, Yogananda writes:

> Bewildered to the point of shock, I rose from my chair and knelt before him. With my customary gesture of re-

spectful greetings at my guru's feet, I touched his shoes. These were a pair familiar to me, of orange-dyed canvas, soled with rope. His ocher swami cloth brushed against me: I distinctly felt not only the texture of his robe, but also the gritty surface of the shoes, and the pressure of his toes within them.[5]

After delivering a message, Sri Yukteswar disappeared with his hand on Yogananda's head in blessing. As the saint faded out, the hand could be felt until it, too, vanished.

Black Elk, Sri Yukteswar, and Padre Pio situate bilocation in a context of universal human experience. To situate the varied forms of this phenomenon (you have noted that Sri Yukteswar's is much more "physical" than young Black Elk's) in some sort of context, let us look at a few phenomena found within Western society. Each is generally below what one can legitimately call bilocation but is perhaps related.

Contact with others through ESP has already been mentioned. Its reality is so generally accepted I need say nothing more on the topic, except to add that as we saw (p. 316), psychic contact may include OOBE with a low-level bilocation.

The next most common phenomenon is the out-of-body experience unrelated to ESP contact with a loved other. Reported in books like Raymond Moody's *Life After Life,* this OOBE is most frequently experienced when very ill or near death. Here the individual finds herself hovering in spirit above the body, perhaps watching efforts to revive it. There are also OOBE unrelated to illness. These usually occur in ecstatic states. Mystic Bl. Henry Suso (1295–1365), for instance, reported he momentarily lost the ability to tell whether he was in or out of his body in his rapturous contemplation of God's splendors. More commonly an individual suddenly experiences a dissolution of ego barriers or personal boundaries to become for a brief time at one with the natural world, all other people, and/or God. Clinical psychologist David Lukoff of San Francisco's Saybrook Institute says studies "consistently found that over one-third of the people in the United States report intense religious experiences which 'lifted them out of themselves.' "[6] Numerous individual testimonies of such experiences exist. Protestant healer Agnes Sanford's twentieth-century account from her teenage years in China is a good example of becoming one with nature†; William James's *Varieties of Religious Experience* and Evelyn Underhill's *Mysticism* both have examples of the specifically God-related type of experience. In some opinions, the OOBE also gets scientific support from studies on its psychophysiological aspects by Charles T. Tart at the University of California at Davis.[7]

In the OOBE related to near death, one *feels* physically outside the body but psychically is self-concerned. In the second type of OOBE, there is a total psychophysical enlargement of one's boundaries with no sense of physical placement whatsoever. Both types of OOBE are relevant to bilocation in the same way: They show a human ability to move out from the boundary of the psychophysical self.

Another category, perhaps slightly related to bilocation but again not close enough to bear the name, is that of the *willed* projection of some nonphysical portion of the self. This seems to happen most often among psychically gifted individuals like Sheila Kalivas, a psychologist friend of mine who once tried projection as an experiment. Telling no one what she was going to do, Sheila lay on her bed and concentrated on "sending herself" to the bedroom in a neighboring home where one of her daughters was sleeping over with a playmate. Eventually she simply fell asleep. However the next morning at the neighbor's, Sheila's daughter's playmate asked her own mother, who is the same height, same build, and also has long blond

† See *Sealed Orders* (p. 29), where she says, "There was no more *me.*"

316

hair like Sheila's, "Mom, why were you standing in the door of my room like that last night? You scared me."

Beyond the psychic experience like Sheila's is a murky area of individuals who seek recognition as "astral projectors." Their first-person accounts often reveal individuals caught up in something from curiosity or looking for excitement—and perhaps the healthy profits their books bring—more than a desire to advance human knowledge or serve others. Like the OOBE of the desperately ill where one hovers over one's body, "astral projecting" is a self-absorbed phenomenon which literally usually fails to get very far geographically. In his *Journeys Out of the Body* self-titled projector Robert A. Monroe reported frustrating attempts to let people know he was there.‡ In a laboratory Monroe was found when "projecting" to be in a state that physiologically resembles the dreaming stage of sleep. Considering that this type of projector is generally neither seen nor heard and by laboratory test appears to be asleep, I don't think it unduly skeptical to propose a lot of these projections (perhaps tapping the limbic brain area) are vivid dreams. Information gained in such cases could be by ESP or clairvoyance, which is not that uncommon for certain types of people in dreams.

I don't say conclusively such projectors never get anywhere, however, for two reasons. The first deals with certain yogis. (I do not speak here of Hindu saints. Patanjali is adamant in the Yoga Sutra that all miraculous powers must be renounced if one is to achieve the highest union with God. When a Hindu saint bilocates, this is, as with all saints, a by-product of the search for God, not a deliberate goal.) Not yet saints, these yogis I speak of are highly disciplined individuals who hone the body to its maximum psychophysical potential as part of the thrust toward God. Hindu authorities I spoke to at the

---

‡ In his two best efforts, he says someone saw something vaporish, and the second felt and was bruised by an invisible pinch. He gives no corroboration from either person.

Hindu temple in Calabasas, California, tell me this includes trying to project. Are they successful, I asked?

"To a very limited degree," was my answer. Paradoxically, as with Western saints, I am told those who eventually succeed in full-fledged bilocation are those who, along the way, drop that goal to seek God instead. Granted, the yogi projector's motive is above that of projectors like Robert A. Monroe, who says he pursued projection primarily for fun and adventure. But if even one yogi learned to project, even on low levels closer to ESP than bilocation, I can't say conclusively that someone like Monroe or Sylvan Muldoon,* another self-proclaimed projector, never succeeded in piercing the body's psychophysical boundaries.

The extremely limited achievements of psychic projectors accomplish one thing at least. They highlight the yogis' finding that the highest psychophysical achievements of our human family, such as bilocation, take place only on the level of spiritual development where ego motives have given way to the search for God alone.

The next type of projector has two things in common with the mystical bilocator. First, a natural psychic, he *discovers* rather than tries to induce projecting abilities. Second and most important, he chooses to use this morally neutral gift to help others.

The most famous recent psychic of this sort is Edgar Cayce (1877–1945), whose paternal grandfather and mother both had psychic capabilities, indicating an inherited talent. Cayce discovered he could go into a kind of sleep and somehow psychically "visit" an ill person hundreds of miles away. He penetrated within the malfunctioning body, it was said, diagnosing its condition and prescribing treatment by answering questions put to him in his comatose state. It is also said many people improved dramatically by following his advice. During World

---

* Author of *The Projection of the Astral Body,* with Hereward Carrington.

War II Cayce gave many of these "readings" for anxious wives and mothers, seemingly able to project himself all over the globe. Always, when he awoke he knew nothing of where he had "been" or what he had said unless he read the transcript a secretary made.†

The best way to see how the high-order bilocation towers above this high-level psychic projection is to contrast Cayce's projections with Padre Pio's bilocations.

Characteristics of Cayce's projections are (1) a deep trance; (2) no one aware of his presence in the place to which he projected; (3) on awakening he had no idea of what he had done or said; (4) the projection was on his own initiative for a purpose of his own, generally to help someone else but not excluding help for himself or for someone in his family; (5) the manner of his psychic projection never varied; and (6) although he "slept," the sessions were energy-draining.

By the time of his spiritual maturity Padre Pio's bilocations frequently (1) showed themselves on the home end no more than an apparent moment of abstraction. (2) In the place to which he bilocated, his presence was known; often he was not only heard and seen but experienced in all ways, including touch, as physically present. (3) By his own statement, he knew what he was doing while he bilocated and afterward had complete recall. (4) He said that God sent him where God willed for God's purposes. If it was a case of the sick, his visit was not for diagnosis. He either came to comfort and spiritually help the dying or the visit announced healing. Having given himself to the service of the human family, he seemed to renounce obtaining special help for his birth family. He rarely bilocated on behalf of relatives,‡ and his infrequent bilocations of a personal nature seemed to take place within a spiritual context. For instance, he was seen in a Naples church listening

† Almost unintelligible, these are disappointing reading.
‡ He did bilocate to the deathbeds of several relatives, but not to heal them.

to a sermon and at St. Peter's in Rome praying at a dead saint's tomb. Whether such jaunts were on his own initiative or a "gift of God" is unknown. (5) The manner of his bilocations varied greatly. Often he was physically present; a few times his disembodied voice boomed out; on many occasions he revealed his presence only by the odor of sanctity; and oddest of all, there are instances when he was apparently fully visible to one person in a group while invisible to others. At times he is said to have carried objects with him that he left with those he visited, and at least once there is excellent evidence that he carried an object away. (6) He did not evidence or ever comment that these travels were any more draining than his normal contacts with people.*

Different as the high-level psychic projection and the full-fledged bilocation are, they may build on the same human sensitivity. As I see it all the phenomena this chapter has looked at point to a latent human ability to pierce one's psychophysical boundaries. Typically, when it actualizes, this latent power takes "psychic" forms. But at the outer boundaries of human development—i.e., sanctity—it may, with a supernatural nudge, become bilocation. Imagine a continuum. Willed projections of one's spirit for power or fun, the most egotistical, would be the lowest level. Unplanned ESP experiences would be next, as these are often not of great import. Above them I would rank the OOBE of the near death, followed by the mystical OOBE, for these peak experiences are spiritually enlarging. Rarer would be inborn neutral psychic ability of unusual magnitude when it is used in the service of humanity. Last, the sanctified body, in the grip of God's towering love, knows no boundaries of time, space, or concern.

---

* We do not know enough yet to distinguish among the types of ecstatic trance. Cade's limited work in this area reveals there are varied types, just as other research (p. 7) shows the yoga prayer "trance" differs greatly from the Zen meditative state. Ecstasy experienced by mystics is life-enhancing and energizing, but whether this is the same trance bilocators experience is unknown. Personally, I doubt it is.

But is the bilocator, then, merely some kind of holy psychic? Not in the crucial sense of having, like Cayce, an inherited gift. Bilocators range from those like Theresa Neumann, born without any psychic tendencies whatsoever, to individuals like Swiss physician Adrienne von Speyr, who was strongly psychic even as a child. Most individuals seem to become psychic, at least to a degree, as they approach holiness. But not all who become psychic, as evidenced by gifts such as reading hearts or foretelling the future, become bilocators. Even among saints bilocation remains a rare phenomenon (although those who do bilocate seem to bilocate frequently).

One wishes a group of psychologists and psychiatrists specializing in mysticism could be formed. Perhaps they could sort out which bilocators had psychic gifts preceding holiness or were unusually empathetic as children.† To correlate the presence and degree of these two factors with the presence and degree of bilocation in the full-blown saint might be instructive. At present we have no data of this nature. But research on nonsaints does exist which will be of interest.

Investigating the levels of human psychospiritual development for his hierarchy of states of awareness, C. Maxwell Cade found so-called psychic events can occur at any level of development. To me this indicates the hereditary factor.

Specific experiments testing clairvoyance (which, you recall, some link to bilocation) and other psychic abilities such as telepathy and precognition showed that although differences remained very strong, individuals' psychic abilities could be increased. Helps were relaxation aids, meditation, and exercises to increase empathy. The last item I find significant, for it implies that as one develops compassion or love in the broad spiritual sense of the word—the foremost virtue of sanctity— one tends to become more psychic.

Psychic abilities, then, seem both to be inherited and, as the

† Padre Pio and Adrienne von Speyr, for two, certainly were.

children's ditty puts it, "to grow as the rest of you grows." This meshes with the contention of mystics of various traditions that increased psychic abilities can be expected as a by-product or "periphery benefit," as Cade puts it, of spiritual growth. Cade also found that at the moment of ESP, performers' electroencephalograms showed brain wave patterns of a high state of consciousness. From his experimental work, the English psychologist believes that "paranormal ability and psychic events . . . [are] a concomitant" of the state of consciousness just above the highest for which he has objective electroencephalographic data.[8] Unfortunately the shortage of holy laboratory specimens makes this difficult to verify experimentally.

Cade's work supports my view that bilocation is related to the human ESP factor not through heredity but in the sense that ESP develops into something rarer at the highest levels of mystical attainment—and in that sense may be regarded as a pure gift of God.

▲

Umbrellaed under the term "bilocation" are a wide variety of phenomena. In some the body appears totally involved, in others the extension of self appears partly physical and partly psychic, and finally there are events at times termed bilocations that appear only psychic. Although this is a book about bodily phenomena, I will give examples of all three types as the only way to do justice to this complex phenomenon. For one thing, there are no neat divisions between "pure" bilocation and mental or sensory phenomena such as clairvoyance or certain types of visions.

But only the more physical forms of dual presence do I consider full-fledged bilocation. As always, there is no correlation of these higher levels with greater sanctity. The same bilocator may bilocate in both very physical and less physical ways.

Oglala Sioux holy man Black Elk's experience, for instance, could be termed a bilocation *or* a vision. He himself, as far as I can tell (since he spoke no English and had to use a translator to share his mystical experiences), called it both a spirit journey and a vision. Below full-fledged bilocation because of his total inability to function at his primary location, Black Elk's experience shows the link I posit between bilocation and ESP contact. The young‡ Oglala Sioux's mother dreamed she saw him on a cloud, while he, experiencing himself as looking down from a cloud, felt she saw him. This is the indirect, shadowy, nonphysical contact of ESP. Black Elk's spirit journey also points up the difficulty of distinguishing the lesser types of bilocation from expanded sensory ability—i.e., far-seeing or the brain state of the so-called visionary.

Now look again (pp. 318–19) at the bilocation of Hindu saint Sri Yukteswar. This type of bilocator is seen and talked to. His physical presence can be demonstrated tactilely as in Yogananda's experience of Yukteswar's hand and toes. This kind of full physical presence is what I call full-fledged bilocation. We will see testimonies that such bilocators may transport material objects from one of their locations to the other.

In between the types of bilocations represented here by Black Elk and Sri Yukteswar are many with mixed elements. For instance, bilocators have appeared against a wall as if projected from a camera and yet spoken. They apparently come in odd dreams as well. In *Nothing Short of a Miracle* I told of an incident involving St. Frances Cabrini, who was in Chicago in the days of travel by slow steamer. An ill nun Mother Cabrini had several years earlier nursed through smallpox in Brazil fell asleep in that South American country with cold compresses on her aching head. She "dreamed" Mother Cabrini appeared

‡ He was nowhere near the height of his spiritual powers.

and, removing the compresses, said, "Why are you lying here, daughter? Get up and go about your duties." Immediately she awoke well. Just a dream—but the compresses, which no one had touched, were gone.[9]

At his primary location, the bilocator's condition may vary greatly: in general, the closer to a psychic projection, the more there is apt to be a deep trance; the more "physical" the bilocation, the less that occurs. To have observers fear one is "dead," as was the case with Black Elk's psychic projection, is rare. For the bilocator to be in a lighter ecstatic trance is common.

For the mystical bilocator not to know where he or she went (as happened with Edgar Cayce) appears extremely rare. I would be surprised if it ever occurs in a full-fledged bilocation. However, in some of the phenomena that are only close to bilocation or its lower forms, I would not want to insist unconsciousness could never occur. For instance Episcopalian healer Agnes Sanford says in *The Healing Gifts of the Spirit:*

> The Lord has . . . guided me to a broader and more subtle way of prayer. It baffles me in a way, because I cannot tell what my spirit does and whither it goes. But that it does travel and that God does work through my spiritual* body even when my mind is quite unaware of it, becomes more and more apparent.[10]

Two other odd cases will be enough to indicate something of the variety and complexity of the question of consciousness at bilocation's lower levels.

Jacinta Marto (1910–20) and the still-living Lucia Abodora were two of three children many Catholics believe repeatedly saw the Virgin Mary at Fatima, Portugal, in 1917. Children though they were, all three gave themselves to God more to-

---

* Note there is nothing physical involved.

tally than many adults. About that time Lucia's cousin, a brilliant but erratic boy, "was missing for weeks" until Jacinta began praying for him. A few days later he was home. Lucia, today a Carmelite nun, reports:

> He told us that, after having spent all that he had stolen from his parents, he wandered about . . . like a tramp until for some reason I have now forgotten, he was put in jail at Torres Novas. . . . He succeeded in escaping one night and fled to the remote hills and unfamiliar pine groves. Realizing that he had completely lost his way, and torn between his fear of being captured and the darkness of the stormy night, he . . . [fell] on his knees [and] . . . began to pray. Some minutes had passed, he affirmed, when Jacinta appeared to him, took him by the hand and led him to the main road which runs from Alqueidao to Reguengo, making a sign for him to continue in that direction. When morning dawned, he found himself on the road to Boleiros. Recognizing the place, . . . he was overcome with emotion and directed his steps straight home to his parents.

Lucia says she asked Jacinta "if it was true that she had gone there to guide him." The little girl replied that she had no idea of the pine woods and hills where he'd been lost. Then she explained, "I only prayed and pleaded very much with Our Lady for him because I felt so sorry for Aunt Vitoria" (the missing boy's frantic mother).

Lucia ends her account: "How then did it happen? I don't know. Only God knows."[11]

In his diary Father Joseph Naber, the parish priest of Theresa Neumann, wrote on May 8, 1931:

> A complete stranger told me yesterday that on Saturday, because of a seemingly unbearable moral and eco-

nomic crisis, he had been on the point of taking his own life. Then Theresa suddenly appeared to him and her warning was enough to keep him from suicide.

When she was in one of her various ecstatic states, Fr. Naber questioned Theresa about what he took for a bilocation. But the Bavarian stigmatic claimed her guardian angel had taken her form to save the suicidal man.[12]

So much for the unresolvable question of consciousness at the phenomenon's lower levels. At least there is no question about the higher levels of bilocation. There, consciousness is total. No deep trance is necessary. The bilocator may appear abstracted for a moment but otherwise continue with his normal activities in apparent† normal consciousness. In the ultimate form of this phenomenon, he *may* go right on talking and working at the primary site while doing the same at the second.

Let me close this chapter with an example of this sort of thing, certainly one of the rarest of human experiences.

Spokesperson for the witnesses is Biagio Valentini, himself known for miracles and holiness. Valentini succeeded St. Gaspar del Bufalo as head of the religious community Gaspar founded. Translated from the Italian, here is Valentini's first-person testimony from the archives of their order:

> I found myself working with him [Gaspar] on a parish mission and in the same church where I was hearing confessions. While I was fulfilling this ministry, about 11 o'clock, there arose a disturbance. Individuals were going back and forth from outdoors into the church and then back out again. They were curious to see whether the Canon [a title of Gaspar's] who was in the confessional

---

† See pp. 15–16 regarding the difficulty in identifying the actual levels of consciousness (there may be more than one at once) in a saint.

was not also preaching at the same time outside in the piazza. With their own eyes they observed this marvelous thing: that the Canon was at the same time both here and there.[13]

Claiming God's guidance is cheap. Many people—including a lot of nuts—do it. But if I find a key to projections of this magnitude, it seems to lie in comments like Agnes Sanford's that say nothing about any decision on her part to pray this way or that but speak matter of factly of God's using her as He wills. If you buy the phenomenon of bilocation in saints, it depicts them, not as men or women putting on a power display, but as humble errand runners for God. Padre Pio once spoke of bilocation briefly to a friend. The phrase he used was "going where God wants." Maybe we'd better let it go at that.

notes

1. Gary Zukaw, *The Dancing Wu Li Masters,* pp. 47–48. See also p. 78.

2. N. Kasturi, *The Life of Bhagavan Sri Sathya Sai Baba,* Vol. 1, pp. 37–41.

3. Carl E. Schmöger, *The Life of Anne Catherine Emmerich,* Vol. 1, p. 71.

4. John G. Neihardt, *Black Elk Speaks,* pp. 191–94.

5. Paramahansa Yogananda, *Autobiography of a Yogi,* p. 216.

6. David Lukoff, "The Diagnosis of Mystical Experiences with Psychotic Features," p. 158.

7. See Tart's articles in *Journal of the American Society for Psychical Research,* 62:1 (Jan. 1968), pp. 3–27; and *International Journal of Parapsychology,* Vol. 9 (1967), pp. 251–58.

8. Described in C. Maxwell Cade and Nona Coxhead, *The Awakened Mind.* See particularly pp. 144–51.

9. Sister Maria Pastorelli's testimony for the *Beatification Process* is found in the *Positio super virtutibus,* p. 364, furnished by Sister Ursula of the Saint's Order, Cabrini College, Radnor, Pa.

10. Agnes Sanford, *The Healing Gifts of the Spirit,* p. 34.

11. Louis Kondor, ed., *Fatima in Lucia's Own Words,* pp. 172–73.

12. Johannes Steiner, *Therese Neumann,* p. 193.

13. Archives of the Congregation of the Most Precious Blood, Rome, furnished by Rev. William Volk. See other bilocations in Amilcare Rey, *Gaspare del Bufalo,* Vol. 2, pp. 489–90, citing the *Process* and other documents.

some
bilocations of
padre pio

B ecause of the holiness the world saw in him, even more than the stigmata he hid as best he could,* Padre Pio was a prisoner of those—of every spiritual persuasion or none—who came to the inaccessible Capuchin friary where he lived, hoping to somehow touch numinous reality through him. To go anywhere from this remote spot in southern Italy is an undertaking. For Pio it was an impossibility. Let there be a rumor he might leave and barricades blocked the road while people from the little town below rushed to cordon off the friary, vowing not to lose "our saint." Except for being driven to the polls to vote, from 1918 to his death in 1968, Padre Pio never left the environs of the friary of Our Lady of Grace. Even his two surgeries were done in the friary.

Yet there are an awful lot of testimonies, as one fellow Cap-

---

* He had, for instance, permission to wear gloves much of the time.

uchin puts it, that during that same half century "Padre Pio was popping up all over the place." As some see it, the saint's back-breaking ministry was further extended by bilocations. Not that Pio consciously learned this skill. He simply found himself sent and obeyed. Due to the immediacy of witnesses who, in most cases, are still alive, I devote this entire chapter to what can only be a minuscule sampling of the bilocations attributed to the stigmatized priest. In particular, I intend to use Padre Pio to show the varied forms this phenomenon may take. While Padre Pio's Cause is still only in progress, the testimonies of many of his bilocations are so complete† I feel they can be presented without qualm. In spite of my efforts‡ to check everything with the Capuchins who knew Pio personally, should one event later prove false, a dozen wait to take its place. Their combined witness that Padre Pio bilocated is the crucial thing, an assertion I find the sheer bulk of evidence makes incontestable.

Among the many sure Padre Pio could be two places at once is Capuchin Agostino Daniele, the saint's intimate friend and confessor. Daniele says a nun in the northern Italian city of Florence told him Padre Pio had appeared to her one day, comforting and blessing her. Skeptical, the next time Daniele went south, he asked Pio about it. Pio only smiled.

"Listen, is it true?" Daniele pressed.

"Yes," Pio admitted.[1]

Pio himself wrote a report in 1905 of what may have been his first bilocation. Far from willed or a planned projection, it appears to have shocked him so much he felt a need to submit the experience to the assessment of his Franciscan spiritual guides. I summarize his account: Praying in the chapel along-

---

† Many with doctors' verification where healing is involved; sometimes other corroborating testimonies, even pertinent photos as in the case of individuals healed of burns or blindness.

‡ At the end of the nineteen eighties, less than half of my correspondence with the friars was reaching them, due to problems in their postal service.

side another friar, the seventeen-year-old seminarian said he "suddenly found myself far away in a wealthy home where the father was dying while a child was being born." Mary, the mother of Christ, appeared as God's messenger, entrusting the spiritual direction of this child to Pio. He was informed he would see her next again in St. Peter's. Afterward she would come to him and he would guide her soul. Then Pio found himself back in the chapel. Imagination? Psychosis?

Corroboration came years later from Leonilde Rizzani, who on that night, 350 miles north of where Pio prayed, gave premature birth to a daughter as the child's father lay dying. Just before labor took the distraught woman by surprise, she suddenly saw a young man in a Capuchin habit kneeling in prayer by the bedside of her unconscious husband. As he abruptly rose and left the room, she followed but he seemed to vanish in thin air.

In 1922 Giovanna, the girl born that night, was in Rome. She went into St. Peter's late one afternoon to go to confession, only to be told that all the priests on duty had left for the day. As she turned to go, a young Capuchin said he would be glad to hear her. She found him a wonderful help with certain theological difficulties, but when she and the friend who accompanied her lingered by the confessional she had just exited to speak to him, no one emerged from the priest's door. Finally a look inside revealed it was empty.

About a year later Giovanna, now in college, went south to see "the holy priest" so many people were talking about. His picture reminded her of the Capuchin confessor but she knew Padre Pio didn't travel. In the mob surrounding Pio, Giovanna was a face among many but to her surprise the saint made his way to her, exclaiming, "Ah Giovanna! I know you. You were born the night your father died."

Startled, the girl—who had never heard of bilocation—could only wonder, as the surging crowd separated them, whether this was an example of those mental gifts one hears saints have. The next day when she entered his confessional, he greeted her with great warmth: "Dear child, at last you've come; I've waited for you many years."

"Excuse me, Padre, you must be mistaking me for someone else," she responded. When he insisted he knew her, she countered she'd never seen him before. Then he told her everything, from her Rome confession to his being asked to guide her soul when she was born. Giovanna was so bewildered she could only wonder aloud, "Does this mean I have to be a nun?" The same year, her mother went to the friary. Her recollections tallied exactly with Pio's report written eighteen years earlier. Assured by Pio that God did not wish her a nun, Giovanna Rizzani married. Today the Marchioness dei Boschi di Cesena, she remains devoted to a spiritual mentor she believes knew her from birth.[2]

A testimony by the Capuchin who in the 1950s headed the friary where Pio lived reveals the saint's "travels" at times could be seen to interfere slightly with his activities. Padre Carmelo tells how he asked Pio to join a group of friars at a concert next door to the friary. Known for his good humor, Pio agreed and seemed to enjoy himself. However during intermission, while others chatted, he seemed tired and put his head down on the seat in front of him for perhaps five minutes.

The next day Padre Carmelo visited an ill man in the neighborhood who said how nice it was that Padre Pio had dropped in the previous evening. Knowing Pio had been at the concert all evening and had returned with the others to the friary, Carmelo asked the time of the visit. The family came up with a time Carmelo found corresponded to those moments Padre Pio seemed to rest.[3]

An American priest, Charles Carty, stayed at the friary for a time to observe Padre Pio, about whom he then wrote a book containing many bilocation testimonies. Carty says:

> I have been able to observe that when one recommends
> [someone to Pio's prayers] . . . his face changes color

and often becomes luminous. He murmurs a prayer, and looking at him carefully, it seems as though he were leaving us and transporting himself to the person of whom we are speaking. . . . It has often happened when speaking to Padre Pio of someone who was far away, that the said person has either smelled his perfume, seen him or felt him to be near them.[4]

Many bilocations were to help individuals die. Carty says Padre Pio "himself admitted, when asked, that he was in Milwaukee, Wisconsin, June 25, 1950, to assist at the death of the father of a Capuchin."[5] There is also testimony Pio was in Uruguay in 1942, keeping a promise to his friend Bishop Damiani of Salto to help him at the hour of death.[6] Martha Gemsch was one of the saint's spiritual children who settled in the little town below the friary. Gemsch tells of her sister Lisa, an x-ray technician, who wanted to bring her knowledge to the third world. Padre Pio advised her not to go. But she went anyway. One day Gemsch noticed Pio, who was just up from an illness, came into the church with a very dark face. He shouted at her, as if upset, to go pray before the tabernacle. And when he left the confessional later he turned away from her without a word. Slightly miffed after all the praying she had done for him during his sickness, Gemsch understood his behavior two days later. Only then did she receive word that Lisa, fatally injured in a car accident in Dar es Salaam, had died in a hospital at those moments Pio was growling at Martha to pray. Pio himself, a Dar es Salaam nun who was present at the death insists, was with Lisa as she died smiling. This witness says Pio said to her, "I feel so sorry about it, but I was here to assist her."[7]

Many bilocations were to heal the sick. I choose as representative the case of Luisa Carnevali of Imola, Italy. With three people present, two did not see Pio. According to the accompanying doctor's statement, Carnevali was in serious condition in 1932 (before antibiotics) after she ended up with gangrene in the lower jaw following dental surgery. Her testimony too long to give in its entirety, I pick it up where she lay in bad shape in a hospital:

> In my room my father was at my bedside, and my eldest son, aged 13, stood at the foot of the bed; all of a sudden I felt someone throw cold water in my face, and I saw our good friend Padre Pio with his hands crossed near my bed. At once I jumped up saying, "Who has thrown cold water on me?"
>
> My father, poor man, thought I was wandering, and told me to keep quiet. "No," I said, "Look!" and putting my fingers on my forehead I showed my fingers dripping with water. I did not say anything to them about Padre Pio. Only afterwards when my mother came did I mention his visit, but we said nothing to the others.
>
> Oh great wonder! The miracle was accomplished. Our good Padre Pio obtained it from the omnipotent Christ so he saved a poor widow with five children. . . . When changing the dressing, Dr. Agostino found that gangrene . . . had oozed out onto the bandage. Delighted, he cried out, "Take courage, you are saved."[8]

The water, of course, *could* be explained away as a sudden outburst of sweat, but not to Luisa Carnevali.

Almost any disease, physicians say, can suddenly be healed under the impetus of a powerful psychospiritual experience. On the other hand, physicians are loath to agree missing body parts can regenerate this way, which makes the well-documented cure* of Giovanni Savino significant.

Savino, a young laborer friend of Pio's, was working in 1949

---

* Pio's intercession is also credited with a new part in the heart of a doomed Irish child. See my *Nothing Short of a Miracle.*

on site preparation for an annex to the friary. A spiritual son, he liked to attend Pio's mass, then ask the holy friar's blessing before starting for the construction site. One day Pio added a big hug and some odd words to their routine. As Savino recalled years later, Pio said, "Courage, I'll pray to God you don't die." The next day and the following, the same anxiety-producing words. But no response when Savino tried to get Padre Pio to explain. Then in the afternoon of the third day a charge of dynamite set to clear a boulder exploded in Savino's face. Before he was rushed to the nearest hospital, twenty-five miles away in Foggia, several witnesses, among them Padre Raffaele, who attempted first aid, saw clearly that the right eyesocket was empty. In Foggia this was confirmed along with the fact that the other eye was so injured it was unlikely it could be saved.

Savino was in the hospital, his head completely bandaged. But every day, by his experience of the odor of sanctity, he believed Padre Pio paid him a visit as the injured worker requested the saint's help interiorly. After ten days Savino awoke in the middle of the night and lay listening to the breathing of the two or three other men asleep in the room. Suddenly someone gave him a gentle slap on the empty eyesocket. And, again, he smelled Padre Pio's characteristic odor of sanctity, "a beautiful smell . . . a smell of heaven," he recalls.

The next morning his head was unbandaged. Doctors were startled to see the shattered, burned face perfectly healed, while Savino cried, "I see you!"

When the ophthalmologist, a man who had no use for outdated ideas like miracles, saints, or God, finally took in that the empty socket now had a fine, functioning eye, it made a believer of him. As for the unslapped left eye, medical effort to restore its vision proved useless.[9]

Although by far the majority of Padre Pio's bilocations were to assist others, occasionally it appears he was taken on a pilgrimage or had a little break from his arduous self-giving. Don Giovanni Miglionico, a fellow friar, says Padre Pio told him, "This morning I felt myself suffocating from the great crowds of men in the sacristy, while I was hearing confessions; not being able to stand it any more I began to walk on the heads of the people [obviously not literally] and I went out on the esplanade for a little fresh air. No one noticed me."[10]

A down-to-earth genius of practical charities, Bl. Luigi Orione is among witnesses that Padre Pio prayed at the tomb of St. Pius X in St. Peter's in Rome while Padre Bonaventure, a Capuchin who was preaching, and many in the congregation saw Pio in a Naples church in 1956.[11]

People often heard Padre Pio's voice, interiorly or aloud, without seeing him. Martha Gemsch (p. 337) says, "Padre Pio gave us [his spiritual children] so many ideas on how to pray. He was capable of entering our minds without being present . . . as a way of guiding us."[12] Sometimes he "came" for other purposes as well. Witness the earliest known incident of this type which took place in 1916 when Padre Pio, unknown as yet to the world, was living in a friary in Foggia. Annitta Rodote, one of his spiritual children, told Capuchin Padre Paolino that while working in her kitchen one afternoon she heard a clear call, "Annina! Annina!"† She knew she was awake. Baffled and increasingly terrified, she heard the speaker urge, "Kneel and pray for me. I'm tormented right now by the devil." As she stood there bewildered, the urgent voice continued: "Quickly! Quickly! Annina, don't doubt because this is Padre Pio who's asking you. Kneel and let's pray the litany of the Madonna together." She fell to her knees and the voice led her in the prayer. Then the disembodied voice said, "Thanks, I'm calm now."

Padre Paolino did not doubt Annitta Rodote's sincerity but he very much doubted her perception. He advised that if any-

† He uses the affectionate diminutive form of her name.

thing like that ever happened again, she should reply that she always prayed for Padre Pio but she didn't like this way of asking for prayer because it could so easily be an illusion. Next day the voice came again. The woman parroted Paolino's words only to be told, "But this is no illusion! I have need of souls to join me in prayer, especially now, when I am tempted by the devil and feel the need acutely. So don't deny me the charity of praying with me."

She prayed again but again consulted Padre Paolino who said she should ask Padre Pio, if this happened any more, from where he was speaking to her. The next day Paolino kept an eye on Pio all afternoon. When Rodote contacted him to say Padre Pio had called her, Paolino had to verify that the young friar had been exactly where he told Rodote he was at the time he "called" her.[13]

Apparently Padre Pio also bilocated at times giving no sign of his presence. On December 10, 1914, for instance, Pio writes in a letter, "A few days ago the Lord permitted me to pay a visit to Giovina [another spiritual child] and by means of me . . . showered many graces upon her. . . . It seemed to me her health was better." He ends his remarks by requesting "Please, no word to Giovina about my visit."[14]

I have mentioned the fact that Pio might be seen by one individual and not by his or her companions. One group of people who considered Pio their spiritual mentor had a meeting and noticed, as had happened before, his spiritual perfume. A five-year-old child present went further, insisting he saw Padre Pio. Five-year-olds are highly imaginative but later several people questioned the saint, "Was it really you that little Giovannino [Trombetta] saw?"

"Who else would it have been?" came the gruff reply from Pio, who was always embarrassed by such questions.[15]

A woman named Maria Campanile, who lived below the friary, rushed up the hill in 1918 to beg Pio's prayers when her sister suffered grave internal injuries in a car accident. He assured her the doctors were wrong: Her sister would live. About eight o'clock that evening Maria and a friend were sitting next to the comatose sister when the friend turned pale and said she could see Padre Pio bending over the bed murmuring, "Poor child."

Maria Campanile, who had never heard of bilocation, didn't know what to think but she did see clearly that after ten minutes when her friend exclaimed, "He's gone," the dying sister suddenly regained consciousness. By the following day she was recovering nicely from her "fatal injuries." Meanwhile Maria had gotten a crash course from her friend on how Padre Pio could be places in spirit as well as in flesh. Still somewhat unsure, Maria went back to the friary.

"What time did you come to my house last night?" she asked without any preliminaries.

"Around eight," Pio answered.[16]

Can a bilocator carry an object from place to place? There are testimonies Pio could. Let me detail the incident of this type I feel most certain of because it concerns Pio's spiritual child Giovanna (pp. 334–36). She was in bed sick at the home of a friend, Margherita Hamilton, in Rome when Margherita brought her a beautiful rose from the garden.

"I'll give it to Padre Pio," Giovanna exclaimed, rather fancifully some would say, and the vase was set on the bedside table next to the framed photo of her spiritual mentor. A third friend arrived and the three sat chatting. The rose was noticed, picked up, and put back in place. A few moments later the visitor suddenly stammered that the flower had vanished. At first it was assumed it had somehow fallen out of the vase. But it wasn't on the floor. Next they got Giovanna out of bed and searched there fruitlessly.

Finally Giovanna said thoughtfully, "It seems Padre Pio has accepted the rose." And everyone tactfully changed the subject.

Almost three weeks later, Margherita and Giovanna went to

San Giovanni Rotondo. Giovanna went straight to Padre Pio, who greeted her with the rose in his hand.

"Thank you very much," he said. "I appreciate it very much."‡

"Oh, Father, give it to me," Giovanna exclaimed. He did, and the framed rose is in her house today.[17]

Call it bilocation or not, Padre Pio also appeared in people's dreams. An engineer from Bologna, for instance, dreamed of a friar standing with stigmatized hands crossed over his breast who looked him deep in the eyes and finally said, "Happy you who have been able to endure my gaze." Only *after* this dream did he learn of Padre Pio. Eight years later, still nagged about his life-style by a dream he should have long forgotten, he arrived, unannounced, at the friary. Taken at his request to Padre Pio, when the door opened, he found himself staring at his dream come to life. Need I say, he changed.[18]

Andre Mandato of North Plainfield, New Jersey, tells how he was trying to emigrate to the United States from Bologna in 1961. Padre Pio was a friend of his. One night he dreamed Pio told him his application for admission to the United States had been rejected. Try again, the dream Pio urged, with a new sponsor and this time all will go well. When he woke up, Mandato didn't know what to think. Then that day he got the official rejection. He tried again with a new sponsor and succeeded.[19]

Italia Betti, a prominent Italian Communist, dreamed of Pio in 1949 shortly after she was told she had incurable cancer. A sister, the only Catholic in the Betti family, had told her of Pio, so it is possible her dream originated in herself, illness triggering a reexamination of her beliefs. Pio would have been merely a symbol of Catholicism or the spiritual in general.

‡ While this incident seems to center around a rose, my guess is Pio was really thanking his spiritual child for something she internally did as the rose was placed by his picture, most likely offering her illness as a prayer for Pio's welfare or some similar gesture of love.

Whatever its origins, Italia saw the dream as a numinous one, a summons from the God she had not known. She answered with a trip to San Giovanni and ended up spending the final ten months of her life there, as passionate a believer in numinous realities as she had been an indefatigable worker for social reform. She is buried by Pio's mother.[20]

There are testimonies that dream appearances of Pio effected healings. In 1944 Gaspare di Prazzo was near death from pernicious malaria. A widow, Mrs. Vaccaro, gave Gaspare's wife a photo of Padre Pio, telling her of this priest who had such marvelous gifts from God. The patient kissed the photo, begging God for a cure.

A few days later Mrs. Vaccaro rushed in, exulting, "The grace has been given. I dreamed of Padre Pio and he said to me 'The grace has been given.' " She could not have been more correct. At eleven the previous night the husband told his wife Padre Pio "is coming." In a dream or a vision the man, who had a high fever—which causes altered states of consciousness, including vivid dreams and delirium certainly— saw Padre Pio and spoke aloud to him. After about ten minutes he told his wife Pio was gone. He described to her having been in spirit with Padre Pio in a church where the saint said mass and he repeated various spiritual counsels Padre Pio gave him after the mass. He ends the account:

> Being thirsty, I asked Padre Pio for water, and he accompanied me to a cistern. I filled a bottle with lovely fresh water; groaning with pain I drank it in one draught, burning with fever. As soon as I had drunk the water I smelt a perfume which resembled vanilla. Then the Padre went away.

All this sounds like a "fever dream," which it may well have been. But to the di Prazzos it is a spiritual event, for when Pio "left," so did the fever and illness. The exultant patient who greeted the excited Mrs. Vaccaro had already seen the physician and knew he was well. Events rooted in the unconscious of a man desperate to live and a compassionate woman? Perhaps, but the di Prazzos and Vaccaro take another view.[21] With this last example I must admit I have snuck up on you. Read it again and you will see that it is possible—we do not have the exact hour of Vaccaro's dream—that besides being in Our Lady of Grace friary and somehow with Gaspare di Prazzo, Padre Pio may also have been making an appearance in Vaccaro's dreams. You groan at the thought that I am proposing trilocation. I groan myself. But it isn't I but Padre Pio who brings the subject up.

There are testimonies from monks who lived with him that they overheard the saint at times talking to people apparently in bilocation.[22] Once, for instance, he was overheard at a certain time giving absolution to someone dying; a letter later arrived thanking Pio for his help with someone's death at that exact time.[23] Padre Costantino, one of the friars who helped care for the old, unwell Pio in his last days openly said to him one day, "Padre, you can't deny now and then you go off to Paris, London, or Berlin, or somewhere else by bilocation, while you're here in San Giovanni Rotondo."

"Whether it's true or not that I'm found in various places by bilocation, trilocation, or whatever, you'll have to ask God, not me," Pio answered. "All I can say is I always try to remain attached to the thread of his will."[24]

He wouldn't mention trilocation if he had no experience of it, would he? I close the chapter with the July 20, 1921, experience of Monsignor D'Indico of Florence. Alone in his study when he sensed someone behind him, D'Indico turned and saw a friar disappearing. When he told another priest about this, it was hinted in a kindly way that, in his anxiety over a sister in a coma, he had hallucinated. A walk was suggested but during the walk the Monsignor D'Indico couldn't keep from stopping at his sister's. He found her out of her coma.

And she had her own tale to tell: At the same hour when her brother had the strange experience, a friar had come to her and said, "Don't be afraid, tomorrow your fever will disappear and after a few days there will be no trace of illness in your body."

"But Padre, are you a saint?" she asked.

"No, I am a creature who serves the Lord through His mercies," she was answered.[25]

As foretold, the illness was gone in a few days. So do we have here dual hallucinations through ESP or one bilocation and one hallucination, or mind-boggling trilocation? One can gasp and cry, "Too much!" or one can take the lighthearted approach of St. Martin de Porres (1579–1639). This black Peruvian bilocator grinned and asked his questioner, "If Jesus could multiply loaves and fishes, why can't God multiply me?"

notes

1. Her name was Suor Beniamina. See the account in C. Bernard Ruffin's *Padre Pio: The True Story,* recommended by the Capuchins who lived with Pio as an authenticated biography, p. 208. Pio also daily for a year blessed Madre Speranza, a mystic under investigation by the Holy Office at the time (1939 or 1940) in Rome, according to her testimony. See *A Padre Pio Profile* by John A. Schug, pp. 45–46. Schug's book is also authenticated by his fellow Capuchins who lived with Padre Pio.

2. Ruffin, op. cit., pp. 57–60.

3. Ibid., p. 272, quoting John McCaffery's *Tales of Padre Pio: The Friar of San Giovanni Rotondo* (Kansas City, 1978), p. 26.

4. Charles Mortimer Carty, *Padre Pio: The Stigmatist,* p. 58. I use material from Carty judiciously as there are some fact errors in this basically excellent work (see note 9, for example). This was his own on-the-spot observation.

5. Ibid., p. 64.

6. The most authentic account is in Ruffin, op. cit., pp. 221–22. Carty's has a few errors.

7. Gemsch's first-person account was given in an interview to John A. Schug. See op. cit., pp. 128–29.

8. Carty, op. cit., pp. 175–77. Her letter is accompanied by the doctor's diagnosis.

9. Savino's first-person testimony, which I have verified with the Capuchins who knew him, is found in Schug, op. cit., pp. 42–44. I find minor discrepancies in other accounts and a big error in Carty, who says sight returned to both eyes.

10. Miglionico's testimony is corroborated by Padre Ludovico, who

was present when Padre Pio made the remark. See Carty, op. cit., p. 65.

11. Carty is among those to cite Don Orione's witness, op. cit., p. 69, while Schug interviewed Padre Bonaventure, op. cit., p. 6.

12. Ibid., p. 127.

13. Ruffin, op. cit., pp. 117–18.

14. Carty, op. cit., pp. 252–54, gives the entire letter.

15. Ibid., pp. 62–63.

16. Ruffin, op. cit., pp. 130–31.

17. Schug, op. cit., pp. 20–21. Schug interviewed Margherita with Giovanna present.

18. Carty says he has been asked not to name the man, op. cit., 99–102.

19. Schug, op. cit., p. 51.

20. Her funeral took place Oct. 27, 1950.

21. Carty, op. cit., pp. 211–14.

22. Ruffin, op. cit., p. 301.

23. Carty, op. cit., p. 78, testimony of Padre Onorato.

24. Ruffin, loc. cit.

25. Carty, op. cit., pp. 67–68. Carty knew D'Indico personally. See also Ruffin, op. cit., pp. 186–87.

▲ 18

those
flaky
ladies

There is a group of women Catholics who incite much suspicion in the arm of their church charged with investigating candidates for the title of saint, and in the average twentieth-century Catholic or non-Catholic as well. Their lives too rich in phenomena for the modern palate, the most far-out of them are the inedics (see chapters 8 and 9).

A number—both eaters and noneaters—carry that other bizarre phenomenon, the bodily marks of crucifixion known as stigmata. With stigmatics like Padre Pio or Gino Burresi, these women suffer, they believe, to help God heal a wounded world.

All of them, including some who have no stigmata, are prone to visions (a phenomenon I discuss in a forthcoming book). They may see Jesus, saints who are dead, or events far removed in time. It is only natural when they also see current events, places, and people that some observers think this also is by a "visionary participation." One suggestion is that these women—whom some derisively and I affectionately call "flaky ladies"—see across miles the way you or I see across a room. Remember, whether we call the thing expanded vision, "visionary participation," or bilocation, we are all labeling a phenomenon or various phenomena, about the mechanics of which we *know nothing*. In the end, however we interpret these mechanics (see pp. 312–16), all we really know is that these stigmatic, visionary women "go" a lot of places.

True, their visits are often of the invisible sort that are related to—may even at times be—clairvoyance, expanded sensory perception or mental visions. But not always. Sometimes they are seen and talked to as well.

There isn't room in any book to examine all these women who allegedly bilocated but we can look at a small sampling: a twentieth-century Bavarian, a late nineteenth-century Palestinian Arab, and a Swiss who died so recently that the thirteen volumes on the extraordinary phenomena of her life are not even available in their original German to the general reader. Briefer reference will also be made to twentieth-century Polish and French women. To these could be added, if space permitted, the Portugese candidate for beatification Alexandrina da Costa (pp. 201–7) and the nineteenth-century housewife from Rome, Bl. Anna Maria Taigi (pp. 119–20). Omitted in spite of much material because they are "too controversial" are a French-Canadian from Rhode Island, a Prussian from Westphalia, and an Englishwoman.* Whatever ails these women, then, is definitely not a local disease.

▲

---

* See Rose Ferron (p. 246), Anne Catherine Emmerich (pp. 315, 358, and 361) and Teresa Higginson (f.n., p. 289).

There are many testimonies that Theresa Neumann, the Bavarian stigmatic visionary, could be somehow in two places at once. Although I have written to the Catholic Church in Konnersreuth, there is no group there doing research. Excellent investigative work, however, was done on the spot during Theresa's lifetime and is reported in great detail in several well-authenticated books in my possession. The one I focus on here is not the most exhaustive or best written, but it has one advantage for you, the reader: It is the only one still in print. By Johannes Steiner, it is based on (1) written and oral accounts of Theresa by observers, including both members of her family and official investigators; (2) her letters; (3) the careful records kept by her pastor-confessor Fr. Joseph Naber; and (4) the author's interviews with the stigmatic and his observations of her from their first meeting in 1929 until her death in 1962.

Now to her bilocations. From Steiner's reports is this quotation from Father Naber's journal, dated December 14, 1930:

> Last week I was in Berlin on pressing business. I really didn't want to go at all. In a state of ecstasy Therese† told me that I would come back satisfied and relaxed, and this really did happen, more than I ever expected. Twice Therese attended my Mass in Berlin, in her ecstatic state. She told me about it right after my return. Even though she had never seen the church in which I celebrated Mass (St. Ansgar's), not even a picture, and had never heard anyone talking about it or even read anything about it, she gave me a very good description of it, size and furnishings and especially the altar.
>
> She told me that I had been unable to open the tabernacle and the server had to come up and tell me how to do it. The second time (she said) the pastor was serving for me.
>
> Actually the first time I said Mass, there was a little

† The translator into English uses the French form of her name.

> purse on the altar with the key I needed to open the taber-
> nacle. When Communion time came, I used it to open the
> tabernacle door. But there was an inner door, made of
> metal, behind the outer wooden door, and I was trying to
> use the same key for both of them. After I'd spent a few
> minutes in this vain attempt, the server stepped up and
> told me there was a special key for the second door, in the
> same little sack as the first.[1]

Father Naber's account goes on to note Theresa was correct:
The pastor did serve the second mass.

Other reports in Naber's journal indicate that Theresa saw
masses in their local church when she was sick at home or
when she was staying in the town of Eichstatt, as well as the
masses her pastor said in Eichstatt when she was at home in
Konnersreuth.

Once when she was in Eichstatt, a friend, professor Wutz,
took down the sermon being preached in Konnersreuth as
Theresa reported it. Then he called Father Naber and asked,
"What did you preach about this morning?" Theresa had it
down cold. She also was correct in statements as to little
things, such as certain flowers beginning to wither.[2] A clever
con artist with confederates could probably have arranged a
deception in such matters, but what would have been the
point? Theresa and her family refused every offer that would
have brought them money or position.

Steiner found the stigmatic also participated invisibly in special church celebrations around the world. These included
events in Lisieux, France; Fatima, Portugal; the healing shrine
of Lourdes; and various events in Rome. One instance:

> At the world Eucharistic Congress in Budapest in 1938,
> her brother Ferdinand from Eichstatt [Germany], without
> her knowledge, had managed to make his way to Budapest

(in those days [under the Nazis] it was legally almost impossible to leave Germany and participate in such a congress). In Budapest he met Cardinal Kaspar from Prague, who was a friend of the Neumann family, and through him managed to secure permission to take pictures in the immediate vicinity of the apostolic nuncio, Cardinal Pacelli.‡ When he got back home to Konnersreuth, Resl [Theresa's nickname] told him, before he could even open his mouth, "You were in Budapest; I saw you there. You were always right out in front."[3]

Theresa participated each year in the pope's Easter blessing, joining the throngs in St. Peter's Square in Rome. In this way she "met" three popes, Pius XI, Pius XII, and John XXIII. According to Steiner, "the last time she had this vision was the year of her death, Easter Sunday, 1962."[4] But was it a vision or is this simply invisible bilocation?

Apparently Steiner never probed for such distinctions. And maybe that would have been useless anyway. He does say Theresa once told him that she got letters from people who said she had appeared before them, talked to them, etc.

"I never pay any attention to such letters," she added. "I just throw them in the fire." Without giving compromising details of name or place, she told him about one letter from a Catholic priest. This man was not only having an illicit affair with a schoolteacher but embezzling church funds. He wrote that one day Theresa appeared before him weeping bitterly. Although she said not a word, her tears and the visible crucifixion wounds on her hands as she daubed at her eyes stuck him like a knife. He wrote to assure her of his changed heart and life.[5]

Of course, if Theresa was an imposter, as some people charged, she could have invented this story. I mentioned in an

‡ Soon elected pope, Pacelli is better known as Pius XII.

earlier chapter that her confessor was approached with a similar one. The individual said he was on the verge of suicide when Theresa appeared to him. What she said changed his mind. When Fr. Naber questioned Theresa, she did not deny it, but said her guardian angel had taken her form to save the young man from his desperate act.

Here is a third instance that Steiner, with a certain illogic, attributes to Theresa's guardian angel and then calls a bilocation:

> When Therese Neumann was in Eichstatt on Easter, 1929, Father Ingbert Naab, who was then guardian for the Capuchin Monastery there, asked her prayers for the mission he was about to preach. . . . There he saw Therese, for about three quarters of an hour, standing in the back in her black dress and white head cloth, while he preached his conference. But Resl had never left Eichstatt. She told her sister Ottile "Today Father Ingbert* begins his mission. We'll have to pray real hard for him."[6]

Padre Pio appeared in two places at once and said it was by "a prolongation of personality." Theresa appeared in two places at once and said, "An angel took my form." Are these two phenomena or one? Do saints who experience something infallibly know *what* they experience? I can only venture my opinion that intellectualizing about the mechanics behind these events is like playing darts in the dark. Even the holy at times make comments like the following from the diary of Polish mystic Sister M. Faustina Kowalska (1905–38), another visionary who is a current candidate for beatification:

---

* On the Nazis' hit list a decade later, Naab owed his life to precisely following Theresa's instructions rechanging hiding places. Eventually one of her brothers, under her guidance, managed the incredible feat of smuggling him safely out of Germany.

> Suddenly I found myself in a strange cottage. A man was dying in great torment. All about the bed was his family. They were crying.

After noting how she prayed and God brought peace to the man, she says:

> At the same moment, I found myself again in my own room. *How this happens I do not know.*[7]

This admission by a mystic will be a comfort as we look again at the little Arab from Galilee, Blessed Mariam Baouardy, who became Carmelite Sister Marie of Jesus Crucified. For Mariam or Sister Marie is more bizarre, in some ways, than even the much-maligned Theresa Neumann. You recall those levitations of hers to the tops of trees. But as a cloistered Carmelite rather than a laywoman, Mariam was at least more easily observed.

Except in the case of bilocations. Here we have only one witness. The testimony is nonetheless worth reporting because Sister Josephine of Jerusalem (d. 1927), foundress of a charitable institution at Kiryath-Yearim in Judea, herself has a reputation for holiness—*and* was cured when she lay near death. Sister Josephine swore to the following strange experience:

In 1876 she was stationed on the island of Cyprus where she fell gravely ill with some oriental fever. She was so close to death that her superior from time to time put a mirror to her lips as the only way to see whether she still breathed. In that condition, at night around eleven o'clock Sister Josephine nevertheless says she was conscious that another nun entered the room where she lay dying.

This sister was elevated off the floor, held her arms out to form a cross, and was enveloped by a vibrant light that lit up the whole room. It was Sister Marie of Jesus Crucified, who before joining the Carmelites had been a postulant of another group of St. Joseph Sisters. (While their mother general, who appreciated her, was out of town, they dismissed her as "too flaky.") I pick up the account, translating Sister Josephine's own words from the French:

> Although I had never seen her, I knew it was she, and I knew she was speaking with the good Lord. I was *not* sleeping. I called her by name and she replied. I said to her then, "Marie, ask the good Lord if I am going to die." She spoke to Our Lord. After several seconds, she said to me, "No, you aren't going to die young; you have a lot of good to do."

Now the account gets vague as Sister Josephine begins asking other questions about her future. Without going into details, she says that "to everything that I asked her pertaining to my soul, she replied."

> Then she disappeared and all that she said has really happened. I was restored from that moment.
> The next year I was able to travel and I left Cyprus for Jaffa. There it happened that the Carmelites of Bethlehem were passing through on their way to Nazareth.† How happy I was to recognize Sister Marie whom I had seen in Cyprus. The good Lord is my witness—it's for him that I'm writing this—she said to me, "St. Joseph loves your order a lot; you won't see me again." She told me she would live only a little longer. Describing her death, she told me the month it would occur. Before God and only for his glory do I say this as solemnly as if I were at the moment of my death.
>
> Jerusalem, Oct. 30, 1895[8]

---

† This was on the voyage from France to establish a new Carmel in the Holy Land. Once set up, they were strictly cloistered, the mode of this contemplative order.

Unquestionably Sister Josephine is sincere. But she certainly leaves a lot of loose ends. I could almost say one recognizes her holiness by her telltale maddening insouciance before the necessity, if one is going to assert such things, of establishing a better case for them than calling God as your witness. Her only worry seems to be someone will think she is tooting her own horn. While she obviously has no doubt‡ she saw Sister Marie on Cyprus while the Carmelite was in France, the rest of us would appreciate it if she could confirm that by asking, "Sister Marie, is it true God had you drop in to heal me that night I was dying?"

In favor of Sister Marie's having bilocated from France to Cyprus is that Josephine recognized the Carmelite later in Bethlehem. (How she recognized her in Cypress is one of those loose ends some will find unresolvable, others credit to a mystical insight.)*

Against bilocation is the undeniable fact that when individuals are very ill, the line between dream and reality blurs and odd dreams that seem real are common. To further cloud the issue, three other things in favor of bilocation must also be acknowledged. First, bilocators do seem to appear at times in dreams. Second, authentic spiritual experiences are also common among all traditions when individuals are very ill, as if consciousness is more permeable. I have mentioned shamans in this regard (see p. 175), as well as Christian mystics. Finally, there is the striking fact that Sister Josephine was close to death one moment and "restored" the next. In the end I do not think we can prove that Sister Marie bilocated to bring God's healing to Sister Josephine. But I wouldn't bet against it either.

‡ Mystical theologians say one mark of an authentic mystical experience is the absolute positiveness one feels about it. Josephine and Marie probably feel no need to ask each other questions.
* Only one photograph appears to have been taken during Blessed Marie's life, and if it existed in 1876, it is unlikely it was circulating.

▲

No two saints describe bilocation exactly the same. I mentioned (p. 311) nineteenth-century stigmatic visionary Anne Catherine Emmerich, who is today discredited among Catholics for saying flaky things like "the angel calls me and I follow him to various places."†

Nineteenth-century rubbish? Listen to this from a recent book on shamanism. After quoting Ruth Benedict that shamanism all over the world generally rests on the concept of spirit helpers, the author writes:

> The main difference between an ordinary person and a shaman with regard to their guardian spirits is that the shaman uses his guardian spirit actively when in an altered state of consciousness. The shaman frequently sees and consults with his guardian spirit, travels with it on the shamanic journey, has it help him, and uses it to help others to recover from illness and injury.[9]

If figures like Anne Catherine are only vestiges of a more gullible age and shamans anachronisms from the race's even more distant past, how do we account for Adrienne von Speyr? A physician herself, cultured and well educated, from a race— the Swiss—not known for imagination, this wife of a university professor who herself authored sixty books, most of them biblical commentaries, draws from her observers, intimates, and Jesuit confessor the same sort of comments many times made of Anne Catherine.

Born at La Choux de Fonds, September 20, 1902, Adrienne, a doctor's daughter, was enormously compassionate toward

---

† She explains elsewhere that this was her guardian angel. Anne Catherine also emphasizes an empathetic link, remarking of one of her experiences: "They drew me to them by prayer [*The Life of Anne Catherine Emmerich*, vol. 2, p. 371].

those who were suffering. Her uncle, another physician who ran a mental hospital, used to let the little girl wander at will among the patients because of the calming effects she produced. Like Anne Catherine, Adrienne from her early years made the flaky claim that she was directed by an angel. And she, too, was a stigmatic and a visionary from childhood. For instance, she was only six when, as she walked up a steep street on Christmas Eve, St. Ignatius Loyola (1491–1556) appeared to take the tiny Protestant child by the hand. As a teenager Mary appeared to Adrienne and left the young girl with a small wound just under the heart, which she knew somehow signified her connection with God. As an adult, like others of these women, her visions eventually became extremely common and she developed the stigmata. She had hardly fit into the fold of Swiss Protestantism. In the twentieth century Catholicism did not exactly welcome the convert with open arms. She was ostracized. Her biblical commentaries could hardly find a reviewer since no one wanted to be associated, even so indirectly, with a figure whose life was such an offense to modern thought.

And while you and I were going about our very unmystical business in the 1960s, in Switzerland Adrienne von Speyr, people of sound minds assert, was also bilocating. Just like nineteenth-century Anne Catherine, who is so laughed at as an utter flake, Adrienne's bilocations were linked to reparatory suffering.

Praying to be taken where she was needed, Adrienne believed she was present, usually invisibly, to help members of the human family by prayer, sacrifices, and vicarious suffering. During World War II she plunged, it is said, into the hell of Nazi concentration camps to comfort and sustain. Other times she helped individuals trying to make confession of misdeeds or priests guiding them. Seminaries, abandoned churches where no one prayed anymore, worldly convents that had lost touch with the truly spiritual—all these were among Adrienne's destinations, according to Father Hans Urs von Balthasar, her spiritual director. And von Balthasar is a world-class theologian,‡ an unlikely candidate to be gulled by some phony mystic.

Again like Anne Catherine, Adrienne could not always give the name of the people or places she visited. But she could always describe the interior state of those to whom she had ministered. To von Balthasar she said she felt herself transposed in her physical body, although she knew that usually her presence was unperceived by those she visited. After the spiritual exertions of her bilocations, he noted that she was physically exhausted. They continued, however, until her death at sixty-five. This woman to whom the numinous had been more real than anything else died in that same mode, her last words a joyous exclamation: *"Que c'est beau de mourir* [How beautiful it is to die]!"[10]

That was September 17, 1967.

Was she a final representative of things we humans have outgrown? I'm afraid not. Rare as it is, the breed shows no signs of dying out. Marthe Robin, for instance, lived until February 6, 1981.

The blind, paralyzed, inedic invalid was known as a down to earth, playful woman who loved to laugh heartily. Even before the illness that opened her soul to spiritual heroism by taking away all of life's normal outlets, analysis of her handwriting shows a person "open to others," "affable," "generous," and, importantly for one in her later situation, an individual "for whom real things take precedence over fanciful ones and who prefers to weigh and measure calmly rather than to be carried away by sentiment. . . ."[11]

As with Adrienne von Speyr, it is not yet possible to gain access to all the material on Marthe, but from the little avail-

---

‡ In recognition of which he was made a cardinal in 1988, but he died shortly before he could be invested.

able there is no doubt in my mind she, too, "got around." I think of the time she remarked in a neighborly sort of way to a woman she knew that the things the woman and her companion had chatted about in their room during a silent retreat the two attended "hadn't been worth" breaking the rules for.[12]

And then there are the odd facts surrounding the mystic's mother's stay in a hospital in the city of Lyon. Although Marthe remained in her blind, paralyzed state in her bed in the little town of Chateauneuf de Galure, she followed her mother's operation for an intestinal obstruction as if she were waiting in the hospital corridor like an ordinary daughter, even asking that someone go open the window of her mother's hospital room after the surgery "because the room's too warm."[13]

Of Marthe, of all the flaky ladies who bilocate, we can borrow the words—nineteenth-century and therefore unafraid of sentiment as they are—of Anne Catherine Emmerich's learned biographer, who perhaps understands what all this is about as well as anyone. After saying that in Anne's bilocations, she was conducted "where she was most needed," he writes, she was ever ready . . . to go wherever the irresistible impulse of pity impelled, for compassion knows neither time nor space.[14]

notes

1. Johannes Steiner, op. cit., pp. 182–83.

2. Ibid., pp. 54–55.

3. Ibid., pp. 55–56.

4. Ibid., p. 56.

5. Ibid., pp. 193–94.

6. Ibid., p. 193.

7. M. Faustina Kowalska, *The Divine Mercy in My Soul,* p. 634.

8. Amédée Brunot, *Mariam: La petite Arabe: Soeur Marie de Jésus Crucifié,* pp. 63–64.

9. Michael Harner, op. cit., p. 55.

10. Hans Urs von Balthasar, *First Glance at Adrienne von Speyr,* pp. 39–40.

11. Handwriting analysis by Jacqueline Genêt, psychologist-graphologist from Valence, quoted by Raymond Peyret in his *Marthe Robin: The Cross and the Joy,* pp. 36 and 135.

12. Ibid., p. 120, quoting a woman from Saint Uze who wishes to remain anonymous. See also a testimony that may be pertinent on p. 17.

13. Ibid., p. 89.

14. Carl E. Schmöger, *The Life of Anne Catherine Emmerich,* Vol. 1, p. 71.

▲ 19

seven
stalwarts—
and a swami

An innkeeper's wife from Oostacker in Belgium testified:

On the fourth of February, 1896, at eleven o'clock in the morning, I suddenly noticed the presence of Father Paul [Francis Luyckx] in my inn, without having seen him enter. He seemed to be in excellent health, yet I reproached him for coming on foot, because, as a rule, I provided a carriage for him, free of charge, whenever he came to Oostacker.

"Oh I feel very well," the Father remarked gaily as he rubbed his hands. I offered him a glass of wine which he declined, saying "No, I shall not take anything, for I am in a hurry and have to make other visits, at the Beguinage [a women's religious community] and at a notary's. You will never see me again; carefully note the day and hour of my visit."

Then he explained the purpose of his visit—it was for her spiritual fortification—and, she says, "took out from beneath his mantle a scapular of rough wool . . . and a handful of medals to distribute among those who would make good use of them." Her testimony concludes:

> Having given me further advice, he strictly forbade me to attend his funeral because, he said, I would not be able to overcome my emotion. After this short conversation of only ten minutes, he said, "Go now to the kitchen and put your potatoes on the fire."
> The potatoes were, as a matter of fact, peeled and ready for boiling. I went to the kitchen and came back to the room after a few minutes but to my great astonishment Father Paul had disappeared.[1]

At the nearby Beguinage religious community in Ghent a nun later confirmed that around the same day—she had not noted the exact date—Father Paul visited her for about half an hour, during which he remarked that he would not be coming back again. Yet Dr. Cyr. Planquaert reports that on February 4 his patient, Abbot Paul, was confined to his room in Termond Abbey, "in such a state of health since January 31 as to absolutely preclude his leaving the monastery." A letter of Father Paul's from Termonde, dated February 4, the day he appeared vigorous and gay in Oostacker, shows the trembling hand of a very ill man, dead twenty days later.[2]

Here is a bilocator who is not an inedic, not a stigmatic. Abbot—an elected office—in the Benedictine order, which prizes moderation, Father Paul is about as far from being "a flake" as one can get. And that is the point of this brief chapter. While stigmatic visionaries like Padre Pio, the living Italian Gino Burresi, and the women of the last chapter seem especially prone to bilocation, bilocation is not limited to that type of mystic. Nor is it limited to so-called archaic spiritualities, like the Huichol healer-shamans of Mexico.[3] Here I present a group of men from the nineteenth and twentieth centuries who meet ordinary ideas of "normality"—and who are bilocators.

As with Padre Pio, the bilocation phenomena attributed to Father Paul took many forms. In the incident just reported, he appeared as a flesh-and-blood presence, able to put a hand in his pocket and hand out palpable objects like scapulars and medals. In the following testimony by a young woman named Louise, we have one of the incidents in which only his voice was heard.

> The reverend mother superior of the convent of the Sacred Heart, opposite our house, sent for Father Paul on behalf of one sister whose back was so afflicted that she could not perform her duties. I accompanied him to the convent. As soon as he came into the presence of the sick sister, he gave her his blessing and she was cured instantaneously.
>
> The mother superior requested Father Paul to say mass at the convent the next morning at half past five; he promised to do so. Then Father Paul said to me, "You shall come to my mass tomorrow."
>
> "No," I replied, "I am tired and half past five is too early. I am not such an early riser."
>
> "But you shall come nevertheless," the reverend father said laughing.
>
> "No, I will not come." With these words I left Father Paul and went home, while he returned to the family where he lodged, some distance from our house. I slept well all night, but towards five o'clock I was awakened by a voice which I recognized as that of Father Paul, and

which said distinctly, "Louise, arise, it is time to come to my mass." Fancying that it was all a dream I tried to sleep again; but I heard the voice a second and a third time, and each time it sounded more determined.

As I did not dare to remain in bed any longer, I arose, dressed hastily and went to mass. After mass Father Paul came to our house for breakfast and said to me with a laugh, "Well, I had to call you three times this morning. I told you yesterday that you would come to my mass."[4]

There is something about saints, approachable as they are, that almost invariably stops questions about the phenomena in their lives cold. But Louise was not easily intimidated. She had seen an instantaneous healing with her own eyes and been so unawed she could tell the miracle worker to buzz off when he suggested she get up early. Now she leaned forward and asked the breakfasting priest, "How were you able to call me? You weren't at our house?"

"The good God," Father Paul answered, "permitted me to make you hear my voice without my being with you."[5] Did he immediately change the subject or was even brash Louise finally awed? Whatever the reason, her account ends here.

Other times, it is said, the Belgian abbot made "visits" with even less sign of his presence. For instance, there is the report of the acquaintance who wanted a keepsake of the man she believed a saint.

[She] asked him repeatedly for a lock of his hair, but in vain. His constant answer was that his hair was too short. [A ruse: saints don't like the idea of others wanting mementos of them as "holy" ones.] One day, at Termond [Abbey], she was bold enough to cut off a lock of his hair at a moment when his attention was drawn elsewhere. As soon as the theft was committed the lock disappeared in the depths of the visitor's pocket.

Father Paul was highly indignant. He threatened to never let his caller visit him again. And he said in a tone so severe it frightened her—but not enough for her to hand back her booty —"You won't keep that lock of hair long."

> As soon as she returned to Ghent, her first thought was to lock up carefully in a drawer the precious relic, having first tied a ribbon around the lock of hair and placed it in a piece of paper.
> About four o'clock the next morning, being in bed, she heard an unusual noise in the house; she got up, went downstairs to investigate, and found the hall door half open. She cast a glance out into the street but saw no one except the night watchman who was making his rounds as usual.

After bawling him out for not ringing her bell when he saw the door was open, she learned that the door had been ajar for two hours but no one had entered or left the house. The watchman consequently had concluded the door had been opened for fresh air by the occupant.

> The lady then went upstairs and looked around to see if anything had been stolen. She opened the drawer in which, the evening before, she had put the lock of hair, and was surprised to find that it had disappeared.

The next time she saw the Benedictine abbot, he asked if she still had the lock of his hair. She said she had lost it. "Oh well, I'll give you one some day," he said, seemingly over his pique.

A year later he did give her a lock of his hair. To her amazement she recognized at once, from the distinctive ribbon she had tied around it, that he was handing her the same lock she had snipped from him.

As she stood there dumbfounded, he said genially, "Now you won't have to reproach yourself with having stolen it."[6]

From this circumstantial evidence, do you deduce bilocation? Or was Abbot Paul in touch with a first-class burglar? If the latter, how did this genius locate a lock of hair in a dark two-story house without ransacking the place? For those who opt for bilocation as an explanation, the comment of a mother superior may be pertinent. She once complained to Fr. Paul, she recalled later, that he seldom came to help her community with his wise counsel.

"Ah," he smiled, "but I am often in the midst of you without your seeing me."[7]

▲

St. John Bosco had similar gifts. For instance, one of Don Bosco's first letters (dated Oct. 20, 1863) to young Fr. Michael Rua (pp. 153–55) after sending him to Mirabello to take charge of a school there says: "You complain that I have not yet written to you, but I visit you daily."[8] That Bosco did not mean this just in the sense of remembering Rua in prayer is clearer in his hasty note to Rua dated Dec. 10, 1863:

> I shall soon be writing again to tell you all the things I observed in the various visits I made to you in my mind on several days of the week and at different times of the day.[9]

Five years later when the saint was in Rome, he kept an eye on his establishments at home in Turin by such visits, announcing beforehand their date and then writing detailed letters of advice based on what he had seen. It is of interest that these visits did not seem to require quiet hours of prayer. On Jan. 24, 1868, for instance, his companion, Fr. J. B. Francesia announces one of these visits at a time when Bosco was so busy that Francesia says the saint could barely find time to eat.

All the recipients of such missives said they were never off base. At instances of a fully authenticated saint announcing ahead of time a bilocation, or as he sometimes put it "a visit in the spirit," at first I thought this evidenced that at least some saints can control this gift. Then on second thought, I realized it could just as easily be that the saint was told in one of his extremely frequent numinous dreams that he would be transported there on such and such a date. Once more, the mechanics of this phenomenon elude.

Any parent of teenagers has undoubtedly wished to bilocate at least once. Don Bosco often found use for this gift as foster father to slum kids whose habits were less than angelic. I've told in another book an incident that shows he apparently could patrol the school while he was also tied up in the church hearing confessions and counseling. When some of his boys took an illegal swim in the local river, they later claimed that as they redressed, a powerful invisible hand blistered their behinds.

On October 14, 1878, Don Bosco was home in Turin. But a French family in the Drôme region of France has left the Salesians well-detailed and corroborated testimony that on that day Don Bosco also came to their house and to the house where their blind, deaf, and dumb infant was being wet-nursed. Appearing within seconds in two houses which were two miles apart, the visitor healed the baby.[10]

Don Bosco only visited Spain once. But Father John Branda, director of the Salesian school at Sarria by Barcelona, gave some interesting Process testimony under oath that makes one look again at the "historical fact."

Father Branda was sleeping in the Spanish boarding school one night during the school year 1885–86 when the voice of Don Bosco woke him with the command "John, get up and follow me." A steady, sensible fellow who knew Don Bosco was in Turin, Italy, he figured he had been dreaming and went back to sleep. A week later the same thing happened again.

This time when he was awakened he saw Don Bosco at the foot of the bed.

"Come now, you're awake," Bosco said, "so get up."

"I'm coming. I'm coming," Branda answered, startled out of any possible drowsiness. Jumping up, he threw on his clothes while Don Bosco stood waiting, the saint's handsome face as usual full of fatherly affection. As soon as the younger priest was dressed, he rushed over to kiss his mentor's hand in a gesture of respect. The hand was solid in his grasp.

"Come, take me on a tour of the house," Don Bosco said. "I need to show you something you don't suspect—a fearsome thing."

Don Branda took his keys and they went through the dormitories where dozens of boys were asleep. Don Bosco pointed out three pupils and told Branda they had been sexually seduced by a staff member. He said Branda "would never believe" who the seducer was "if I hadn't come to tell you. You think he's good. And he seems good on the outside. It's . . ." and he named a fellow Salesian, a lay brother.

Branda was dumbfounded. The man Bosco said was using his religious habit as a way to a steady supply of young boys seemed impeccable. And now Don Bosco was saying, "Send him away immediately."

Meanwhile they continued touring the whole house, Don Bosco moving swiftly as if he were in his forties (he was actually an exhausted seventy). Each area—dormitories, stairs, rooms, playground—lit up as if it were day as they passed.

Finally they returned to Branda's room. There in a corner, as if a film were being projected on the wall, appeared the three boys. Beside them, his head hanging, ashamed and afraid, appeared the abuser. Then a seminarian appeared on this "screen." He, too, was involved and must go, Bosco said.

"But I don't know," sputtered Branda, "how I can act on your orders. I have no proof of what you say. Can't you let someone else handle this?"

But without more discussion, Don Bosco turned and left. Instantly the room, brightly lit without any lamps, plunged into darkness. It was two hours before Branda's rising time. Too stirred to sleep, he prayed in great agitation until it was time to go downstairs for mass. He felt he could not, in justice, expel the brother or the seminarian. Yet an inner voice seemed to insist, "Act!"

To quiet it, he called in his assistants and cautioned them to keep their eyes open without saying anything specific. For a few days he was at peace, feeling he had done the right thing in going no further regarding what was probably some strange kind of hallucination. Still every time he began to celebrate mass, he was seized by a kind of horror that made him tremble.

Then he received a letter from Don Bosco's right-hand man, Don Rua. Rua said, "I was out walking with Don Bosco this evening and he told me he paid you a visit. But perhaps you were asleep at the time."

Panic seized him again. But Branda was not one to act capriciously. He still saw no grounds to accuse anyone of anything in spite of careful observation. And he still thought he must have hallucinated.

Four or five days later he went to celebrate mass in the home of a saintly woman who was a great benefactor of the Salesians.

"Guess what?" she greeted him. "I dreamed of Don Bosco last night."

"Excuse me. I have to start Mass immediately this morning," cried Branda, rushing away. He was suddenly afraid of what she might say. In turmoil he put on his vestments and approached the altar. As he bent to kiss it, he heard an interior voice: "Do what Don Bosco told you to do immediately or this is your last mass."

That did it.

Back at the boarding school, he met with each boy individually. Although he was careful not to mention the brother, he assumed the air of a man who knows what is going on. The boys responded. It was they who named the man Bosco had said must go and his accomplice, the seminarian.

When Branda sent for the brother and detailed all the boys had revealed, the man's response was interesting: "Did Don Bosco write you?" he asked.

"No. He came in person to tell me," Branda answered truthfully.[11]

▲

Did the French parish priest Jean Edouard Lamy, who had so many other spiritual gifts, also bilocate? Eugene Gengenwin, for whom Lamy was a spiritual mentor, thinks he did. Gengenwin writes:

> At Bordeaux one Sunday night, June 10, 1928, I broke a wine glass, getting a splinter into the right eye. At once it started weeping. How could I get an oculist at that time of night and on a Sunday too, to get it out? An idea! I asked my Guardian angel to go and get Père Lamy to pray for me. In bed an hour later, I [prayed] . . . and put a wet compress of . . . water [that had been blessed] on my eyes. Then I slept.
>
> The next morning, I felt no more pain, and called them all to look at my eye. Nothing to be seen. Up in my room making the bed, I took up a picture of Our Lady . . . which I had put under my pillow. Guess my wonder at finding the glass splinter *under* the picture. Not a doubt of it. An Unseen hand had taken out the splinter and put it under the picture while I slept. I heard nothing; saw nothing.
>
> At once I sent a little word of thanks to the Abbé at Pailly just then. He assured me later on that the errand

had been given him by my Guardian angel, and how urgent it was to get the splinter out.[12]

Gengenwin may find it natural to say "not a doubt of it," but how does even a bilocator get a splinter out of a closed eye and place it *under* a picture which is *under* the pillow of a sleeping man? It's simpler to believe Gengenwin a lunatic whom Père Lamy humored. Of course, that still leaves the problem of how the splinter, if it simply fell out in the night, got under the picture. You work on that.

▲

On August 27, 1849, the great heart of Bl. Dominic Barberi gave out in the packed third-class car of an English train. Although the physician hastily summoned from first class assured the passengers that the foreigner did not have the cholera rampant in London, the dying Italian was unceremoniously dumped off the coach at the next stop. Gasping in agonizing pain, he lay on the cement railway platform, a bundle of straw under his head. No one would take him in. Finally he was hoisted onto another train, jolted and bumped to the next stop, and carted off there to a hotel that consented to give him a bed to die in. Another five hours of agony and it was over.

It was a somehow fitting end for the Passionist priest. He belonged, after all, to the Catholic religious order that preaches and meditates unceasingly on the Passion of Christ. And laboring to bring the Catholic tradition once more to England, he had been cursed, stoned, pelted with rubbish and mud balls, abused verbally, and assaulted physically just walking English streets in his black Passionist cassock and sandals.

The Church's investigation after his death uncovered the fact that through eight years in England his response to everything had been love, love, and more love. That love and joy in, not because of, suffering finally won over most of those who had pelted him in his daily rounds. The town of Stone where he endured his worst persecutions turned out en masse to stand, hats off, in silent tribute as his coffin was carried from the church to the local cemetery.

People in other towns grieved too. And laughed, recalling his fractured English and his irrepressible sense of humor. A group of nuns remembered how he listened to their fears of having to give instructions to young men. "Don't worry," he said, the twinkle just barely visible in his dark eyes, "you are all so ugly, it should present no problem." Another mourner was John Henry Newman, former pastor of St. Mary's Anglican church in Oxford who would become a Catholic cardinal. He wrote of the man who received him into the Catholic tradition:

> His very look had about it something holy. When his form came into sight, I was moved to the depths in the strangest way. The gaiety and affability of his manner in the midst of all his sanctity was in itself a holy sermon.[13]

Other testimonies spoke of mystical phenomena, including bilocation. Here, from the Beatification Process, are two reminiscences under oath by Teresa Margherita Torti, abbess of the Poor Clare convent at Anagni, Italy:

> At the time Father Dominic was to leave [Italy] for Belgium, he wrote me a letter from Rome, in which he said he would be on his way the following Monday. This letter arrived Friday, just when I was in great need to discuss a certain matter with him and had been thinking about sending him a letter requesting his advice. I felt bewildered by the news of his departure, especially because any letter I wrote most likely would not arrive in time to reach him. Nevertheless with faith in sweet provi-

dence, I wrote him on Saturday revealing my need for his counsel.

In the very same day, around the hour of Vespers, I was in the parlor with some officials conducting a business matter of the convent, when I suddenly heard the bell at the door. As I was acting as Portress (the regular portress was in choir), I went to see who it was. To my great surprise I heard the voice of Father Dominic [the end of this testimony makes clear she also saw him] who said, "Mother Abbess, I have come purposely for you." I replied that I was carrying with me a letter for him which I had been planning to give the postman. But without giving me time to say what I might have been writing him about, he began to talk about my concerns, giving me opportune counsels. He consoled my heart so that I wanted to detain him but he replied that he had come just to deal with my need and could not stay. After those words, before my very eyes he vanished.[14]

Sometime before the incident just reported, Father Dominic gave a retreat to the nuns. His holiness made a deep impression. Afterward when a young sister was slowly losing ground to tuberculosis, she found comfort in Father Dominic's assurance that he hoped, in God, to be there to help her with her death. That and her faith in God kept her going until the last stage of the disease. Then suddenly she fell into such an anxiety state she could not bear any talk that she might not recover.

The abbess wrote Father Dominic, begging more prayers. When the reply came, she went with it to the sickroom, where she unexpectedly found the patient looking extremely serene.

"I wrote Father Dominic at Pugliano," the abbess began, "and he has sent you his blessing."

"And what a blessing!" came the reply.

"What do you mean?"

"Didn't you see him?" The patient was perplexed. "Didn't you open the door of the cloister? He came himself, as he promised. He spoke about death so well I don't care to live any longer. Not by a letter—*in person,* he has quieted me completely. I'm not thinking anymore about living," she repeated. "Father Dominic assures me God wills that I die and that I die *soon,* so I *wish* to die—not when I desire but when God wills, that is right now."

Before this instant mutation of attitude and its circumstances, the other sisters insisted on hearing from the lips of the young nun what had happened. The event, the account says, consoled the entire community greatly. The abbess's account of what the Poor Clares call "a bilocation by Father Dominic" concludes with the assurance that the tubercular nun "died as tranquilly as an angel."[15]

But why do the nuns insist this was a bilocation? Couldn't Father Dominic have simply made a quick trip to the convent? Hardly. First, he was apparently geographically some place from which he could not have reached the convent between penning his letter and his appearance to the dying nun. Equally important is the fact that the Poor Clares were contemplative nuns whose nineteenth-century convent was strictly cloistered. Like a fortress, it was not accessible for "slipping in" via an unlocked door or open window. High walls and grills protected privacy. The young sister asked in surprise, "Didn't you open the door of the cloister?" because only the abbess had the right—and more important, the key—to admit anyone from the convent's public rooms to the living quarters where the Poor Clares, by choice, sought God walled off from exterior distraction.

The Beatification Process also mentions a bilocation to another convent, commonly called the Duchesses, in Viterbo, where a Sister Serpieri, in spiritual anguish, complained she wished Father Dominic could be with her. He was not anywhere near the area. But shortly thereafter she was called to the visitor's parlor and, to her surprise, found the Passionist priest waiting for her.[16]

In the light of the miracles Father Dominic worked, his foreknowledge of the future, and his ability to read hearts, bilocation isn't such big stuff. A greater wonder is his legendary joy. Even in the terrible persecutions he suffered in England the mystic admitted he often "felt like singing in the depths of my soul."

▲

Padre Pio is definitely not the only saint of modern times to apparently project himself into others' dreams. Not a subject I can pursue at length, here is an example from the life of St. Pius X. Like Pio, Pius (Giuseppe Sarto) was a miracle worker, a prophet (he died of a broken heart in the opening days of World War I, which he saw in all its dreadful detail of extent, duration, and suffering), and a great healer. Modestly, he disassociated himself from his wonders—which when he became pope were suddenly conspicuous—by attributing them to the power of his papal office.

On one occasion at least, Pius' appearance in someone's dream had dramatic results and an intriguing sequel.

> The mother superior general of the Franciscan nuns in the Via Castro Pretorio [in] Rome, had a serious throat complaint which endangered her life. Human science could only suggest a tracheotomy, the results of which would be at best doubtful. The sister had great confidence in the power of Pius X [then pope], of which she often spoke familiarly to her nurse. One night when her suffering reached its climax and she was scarcely able to breathe, Pius X appeared to her in a dream and assured her that she would be cured.
>
> Next morning she took up her place in the chapel for

meditation with the other sisters, much to their astonishment. At breakfast she related the miraculous dream with which she had been privileged.

There is no doubt that physical illness can suddenly take a dramatic turn for the better. The sister could simply have had a dream of the pope, who was a symbol of power and healing, at the moment when her body realized its victory over her illness. However, there is this odd sequel:

> A few days later she went to see the pope to thank him personally for the favor that had been granted her. He did not give her a chance to speak, but addressed her by name and said, "You are the sister that I have healed."[17]

In the context of Pius' extreme modesty and his desire not to mention his "miracles" (he used to snort, "you are confusing your consonants: It is Sarto, not Santo"* when called a saint), one may conclude the pope was speaking before the nun could burst out with something that would start tongues wagging in the crowded audience hall. If so, had he heard of the cure? Or did he know by his personal involvement?

Another canonized bilocator with nothing of the flake about him is St. Francis Xavier Bianchi, who died in 1815 in Naples. This namesake of an earlier Catholic saint overcame his father's objections to become a priest in the order known familiarly as the Barnabites. While serving as president of two colleges, he became known for his holiness, miracles, and gifts of prophecy. Taken from the authenticated testimonies included in the Church's study of his life, here is a bilocation sworn to by a fellow priest, Agnellus Coppola.

Being a priest in any tradition in itself is no guarantee of holiness—or even of serenity. Seriously ill, Coppola was very

---

* "Saint" in Italian.

devout but also anxious and self-pitying. Bianchi assured him he would be healed. Coppola wanted to believe but quivered nevertheless with uncertainty.

"Listen," said Bianchi compassionately, "call to me with trust when you are sad and I will comfort you and bless you." Coppola did this a number of times, he says, always with "comforting results."

On the occasion in question the ill, anxious priest was praying alone at home and apparently not thinking of Bianchi but just feeling sorry for himself when suddenly a "wonderful light" flooded his room. In its midst appeared Bianchi, his face luminous.

"You're feeling so sad; don't you see what I suffer?" the visitor asked. Then Bianchi lifted up his cassock and Coppola saw his feet and ankles were bandaged. Undoing the cloths, the saint revealed red, swollen feet with matter oozing from large, black boils.

The sight of this "hidden cross," he says, flooded Coppola "with an overwhelming joy" that went on for five hours. Aroused finally when someone, worried about him alone and silent in his room for so long, pounded on the door, Coppola was surprised that more than seconds had passed. He had been occupied, he testified, with the words "Awaken my soul."

The next day he hurried to visit Bianchi, whose feet he had never seen nor heard talked about.

Bianchi welcomed him with the knowing grin Coppola recognized from other occasions when wondrous things had occurred. Embarrassed and taken aback, Coppola nevertheless stammered out his desire to see Father Bianchi's feet. The saint laughed good-naturedly, "Eh here you are like Thomas to see with your eyes and feel with your hands."† Then he

---

† Coppola refers to Christ's disciple who said he would only believe in the resurrection if he personally could see and touch the crucifixion wounds (John 20:24).

permitted his feet to be unwrapped so Coppola could see they were precisely as he had seen them in his own room.[18]

▲

Father Aloysius Ellacuria was a bilocator, I am told by people who knew him. His friend Francis Levy (p. 224) has told of a troubled night when Levy's first wife, Marion, was dying of breast cancer in their Southern Californian home barely two years after the birth of the couple's sixth child:

> Because of the great discomfort that Marion experienced with her illness, it was often difficult for her to sleep. In order for me to get adequate rest before going to work, I frequently slept in another room. About four o'clock one morning, I was startled by an overpowering sensation that I was not alone; rather, Father was there with me, putting me at peace. When I had the opportunity, I questioned him as to whether he had bilocated at that time. He answered with his usual downward glance and smile that he was not aware of it, but that other people had also told him of similar experiences.[19]

"Peace" is not something tangible and the reader may feel Levy imagined or dreamed his friend's presence. Physical healing, however, is harder to dismiss. And healing is the crux of an incident shared with me by Mother Marguerite Carter, who you may recall (p. 256) knew the Claretian priest for almost forty years. Mother Marguerite says:

> I was in San Diego when I received a telephone call from my brother in Boston. He said my sister Mary, who had had leukemia for a long time and was now in the last stages, was dying. I should get on a plane and come at once.

When I arrived, Mary looked terrible. Doctors said she had only two or three hours to live when I phoned from Boston to Los Angeles to Father Aloysius to ask his prayers for her.

I phoned at five o'clock in the evening. At seven o'clock Mary saw a man on the veranda outside her hospital room.

Although she had never met Father Aloysius, I had told her a lot over the years about Father's unusual mystical gifts and healing power. Somehow she knew this man looking in at her through the window was he. Later she told me, "He looked like a little old wine merchant." [From his photographs, not a bad description of the chunky little Basque.]

He said nothing. But he bowed to her and smiled. That was all. She felt no strange sensations in her body or anything. But in a couple of hours when she should have been dead, she wasn't. She not only lived through the night but in the morning she was able to keep food down, something she had not been able to do.

That night Father Aloysius again appeared on the veranda outside Mary's window. Again he bowed and smiled. And the next morning Mary was able to keep her medicine down, as well as her food.

The third night he came again. One last bow. One final, healing smile.

The next day Mary was up and walking around, feeling fine.

The following day she went home.[20]

Mother Marguerite's sister, Mary Lynch, came to California and met the man she swore had bilocated across the country faster than any plane could travel to prolong her life. And prolong it he certainly had: She lived another fifteen years, dying in 1983 two years after he did.

▲

Is anybody bilocating today? Considering that bilocation is found in mystics of every era, I think we need not fear Father Aloysius was the last of a breed. Catholics can point to Gino Burresi as one living bilocator. There is talk (see pp. 234 and 238 for possible instances) that Father Gino, who has never left Italy, has "visited" the United States. But stigmatics like Burresi are not the subject of this chapter. And anyway, rather than describing one more Catholic, in apology to those traditions I have had to ignore for want of skills to research in their languages, let me end these pages by sharing an incident regarding a living Hindu saint, swami Saraswati Prakashanand.

In 1977 Isabel Cade had an unforgettable experience while participating in her husband C. Maxwell Cade's research on the physiological effects of meditation. This particular day subjects were being measured for response to the meditation on divine love taught by the swami, who was present. Hooked up to electroencephalographs and to skin resistance meters, the group were listening to the Hindu's taped chant.

Although she was an experienced meditator, Isabel was not doing much according to either her own evaluation or the gauges, when the swami suddenly put his hand on her head. I have written in other places of the ability of some saints (Don Bosco, for instance) to dramatically alter consciousness or heal by this simple physical contact. Touched by the swami, Isabel Cade immediately shot into a euphoric state, which registered on the monitors as a great leap.‡ After a bit the euphoria faltered. The swami put his hand on her head again. This time the state lasted three days, coolly observed by Isabel's scientist husband.

Eight years later when we talked, Isabel could point to last-

‡ Her husband mentions the experiment in *The Awakened Mind* (p. 163), giving the precise physiological measurements.

ing results. First, her hands, which up to that time were usually cold, are now habitually warm, a fact this writer experienced. Second, as her pleasantly warm hands reflect, she has a relaxed, peaceful attitude toward life, which she dates from that incident.

Naturally Isabel had a high regard for the swami. When the six weeks of his involvement in her husband's researches ended, she kept in touch. He had left England, when one day as she was meditating he suddenly was with her. The spiritual aspects of this visit are not something she wishes to share for publication, but she will say she is quite sure that he was present* because he left behind a wonderful perfume vaguely reminiscent of freesias, a delicate spring flower.[21]

---

* Her husband, as a good scientist and a mystic who follows Buddha in such matters, called the experience a hallucination.

379

notes

1. Edward van Speybrouck, *Father Paul of Moll,* pp. 174–75. The Benedictines can vouch for Fr. Paul's holiness and his biographer's integrity; they cannot, obviously, guarantee the veracity of every witness.

2. Ibid., pp. 175–76.

3. Prem Das, "The Singing Earth: A Look at Shamanism," *Yoga Journal,* No. 52, (Sept./Oct. 1983), pp. 19–25.

4. Edward van Speybrouck, op. cit., pp. 98–99.

5. Ibid.

6. Ibid., pp. 196–98.

7. Ibid., p. 240.

8. John Baptist Lemoyne, *The Biographical Memoirs of St. John Bosco,* vol. 7, p. 328.

9. Ibid., p. 346.

10. Ibid., vol. 14, pp. 552–55.

11. Eugenio Ceria, *Memorie Biografiche di San Giovanni Bosco,* vol. 18, pp. 34–39. Don Ceria not only had Branda's *Process* testimony from the *Positio super introductione causae,* Rome, 1907, vol. 5, pp. 782–89, he personally heard the incident from Branda.

12. Paul Biver, *Père Lamy,* pp. 199–200. Verified by the present head of the order Lamy founded.

13. Quoted in Jude Mead's *Shepherd of the Second Spring,* p. 207.

Based on primary materials, this book was supplied to me by the Passionists.

14. I have translated from the Italian of the *Process,* pp. 497–98, supplied by the Passionists, Rome.

15. Ibid., pp. 496–97.

16. Ibid., p. 863.

17. Hieronymo Dal-Gal, *Saint Pius X,* pp. 213–14. This "guarigione prodigiosa" verified by the Congregation for the Causes of Saints. May 22, 1989, letter to me, citing *Processo Ordinario Romano* (1923–31), vol. 2, f. 608.

18. *Summarium Super Virtutibus,* p. 297, reported in *Wunder sind Tatsachen* by Wilhelm Schamoni, pp. 350–51.

19. Francis Levy, *Our Guide,* pp. 22–24.

20. My series of interviews with Mother Marguerite in Southern California were in Oct.–Nov. 1988.

21. My interviews with Isabel Cade in London were in Apr. 1985.

afterword

Do the bodily phenomena of mysticism have a place only in the almanacs of human oddity? Or do they have some relevance for us? I think they do or I would not have spent years on this book. Oddities are of no interest to me. Signs directing me to things of value are distinctly worth my time. For the six signs, to use Jesus' term, of this book, I claim the relevance of *Swan Lake* and Olympiad-level running, of *La Bohème* and medieval madrigals, of *The Brothers Karamazov* and Henry James' *Portrait of a Lady.* Each of these, beyond its unique message, is a medium or sign speaking to me of human capacities. From great ballet like *Swan Lake,* I know beyond a shadow of doubt that physical grace and power are part of my human heritage. While runners win personal prizes, they gain for our human race certainties that breathtaking speed and dauntless stamina are not just myth or legend. *La Bohème* and madrigal alike sing not only their own haunting or crystal melodies but also humankind's capacity for lyrical creativity. *The Brothers Karamazov* tells a tale not only of human personalities but of the creativity of the written word which is so distinctly and uniquely human. James' great portrait of human psychology is irrefutable evidence our species has enormous potential for both nuances of expression and penetrating insight.

Because they are signs of so much beyond themselves, phenomena as disparate as opera, world-class running, and the novel broaden and deepen my humanness. The six physical mystical phenomena of this book speak to me of still another human capacity, the ability to enter another reality, the spiritual dimension, and be engaged there in a passionate relationship.

Authenticated, well-studied phenomena are bodily or physical signs that sanctity is a real state. In turn the reality of sanctity is a reliable sign that the spiritual dimension is not a fairy tale from the past or a myth which, as primitive peoples become civilized, is recognized for no more than rich, symbolic representations of psychological conditions. Saint and mystical phenomenon both hymn the profound encounter with the numinous One who has created galaxies, grasshoppers, and the human spirit. That One, wrapped in the glory of His own being, bathed in the bliss of Her own sound, yet receives human love with an eagerness that presses the lover rapturously to one's breast in an ecstasy of delight given and received. Because phenomena like luminosity and levitation are observable signs of this passion between a human body-mind-soul that has reached heights of human goodness or wholeness and the numinous One, I am not entirely whistling in the dark to believe there is a god who loves me and each human being and calls us to wholeness.

I will never be a Verdi, a Dostoevski, or a world-class runner but by acknowledging myself as a creature with impulses to creativity and movement, I enrich my life. Without being a ballerina, from the greats of dance I learned the possibility of moving my body for delight. What matter that I dance for myself, rather than to applause. I dance. Because all my life I have heard music, I know singing is possible. I sing with gusto and not a whit of shame that no one shouts, "Encore."

From the saints I learn that my spiritual dimension is as real and in need of friendly attention as my creative and body urges. If I want to move toward wholeness, I must nourish my soul as well as my body, my emotional life, and my rational powers. Nor am I to be discouraged by the discrepancy between the saint's love of God and my own puny reach toward him. St. Therese of Lisieux as a youngster once asked her older sister if it were not unfair that some souls should have more glory in the numinous realms beyond this life. In silent answer the sister filled before her a tiny cup and huge mug. Therese got the message. Each was full within its capacity to receive. One may be only a thimble next to the barrels and still be filled to overflowing.

From those whose spiritual greatness flowered into full "resurrection life" in the physical body, I could expect a scolding for writing on levitation instead of the divine lover who swoops the saint into the air. All phenomena are a distraction from the way and should be resolutely ignored, the Buddha directed. "But a small number are confirmed in faith by wonders," counters Père Lamy. And Jesus urged crowds to believe because of his "works" of mystical power if they could believe for no other reason (John 10:37–38). I wrote in the same hope that mystical phenomena sign God's reality, love, and power to transform even the dullest of us into people seized by joy. Still in my nightmares I see someone reading this book and taking the sign that points beyond itself for the whole message. My dream phantom writes me for the whereabouts of a workshop of bilocation or to know if the perfume saint takes pupils. As Juan Mascaro puts it in his introduction to the Upanishads, such a "lover of the physical miracle is in fact a Materialist: Instead of making material things spiritual, as . . . the spiritual man does, he simply makes spiritual things material, . . . the source of all idolatry and superstition."

Of course, if one is more fascinated by levitation than the love that lies behind it, more wishful to bilocate than to have the complete openness to God's will of the bilocator, one cannot change such facts. Many of us have gone through that stage. One keeps moving by naming it frankly to oneself as the kindergarten spirituality it is—and laughing about it. This saves from being permanently distracted, as Buddha so wisely put it, from the true path. And it encourages at least *anticipating* moving down the road where fascination with the saints themselves and the meaning of sanctity leads to the numinous One, whose mark they bear, the by-all, in-all, and end-all, who waits with living waters to quench our deepest thirsts.

selected
bibliography

Where both hardcover and paperback editions are cited, pagination is from the paperback reprint. Wherever full references are given in the endnotes, as for instance with Process testimonies and other Cause documents, interviews conducted for this book, or newspaper excerpts, I have not repeated citations here. If nothing is listed here regarding a particular saint, refer to those endnotes. Where there are many biographies on an individual, rather than all those read I list only the one or two that the authorities on the individual recommend. Where I deem a book worthwhile but it still contains one or more significant fact errors, an asterisk will note it is recommended with qualifications. On mystical phenomena in general I list few books, because most contain serious inaccuracies and misrepresentations. Almost all, even those listed here, to a greater or lesser degree, further the idea that only the tradition of the writer or those spiritualities the writer favors produce "real" mystics. If both a foreign-language and English citation are given for the same book, I worked from the original foreign source, usually because my work predated translation.

Arintero, Fr. John G., O.P. *The Mystical Evolution in the Development and Vitality of the Church.* 2 vols. St. Louis: B. Herder Book Co., 1949. Reprint. Rockford, Ill.: TAN Books & Publishers, 1978.

Auffray, A., S.D.B. *Saint John Bosco.* Blaisdon, Longhope, England: Salesian Publications, 1930.

Ayers, John, S.D.B. *Blessed Michael Rua.* Homebush, N.S.W., Australia: Saint Paul Publications, 1974.

Bakhtiar, Laleh. *Sufi: Expressions of the Mystic Quest.* New York: Avon, 1976.

Beevers, John. *Storm of Glory: The Story of St. Therese of Lisieux.* Garden City, N.Y.: Image Books/Doubleday, 1955.

Benson, Joachim, S.T. *The Judgments of Father Judge.* New York: Macmillan Co., 1934. Reprinted as *Father Judge: Man on Fire.* Holy Trinity, Ala.: The Cenacle Press, 1978.

Bergeron, Henri-Paul, C.S.C. *Brother André, C.S.C.: The Wonder Man of Mount Royal.* Rev. ed. Trans. Real Boudreau, C.S.C. Montreal: Saint Joseph's Oratory, n.d.

Bessières, Albert, S.J. *Wife, Mother and Mystic.* Trans. Stephen Rigby. London: Sands & Co., 1952. Reprint. Rockford, Ill.: TAN Books & Publishers, n.d.

Biver, Comte Paul. *Père Lamy.* Dublin: Clonmore & Reynolds, 1950. Reprint. Rockford, Ill.: TAN Books & Publishers, 1973.

Blin de Bourdon, Françoise. *Vie de Julie Billiart par sa première compagne, Françoise Blin de Bourdon, ou les Mémoires de Mère Saint-Joseph.* Rome, n.p., 1978.

Bonaventure, St. *The Life of St. Francis.* In *Bonaventure,* trans. Ewert Cousins. Classics of Western Spirituality series. New York: Paulist Press, 1978.

Brunot, Amédée, S.C.J. *Mariam: La petite Arabe: Soeur Marie de Jésus Crucifié.* Mulhouse (France): Éditions Salvator, 1981. Reprint. *Mariam, The Little Arab: Sister Marie of Jesus Crucified.* Trans. Jeanne Dumais, O.C.D.S., and Sr. Miriam of Jesus, O.C.D. Eugene, Oreg.: The Carmel of Maria Regina, 1984.

Brunton, Paul. *A Search in Secret India.* London: Rider & Co., 1934. Reprint. York Beach, Maine: Samuel Weiser, 1985.

Burton, Katherine. *The Great Mantle: The Life of Giuseppe Melchiore Sarto, Pope Pius X.* Dublin: Clonmore & Reynolds, 1950.

Cade, C. Maxwell, and Coxhead, Nona. *The Awakened Mind: Biofeedback and the Development of Higher States of Awareness.* New York: Eleanor Friede/Delacorte Press, 1979.

Capra, Fritjof. *The Tao of Physics.* Boulder, Colo.: Shambala, 1975.

Carrouges, Michel. *Père Jacques.* Trans. Salvator Attanasio. New York: Macmillan, 1961.

*Carty, Rev. Charles Mortimer. *Padre Pio: The Stigmatist.* St. Paul, Minn.: Radio Replies Press, 1963. Reprint. Rockford, Ill.: TAN Books & Publishers, 1971.

————. *Who Is Teresa Neumann?* St. Paul, Minn.: Radio Replies Press, 1956. Reprint. Rockford, Ill.: TAN Books & Publishers, 1974.

Catta, Étienne. *Le Frère André (1845–1937) et l'Oratoire Saint-Joseph du Mont-Royal.* Montreal and Paris: Fides, 1965.

Claret, St. Anthony. *The Autobiography of Saint Anthony Mary Claret.* Ed. Jose Maria Vinas, C.M.F., Director Studium Claretianum, Rome. Chicago: Claretian Publications, 1976.

The Cloud of Unknowing. Harmondsworth, Middlesex, England: Penguin, 1961.

Cousins, Norman. *Anatomy of an Illness.* New York: W. W. Norton & Co., 1979.

Cranston, Ruth. *The Miracle of Lourdes,* Rev. ed. New York: Image Books/Doubleday, 1988.

Crookall, Robert. *The Techniques of Astral Projection.* Aquarian Press, 1964. Reprint. New York: Samuel Weiser, 1977.

————. *The Study and Practice of Astral Projection.* New York: University Books, 1966.

————. *Out of the Body Experiences: A Fourth Analysis.* New York: University Books, 1970.

Curley, Michael J., C.SS.R. *Cheerful Ascetic: The Life of Francis Xavier Seelos.* New Orleans: The Redemptorist Fathers New Orleans Vice Province, 1969.

Daher, Père Paul. *Charbel: un Homme ivre de Dieu.* Jbail, Lebanon: Monastère S. Maron d'Annaya, 1965.

Dal-Gal, Fr. Hieronymo. *Saint Pius X.* Trans. and adap. Rev. Thomas F. Murray, Dublin: M. H. Gill & Son, 1959.

DeCelles, Charles. *The Unbound Spirit: God's Universal Sanctifying Work.* Staten Island, N.Y.: Alba House, 1985.

De Libero, Giuseppe. *S. Gaspare del Bufalo.* Rome: Curia Generalizia della Congregazione del Preziosissimo Sangue, 1954.

De Maria, Saverio. *Mother Frances Xavier Cabrini.* Trans. and ed. Rose Basile Green. Chicago: Missionary Sisters of the Most Sacred Heart, 1984.

Dempsey, Rev. Martin. *Champion of the Blessed Sacrament: Saint Peter Julian Eymard.* Blessed Sacrament Fathers, n.d.

Du Plessis, David. *A Man Called Mr. Pentecost.* Plainfield, N.J.: Logos International, 1977.

Eliach, Yaffa. *Hasidic Tales of the Holocaust.* New York: Avon, 1982.

Eliade, Mircea. *Shamanism: Archaic Techniques of Ecstasy.* Princeton, N.J.: Princeton University Press, 1972.

Fox, Rev. Robert J. *The Call of Heaven: Br. Gino, Stigmatist.* Front Royal, Va.: Christendom Publications, 1982.

Friedman, Meyer, M.D., and Rosenman, Ray H., M.D. *Type A Behavior and your Heart.* New York: Alfred A. Knopf, 1974.

Germano di S. Stanislao. *S. Gemma Galgani.* 10th ed. Rome: Postulazione dei PP. Passionisti, 1983.

Goleman, Daniel, and Davidson, Richard J. eds. *Consciousness: Brain, States of Awareness, and Mysticism.* New York: Harper & Row, 1979.

Grashoff, Raphael, C.P. *A Good Shepherd He Was: The Life of Saint Pius X.* St. Meinrad, Ind.: Grail Publications, 1952.

Grassiano, M. Domenica. *My Decision Is Irrevocable: A Spiritual Portrait of Sr. Teresa Valsé-Pantellini.* Rome: Daughters of Mary Help of Christians, 1971.

Green, Arthur, ed. *Jewish Spirituality.* 2 vols. New York: Crossroad, 1987–1988.

Griffiths, Bede, O.S.B. *The Golden String.* Garden City, N.Y.: Image Books/Doubleday, 1964.

———. *The Marriage of East and West.* Springfield, Ill.: Templegate, 1982.

Groeneveld, Albert, O. Carm. *A Heart on Fire: An Outline of the*

Saintly Life and Heroic Death of Father Titus Brandsma. Faversham, Kent, England: Carmelite Press, 1954.

Guitton, Jean. *Portrait de Marthe Robin.* Editions Grasset & Fasquelle, 1985.

Hanley, Boniface, O.F.M. *Brother André.* Montreal: St. Joseph's Oratory, n.d.

—————. *No Strangers to Violence, No Strangers to Love.* Notre Dame, Ind.: Ave Maria Press, 1983.

—————. *Through a Dark Tunnel.* Reprint from article in *The Anthonian.* Paterson, N.J.: St. Anthony Guild, n.d.

Harner, Michael. *The Way of the Shaman.* New York: Harper & Row, 1980. Reprint. New York: Bantam, 1982.

Houselander, Caryll. *A Rocking-Horse Catholic.* New York: Sheed & Ward, 1955.

James, William. *The Varieties of Religious Experience.* 2nd ed. London: Longmans, Green & Co., 1929.

Jeans, Sir James. *The Universe Around Us.* Philadelphia: Ridgeway Books, 1929.

—————. *The Mysterious Universe.* New York: Macmillan, 1932.

Johnston, Francis. *Alexandrina.* Dublin: Veritas Publications, 1979. Reprint. Rockford, Ill.: TAN Books & Publishers, 1982.

Johnston, William. *The Mirror Mind: Spirituality and Transformation.* San Francisco: Harper & Row, 1981.

———. *Silent Music: The Science of Meditation.* New York: Harper & Row, 1974.

———. *The Still Point: Reflections on Zen and Christian Mysticism.* New York: Fordham University Press, 1970.

Kaoloubovsky, E., and Palmer, G.E.H., eds. and trans. *Early Fathers from the Philokalia* from the Russian *Dobrotolubiye.* London: Faber & Faber, 1954.

Karagulla, Sharafica, M.D. *Breakthrough to Creativity.* Santa Monica, Calif.: DeVorss & Co., 1967.

Kasturi, N., *The Life of Bhagavan Sri Sathya Sai Baba.* Bombay: Sri Sathya Sai Educational Foundation, 1969. American ed. 4 vols. Tustin, Calif.: Sai Baba Society, 1971.

Keddie, Nikki R., ed. *Scholars, Saints, and Sufis: Muslim Religious Institutions Since 1500.* Berkeley: University of California Press, 1978.

Keene, M. Lamar. *The Psychic Mafia.* New York: St. Martin's Press, 1976. Reprint. New York: Dell, 1977.

Kelsey, Morton T. *The Christian and the Supernatural.* Minneapolis: Augsburg Publishing House, 1976.

———. *Encounter with God.* Minneapolis: Bethany, 1972.

———. *The Other Side of Silence.* New York: Paulist Press, 1976.

Kleber, Albert, O.S.B. *A Bentivoglio of the Bentivoglios: The Servant of God Mary Maddalena of the Sacred Heart of Jesus: Countess Annetta Bentivoglio.* Evansville, Ind.: Monastery of St. Clare, 1984.

Knowles, Leo. *Candidates for Sainthood.* St. Paul, Minn.: Carillon Books, 1978.

Kondor, Louis, S.V.D., ed. *Fatima in Lucia's Own Words: Sister Lucia's Memoirs,* Fatima, Portugal: Postulation Centre, 1976.

Kowalska, M. Faustina. *Divine Mercy in My Soul: The Diary of the Servant of God Sister Mary M. Faustina Kowalska.* Stockbridge, Mass.: Marian Press, 1987.

Lambertini, Prospero [Benedict XIV]. *De servorum Dei beatificatione et beatorum canonizatione.* Bologna: 1734.

Lappin, Peter. *Sunshine in the Shadow: Mama Margaret, Mother of St. John Bosco.* New Rochelle, N.Y.: Don Bosco Publications, 1980.

————. *The Wine in the Chalice.* International ed., 1972; distributed by Salesiana, New Rochelle, N.Y.

Le Deaut, Roger, C.S.Sp., Jaubert, Annie, and Hruby, Kurt. *The Spirituality of Judaism.* Trans. Paul Barrett, O.F.M., Cap. St. Meinrad, Ind.: Abbey Press, 1977.

Legere, J. Roy. *Be My Son.* Notre Dame, Ind.: Ave Maria Press, 1976. Reprint. Rockford, Ill.: TAN Books & Publishers, 1982.

Le Joly, Edward. *Mother Teresa and Her Missionaries of Charity.* San Francisco: Harper & Row, 1977.

Lemoyne, John Baptist, S.D.B. *The Venerable Don Bosco: A Character Sketch.* New Rochelle, N.Y.: Salesian Press, 1927.

Levy, Francis X. *Our Guide.* Rev. ed. Privately pub., 1986.

Life of Marcellin-Joseph-Benedict Champagnat by one of his first dis-

ciples. Paris, Tournai, Rome: Society of St. John The Evangelist, 1947.

Louf, André. *Teach Us to Pray.* New York: Paulist Press, 1974.

Lozano, Juan Maria, C.M.F. *Mystic and Man of Action: Saint Anthony Mary Claret: A Study in the Development of His Spiritual Experience and Doctrine.* Trans. Joseph Daries, C.M.F. Chicago: Claretian Publications, 1977.

Lukoff, David. "The Diagnosis of Mystical Experiences with Psychotic Features." *The Journal of Transpersonal Psychiatry* 17, no. 2 (1985): 157–58.

MacAdam, Eily. *Venerable Francis Libermann of the Holy Ghost Fathers.* Dublin: The Anthonian Press, 1941.

McCluskey, Neil G., S.J. "Darkness and Light over Konnersreuth." *The Priest* (Sept. 1954): 765–74.

Maloney, George, S.J. *Following Jesus in the Real World: Asceticism Today.* Albany, N.Y.: Clarity, 1979.

Martin, St. Thérèse. *Autobiography of St. Thérèse of Lisieux: The Story of a Soul.* Trans. John Beevers. Garden City, N.Y.: Image Books/Doubleday, 1957.

Matin, Thomas, C.M.F. *The Mystery of Konnersreuth.* Privately pub., 1961.

Mead, Jude, C.P. *Shepherd of the Second Spring: The Life of Blessed Dominic Barberi, C.P.* Paterson, N.J.: St. Anthony Guild Press, 1968.

Memorie Biografiche di San Giovanni Bosco. Vols. 1–9 by Giovanni

Battista Lemoyne, S.D.B.; vol. 10 by Angelo Amadei, S.D.B.; vols. 11–19 by Eugenio Ceria, S.D.B.; vol. 20 *(Indice Analitico delle Memorie Biografiche di S. Giovanni Bosco nei 19 volumi)* compiled by Ernesto Foglio, S.D.B. in 1948. Turin: Società Editrice Internazionale, 1898–1939, 1948. Trans. as *The Biographical Memoirs of Saint John Bosco.* 15 of the 20 vols. available in trans. as of 1989. Trans. ed. Diego Borgatello, S.D.B. New Rochelle, N.Y.: Salesiana Publishers, 1965– .

Merton, Thomas. *The Seven Storey Mountain.* New York: Harcourt, Brace & Co., 1948.

Monroe, Robert A. *Journeys Out of the Body.* Garden City, N.Y.: Anchor Books/Doubleday, 1973.

Moody, Raymond A., Jr. *Life After Life.* Harrisburg, Pa.: Stackpole, 1976.

Moss, Thelma. *The Probability of the Impossible.* Los Angeles: J. P. Tarcher, 1974. Reprint. New York: Plume/New American Library, 1975.

Muggeridge, Malcolm. *Something Beautiful for God.* New York: Harper & Row, 1971. Paperback reprint. San Francisco: Harper & Row, 1986.

Muldoon, Sylvan, and Carrington, Hereward. *The Projections of the Astral Body.* New York: Weiser, 1973.

Neihardt, John G. *Black Elk Speaks: Being the Life Story of a Holy Man of the Oglala Sioux.* New York: William Morrow & Co., 1932. Reprint. New York: Pocket, 1972.

O'Carroll, Michael, C.S.Sp. *Blessed Jacques Désiré Laval.* Dublin, n.d.

———. *The Venerable Francis Libermann.* Long Island City, N.Y.: Ven. Libermann Guild, n.d.

Olive, Martin-Maria, O.P. *Práxedes: Wife, Mother, Widow and Lay Dominican 1886–1936.* Madrid: Secretariado Práxedes, 1980. Reprint. Trans. Maria Maez., O.P. Rockford, Ill.: TAN Books & Publishers, 1987.

O'Mahoney, Christopher, O.C.D., ed. and trans. *St. Thérèse of Lisieux by Those Who Knew Her.* Huntington, Ind.: Our Sunday Visitor, 1975.

Ostrander, Sheila, and Schroeder, Lynn. *Handbook for Psi Discoveries.* New York: Berkley Publishing, 1974.

———. *Psychic Discoveries Behind the Iron Curtain.* Englewood Cliffs, N.J.: Prentice-Hall, 1970. Reprint. New York: Bantam, 1971.

Palm, John Baptist, S.J. *Tape-Recorded Little Rose Testimonies.* Transcribed and privately pub. by Fr. Palm. Taiwan: n.d.

Parker, William R., and St. Johns, Elaine. *Prayer Can Change Your Life.* Englewood Cliffs, N.J.: Prentice-Hall, 1957.

Peck, M. Scott. *People of the Lie.* New York: Simon & Schuster, 1983.

———. *The Road Less Traveled.* New York: Simon & Schuster, 1985.

Peers, E. Allison, ed. and trans. *The Autobiography of St. Teresa of Avila.* Garden City, N.Y.: Image Books/Doubleday, 1960.

Pelletier, Kenneth R. *Mind as Healer, Mind as Slayer.* New York: Seymour Laurence/Delacorte Press, 1977.

Peyret, Rev. Raymond. *Petite vie de Marthe Robin.* Paris: Desclee de Brouwer, 1988.

————. *Marthe Robin: The Cross and the Joy.* Trans. Clare Will Faulhaber. Staten Island, N.Y.: Alba House, 1983.

Rahman, Fazlur. *Islam.* 2nd ed. Chicago: University of Chicago Press, 1979.

Rauscher, William V. "The Mystical and the Psychical." In *Frontiers of the Spirit,* ed. Paul L. Higgins. Minn.: T. S. Denison & Co., 1976.

Rees, Joseph. *Titus Brandsma: A Modern Martyr.* London: Sidgwick & Jackson, 1971.

Rey, Amilcare. *Gaspare del Bufalo.* 2 vols. Rome: Edizioni Primavera Missionaria, n.d.

*Ricciardi, A. *Beato Massimiliano Maria Kolbe.* Rome: Postulazione Generale dell'Ordine dei Frati Minori Conventuali, 1971. Reprinted as *St. Maximilian Kolbe: Apostle of Our Difficult Age.* Trans. and adapted by the Daughters of St. Paul. Boston: The Daughters of St. Paul, 1982.

Rinaldi, Peter M., S.D.B. *By Love Compelled: The Life of Father Philip Rinaldi, Third Successor of St. John Bosco,* New Rochelle, N.Y.: Salesiana Publishers, n.d.

Rohrbach, Peter-Thomas, O.C.D. *The Search for St. Therese.* Garden City, N.Y.: Hanover House, 1961.

Ruffin, C. Bernard. *Padre Pio: The True Story.* Huntington, Ind.: Our Sunday Visitor, 1982.

Rumble, L., M.S.C. *Spiritualism and Psychical Research.* St. Paul, Minn.: Radio Replies Press, 1957.

Salotti, Cardinal Carlo. *La Beata Anna Maria Taigi: Madre di Famiglia,* 3rd ed. Roma: Postulazione dei Trinitari, 1937.

———. *La Beata Maria Taigi.* Rome: Libreria Editrice Religiosa Francesco Ferrari, 1922.

———. *Suor Maria Assunta Pallotta delle Francescane Missionarie di Maria.* Rome: Franciscan Missionaries of Mary, 1929.

Sanford, Agnes. *Creation Waits.* Plainfield, N.J.: Logos International, 1978.

———. *Sealed Orders.* Plainfield, N.J.: Logos International, 1972.

Sanford, John. *Healing and Wholeness.* New York: Paulist Press, 1977.

Sardi, Monsignor Vincent. *Gaspar del Bufalo.* Adapted and trans. Edwin G. Kaiser, C.PP.S. Carthagena, Ohio: The Messenger Press, 1954.

Schamoni, Wilhelm. *Wunder sind Tatsachen: eine Dokumentation aus Heiligsprechungsakten.* Wurzburg: Johann Wilhelm Naumann, 1976.

Schaya, Leo. *The Universal Meaning of the Kabbalah.* Trans. Nancy Pearson. Baltimore: Penguin, 1973.

Scholem, Gershom G. *Major Trends in Jewish Mysticism.* Jerusalem: Schocken Publishing House, 1941. Reprint of 3rd rev. ed. New York: Schocken Books, 1961.

Schug, John A., O.F.M. Cap. *A Padre Pio Profile.* Petersham, Mass.: St. Bede's Publications, 1987.

Poor Clare Nuns. *Seed Sown in Sorrow: Mother Mary Magdalen Bentivoglio.* St. Louis: Poor Clare Nuns, n.d.

Shakarian, Demos. *The Happiest People on Earth.* Chosen Books, 1975.

Sheridan, John V. *Saints in Times of Turmoil.* New York: Paulist Press, 1977.

Siegel, Bernie S. *Love, Medicine, & Miracles.* New York: Harper & Row, 1986.

Sister Saint Michael, S.S.J. *Portrait of Saint Gemma.* New York: P. J. Kenedy & Sons, 1950.

Skoglund, Elizabeth R. *The Whole Christian: How You Can Find Physical, Mental, and Spiritual Health.* New York: Harper & Row, 1976.

S.M.C. of The English Dominican Congregation of Saint Catherine of Siena. *Steward of Souls: A Portrait of Mother Margaret Hallahan.* London: Longmans, Green & Co., 1952.

Statler, Oliver. *Japanese Pilgrimage.* New York: William Morrow & Co., 1983.

Stearn, Jess. *Edgar Cayce: The Sleeping Prophet.* New York: Doubleday & Co., 1967.

Steiner, Johannes. *Therese Neumann: A Portrait Based on Authentic Accounts, Journals and Documents.* Staten Island, N.Y.: Alba House, 1967.

Stolz, Benedikt, O.S.B. *Pater Paul von Moll: Der Sänger der göttlichen Liebe und grosse Nothelfer.* Wels (Austria): Verlagsbuchhandlung Franz Reisinger, 1979.

Sugrue, Thomas. *There Is a River: The Story of Edgar Cayce.* New York: Holt, Rinehart & Winston, 1942.

Ten Boom, Corrie. *The Hiding Place.* Washington Depot, Conn.: Chosen Books, 1971.

Teodorowicz, Joseph. *Mystical Phenomena in the Life of Theresa Neumann.* Trans. Rudolph Kraus, St. Louis: B. Herder Book Co., 1940.

Tesnière, Albert, S.S.S. *Saint Peter Julian Eymard.* New York: Eymard League, 1962.

The Life of Blessed Julie Billiart Foundress of the Institute of Sisters of Notre Dame by a Member of the Same Society. Ed. Father James Clare, S.J. Edinburgh: Sands & Co., 1909.

The Theme Song of Assunta [Pallotta] by One of Her Sisters. St. Francis of Assisi Province, U.S.A.: Franciscan Missionaries of Mary, 1956.

Thurston, Herbert, S.J., ed. J. H. Crehan, S.J. *The Physical Phenomena of Mysticism.* Chicago: Henry Regnery Co., 1952.

Thurston, Herbert J., S.J., and Attwater, Donald, eds. *Butler's Lives of the Saints.* Westminister, Md.: Christian Classics, 1981 edition.

Treece, Patricia. *Nothing Short of a Miracle: The Healing Power of the Saints.* New York: Image Books/Doubleday, 1988.

————. *A Man for Others: Maximilian Kolbe, Saint of Auschwitz, in the Words of Those Who Knew Him.* San Francisco: Harper & Row, 1982.

Trochu, Abbé Francis. *The Curé d'Ars: St. Jean-Marie-Baptiste Vianney According to the Acts of the Process of Canonization and Numerous Hitherto Unpublished Documents.* Lyons and Paris: Librairie Catholique Emmanuel Vitte, 1927. Reprint. Trans. Dom Ernest Graf, O.S.B. Westminister, Md.: The Newman Press, 1960.

————. *Saint Jeanne Antide Thouret.* Trans. and adapted by John Joyce, S.J. London: Sands & Co., 1966.

Una Carmelitana Scalza. . . . *Quello che fa l'amore: Suor M. Giuseppina di Gesú Crocifisso.* Rome: Postulazione Generale dei Carmelitani Scalzi, 1976.

Underhill, Evelyn. *The Essentials of Mysticism and Other Essays.* London, 1920. Reprint. New York: E. P. Dutton & Co., 1960.

————. *The Life of the Spirit and the Life of Today.* London, 1922. Reprint. San Francisco: Harper & Row, 1986.

————. *Mysticism.* 1911. Reprint. New York: E. P. Dutton & Co., 1961.

Un Religieux du Très Saint Sacrement. *Le Bienheureux Pierre-Julien Eymard d'après les pièces du Procès de Béatification et de nombreux documents in édits.* 2 vols. Paris: Imprimerie-Librairie Saint-Paul, 1927.

The Upanishads, Translations from the Sanskrit, Juan Mascaró. Baltimore: Penguin, 1965.

Van Kaam, Adrian L., C.S.Sp. *A Light to the Gentiles: The Life-Story of the Venerable Francis Libermann.* Duquesne University, 1959. Reprint. Milwaukee: The Bruce Publishing Co., n.d.

Van Speybrouck, Edward. *Father Paul of Moll.* Clyde, Mo.: Benedictine Convent, 1910 (previously published in Belgium). Reprint, Rockford, Ill.: TAN Books & Publishers, 1979.

Von Balthasar, Hans Urs, S.J. Erster Blick auf Adrienne von Speyr. Einsiedeln: Johannes Verlag, 1968. Trans. as *First Glance at Adrienne von Speyr.* Trans. Antje Lawry and Sister Sergia Englund, O.C.D. San Francisco: Ignatius Press, 1981.

Ward, Maisie. *Caryl Houselander, That Divine Eccentric.* New York: Sheed & Ward, 1962.

Weiner, Herbert. *9 1/2 Mystics: The Kabbala Today.* New York: Holt, Rinehart & Winston, 1969. Reprint. New York: Collier Books, 1971.

Wilkerson, Ralph. *Beyond and Back: Those Who Died and Lived to Tell It.* Anaheim, Calif.: Melodyland Productions, 1977.

Yogananda, Paramahansa. *Autobiography of a Yogi.* Los Angeles: Self-Realization Fellowship, 1972.

Zukaw, Gary. *The Dancing Wu Li Masters: An Overview of the New Physics.* New York: William Morrow & Co., 1979. Reprint. New York: Bantam, 1980.

about the author

Patricia Treece holds degrees in Journalism, Anthropology and French and is the author of *Nothing Short of a Miracle* and *A Man for Others* (a biography of Maximilian Kolbe). She resides with her husband and two children in Calabasas, California.